THE ASSOCIATION FOR SCOTTISH LITERARY STUDIES

NUMBER SIX

WILLIAM DRUMMOND

OF HAWTHORNDEN

POEMS and PROSE

THE ASSOCIATION FOR SCOTTISH LITERARY STUDIES

WILLIAM DRUMMOND

OF HAWTHORNDEN

POEMS and PROSE

EDITED BY
ROBERT H. MACDONALD

SCOTTISH ACADEMIC PRESS
EDINBURGH & LONDON
1976

Published by
Scottish Academic Press Ltd
33 Montgomery Street, Edinburgh EH7 5JX
and distributed by
Chatto & Windus Ltd
40 William IV Street
London WC2

First published 1976
SBN 7011 2192 0

Printed in Great Britain by
Western Printing Services Ltd, Bristol

ACKNOWLEDGEMENTS

The editor would like to thank The Canada Council for the award of a Leave Fellowship, during the tenure of which much of the work for this edition was done. He would also like to acknowledge the financial assistance given him by the Faculty of Graduate Studies and the Dean's Fund of Carleton University. He also wishes to thank Dr Barbara Garner for her most helpful advice and patient criticism.

CONTENTS

INTRODUCTION

Drummond of Hawthornden, it could be argued, was the best poet
Scotland produced between Douglas and Ramsay. Certainly he ranks
higher than any other Scot of the seventeenth century, and looking
south, he holds his own as one of the superior craftsmen of his age.
Yet his work has been much neglected, and since the root of this neglect
lies in the obscuring prejudices of fashion, it is not too late now to seek
a remedy.

Drummond suffered from the times he lived in, from the want of a
cultural centre in Scotland and the civil wars that came with the
English connection. His early poetry, preferring European models,
invited unfavourable comparison with the metaphysical innovations
of England; his enlightened commentaries on history and politics were
silenced by the realities of extremism. After his death his works
continued to be unfashionable: his poetry out of date, his prose
controversial and a little too self-righteously correct. His first biog-
rapher, Bishop Sage, in 1711, rescued Drummond for the cause of
Toryism, and claimed him as a patriot and an upholder of monarchy.[1]
David Masson, in his Victorian biography,[2] emphasized the romantic
poet, and in our time, French Rowe Fogle has made a sentimental
tragedy of the young Scot in love.[3]

The real Drummond, in addition, has been obscured for other
reasons. Regarding him as one of the first traitors to the Scots language
—for he began writing in English very early on—the modern Scot
may have had the feeling that neglect was the kindest fate for such a
case. His famous "Conversations" with Ben Jonson earned him only
a place at the coattails of that poet. Lastly, his extraordinary extant
literary remains, his library and his collection of manuscripts,[4] may
in a way have done something to shadow his reputation: with so
extensive a record of his life's interests at hand, attention has been
diverted a little from the actual product of these interests.

The aim of this volume is to restore a balance. By setting out a selection of his best work, both poems and prose, and by reminding the reader to judge this work as it is, for what it is, we hope to foster an appreciation of Drummond's real worth. His work needs setting in its historical context: before we approach it we must understand the traditions and conventions within which he worked. If we do not, we will end up with yet another imaginary Drummond.

William Drummond was born in 1585, the son of a minor official at the Scottish court. The family owned the lands of Hawthornden near Lasswade in Midlothian. Drummond was sent to the Tounis College (Edinburgh University) where he studied in Latin the usual university subjects of his time: a great deal of Aristotle (logic, natural science, metaphysics), theology and humanities. He graduated in 1605. He then went travelling, first to London, and afterwards to France where he stayed some two years. At the University of Bourges he attended lectures in civil law, though it is doubtful whether he ever seriously intended to qualify himself in the profession. He visited Paris, and in the time he was abroad and in London on the way home, he bought many books, beginning then his large collection of literary works in French, Italian, English and Spanish. His father died in 1610, and Drummond succeeded as laird. As far as we know, he never left Scotland after this date; and indeed, apart from visits to his brother-in-law Sir John Scot, in Fife, he seems to have spent most of his time at Hawthornden.

Drummond began writing seriously sometime after 1611, and in 1613 at the age of twenty-eight published his first poem, a formal lament for the death of Prince Henry, the heir to the thrones of England and Scotland. His sonnet sequence, his next work, seems to have been more or less complete in 1614, and was published in its finished form two years later. In 1617 he wrote another occasional poem, this time for the return of James VI to Scotland. In 1623 he published his last major poetical work the *Flowres of Sion*, and added to it a prose meditation, *A Cypresse Grove*, itself probably written some years before.[5]

There is then a gap in Drummond's literary activity. He produced an "entertainment" for the welcome of Charles I to Edinburgh in 1633, and was probably by that time at work on his history of Scotland. The history was however a lengthy project—there are several scroll copies in the Hawthornden MSS—which began as the civil war approached to take on a political tone, but he did not see it published.

In his last years he turned directly to polemics, and produced a number of tracts and satires on the civil troubles, all of them unpublished, but some perhaps circulated in manuscript. He died in 1649. Of Drummond's private life we know little. His biographers speak of him as leading a retiring life among his books and music; his books have largely survived and there is a record in his manuscripts of his interest in madrigals. He probably played the lute. In his thirties he took a mistress, and by her had three natural children; one son Ludovick lived to maturity. At the age of forty-five Drummond married and fathered nine children: his diary or "Memorialls" records their births, christenings, illnesses and burials. A daughter, Eliza, and two sons survived him.[6]

These few facts suggest something of Drummond's character: he had no taste for public life, he was studious, retiring, solitary. His portraits suggest a melancholic:[7] in his youth this may have been a reflection of his poetic stance; in old age the civil wars were the more immediate cause. He fell into poverty and debt, took to the law courts, became dependent on protectors such as the Earl of Perth. His last unpublished letters show him as irascible, querulous and self-righteous, a man whose pride made it difficult for him to accept a condition of dependency.[8]

As a young man he had formed a quite definite literary *persona*. He cultivated the image of the poet as a lonely, pensive figure, a "romantic," wandering alone by the river Esk while the nightingale sang in the woods around.[9] On the rebuilding of his house at Hawthornden he inscribed the words "ut honesto otio quiesceret" above the door,[10] and indeed attempted to repose there in honest leisure for the rest of his days. He took great pride in his calling of poet, and (at least in his dreams) aimed high.

The most extraordinary and most revealing evidence of this vision of the artist as a young poet lies buried in his manuscripts. There in rough draft is a eulogy, or rather, the notes for a eulogy, in which he compares himself to Orpheus, and his verses to the songs angels sing in heaven. "Δρουμμονδος" [that is, Drummond] . . . describing earthly Beautye and love . . . left all other of the Muses of Albion behind him . . . Now writing of heavenlye beauty and love and praising the eternal king of this universe he hath over-runne and out-matched himselfe . . . If Albions language were by tyme to perish it . . . should be preserved by thes . . . noble poems,"[11] This effusion must refer to his divine poems, *Flowres of Sion*. It was only fancy, but it does mark the

xi

humanistic Petrarchan tradition he saw himself in: he is among the immortals, and notably, he is one of the Muses of Albion.

There is in the production of his poems however an attention to detail, a caring for excellence, for the right word and the look of the book, that is evidence of his superior concept of poetry itself. His poems were put out by the Edinburgh printer, Andrew Hart, and considering the limitations of Hart's press, they are what we might call today prestige productions, tastefully printed with nice ornaments, plenty of white paper, and elegant cuts. They came in several issues, and Drummond revised between printings. He had several copies gilt bound for gift presentations to special acquaintances, and seems on the whole to have devoted much time (and probably money) to having everything done right.[12]

His self-image as a poet clearly matured with him, for by 1633 and his production of the entertainment for the King's visit, he was the unofficial Scottish poet laureate, a gentleman ready to advise the Town of Edinburgh on matters poetical, literary or cultural. He had earned his honour long before, and indeed the best mark of his ability is not such official recognition, but the very real reputation he had established amongst his fellow writers. His friendships with Ben Jonson and Michael Drayton, though expressed in formal terms, were based on mutual admiration: Jonson may have been gossipy and irreverent in the "Conversations" but he respected Drummond's work. With his fellow Scots he was on a more familiar footing: he corresponded with Sir William Alexander, Sir Robert Kerr and others at the court, and though there is a note in the letters from Drummond of deference to his friends' high rank, there is no condescension in theirs to him.[13] He was too a corresponding member of King James's psalm-versifying school, and with Alexander and Kerr shared a realistic understanding of their leader's prerogative.[14]

What motivated Drummond in the larger sense, what inspired his sense of quality in its various forms, was the humanistic spirit which he found first in the classics and later diffused in the vernaculars. His formal education was in the usual way scholastic; his inclinations and self-learning were for belles-lettres. In the Hawthornden MSS is the detailed evidence of his real enthusiasm for literature: he kept lists of the books he bought, and copious notes of the books he read.[15] He took first to English romances, Sidney's *Arcadia* and Lyly's *Euphues*, and later turned to French with the *Amadis* and d'Urfé's *Astrée*. He read widely in the English poets of the day, then systematically in French and Italian, and by the end of his apprenticeship he had mastered Spanish. His ambition was to embrace the best of European vernacular literature, to be as familiar with Bembo as Ronsard, with Garcilaso as Du Bellay, with Daniel as Tasso. He read anthologies and encyclopaedias, handbooks and commentaries; commonplace books, and courtesy books. He had had some formal training in classical letters; he kept up his Cicero and Quintilian. As he read he learned. He took direction from Castiglione or Pasquier: how to behave, what to read. His poetry and prose are evidence of his industry, for they are a distillation of some of the best work of an age; a purification in their own form of two hundred years and more of artistic convention, and everywhere distinguished by the high ideals of humanism. Drummond was one of the most European of writers, a man for whom national boundaries had no meaning and formed no obstacles.

His interests were catholic. In 1608 in Bourges he attended some plays put on by an Italian commedia dell'arte company, and afterwards stayed to watch a longer season performed by a rival French troupe. He took copious notes of the performances, giving accounts of the prologues, the plots and even the players, incidentally thus providing us with original information on the early French theatre.[16]

Enjoying his 'honest repose' at Hawthornden he picked up the courtly pastimes of his poet-uncle, William Fowler. Fowler had left his manuscripts sprinkled with anagrams (among them DANISMERCA/ CANIS MERDA—a joke against his employer and patron, Queen Anne of Denmark). Drummond composed dozens more, many witty, many scurrilous. In WARISTON he found UN VRAI SOT, from IHON SMITH, SHIT ON HIM. To get anything from these now we have to remember the almost mystic, sometimes superstitious significance given to the power of the word, with the idea that a secret but real meaning lay concealed within. In his wife's name Drummond found the imperfect anagram BETH LOVELY AND GAY (from Elizabeth Logan) and turned himself into a Spanish cavalier, DON GEMMA DE MURAVILL, alias DON MURMIDUMILLA.[17] He was interested too in impresas, those mottos and emblems of the aristocracy and literati, and wrote an essay defining their art to his kinsman, the Earl of Perth.[18]

His own memory he nursed along with notes on every subject; he was a collector, a hoarder, a kind of literary squirrel who saved anything that came his way. One volume of his manuscripts he labelled "Democritie. A Labyrinth of delight or worke preparative for the apologie of Democritus. Containing pasquills apotheames impresas

anagrames epitaphes epigrames of this and the late age before."
Named for the laughing philosopher, this collection has dozens of
what Drummond's son later characterized as "mirrie jests":

> At Oxford a professour having put on a new gown, and some
> about saying it was too short, answered let it alone, it will be
> long enough ere I get an other.
>
> King James loosing a stagge at hunting and meeting a man
> with a syde beard cryed hee had found wher the stagge was and
> willed the mans beard by his footemen to be searched.
>
> When King James went to see his Queene Anne to Denmarke
> and was tossed by the windes on the sea, sundrye of these
> attended him, perplexed with the tempestes desired earnestly
> hee would turn his course homeward againe. But when they
> could not prevaile, a merry disposed gentleman said, apperingly
> his pricke was touched with a magnet, it would not stand but
> toward the north.[19]

The epigrams are much the same. Sir Jocelyn Percy, the Elizabethan
courtier, is credited with

> The Queen is to make two knights of
> the Garter
> The one is a greate foole the other a
> greater farter.[20]

This sort of thing must have circulated in manuscript, or was passed
about by word of mouth. (Many of Drummond's stories were given
him by Jonson). King James is the subject of many witticisms, Sir
Edward Dyer, Sir Francis Raleigh, Sir Francis Bacon, John Donne and
Tobie Matthew appear in others. Hawthornden may have been far
from the court, but it was not entirely cut off.

Drummond had other closet pursuits. There is the enigma of his
patent in 1627 of some sixteen frightful inventions of war, each dignified
with an appropriate classical title. These included machine guns, a
salt-water converter, and a perpetual motion machine. Drummond's
description of the "Elephant" is typical of the rest:

> A sort of machine, not unlike the *Helepolis* of the ancients, or
> rather the *Helepolis* itself adapted to modern warfare, and both
> for storming forts, and defending the same; by the help of which,
> in sieges of towns, rapid approaches may be made to an inner

fortification. .... This machine, on account of its likeness to that part of a fortification which is commonly called the *Cavalier*, and because it carries several soldiers and is moveable, may be named Προβοληκινητος, vulgarly The Elephant, or The Cavalier Errant.[21]

It is hard to believe that such schemes ever got further than his library, for his interests were literary rather than practical.

Occasionally the outside world touched him. As he grew old he developed an interest in genealogy, and did research on the family name for his noble relation the Earl of Perth, and in the same line of business advised the Marquis of Douglas how to protect his reputation. He seems too to have corresponded with the Marquis of Montrose, who in 1645 led the royalist army, and there was some talk of his pamphlets (particularly the *Irene*) being used to help the royalist cause. But it all came to nothing.

My last impression is of the recluse, an embittered, impoverished man in a world apparently gone mad, his fine humanist ideals and civilized interests threatened by sectarian self-interest and civil strife. One of his last writings before his death in 1649, a half-finished prophetic satire in very rough draft, epitomizes his mood. Called the "Amauria" (the land of obscurity), and modelled vaguely on More's *Utopia*, this piece describes a land "latlie turned most part Mad."[22] Sailing north towards this Scotland are men from Anticyra (England) bearing a cargo of hellebore (the herb that cures madness). They are met on landing with a number of "apparitions:" various Amaurians (Scots) exposed in their madness, worshipping (like the Israelites) a "calfe anant" (the Covenant), an object looking like gold but made of paper. They see other apparitions—civil wars, the beheading of "some of the wisest" Amaurians, and the beheading of the king himself by "his owne subjects." The manuscript ends in obscurities; it was in any case unpublishable, and probably even dangerous to write.

This concludes my account of Drummond's varied interests. I have presented them in some detail in the belief that they are part of the necessary background to an understanding of his work. He was essentially in his ambitions and culture a Renaissance man. He took all learning as his province; his very instincts were ultra-national. If we celebrate him now as a Scottish writer, it is as a Scot who was by election a writer of the world.

★   ★   ★

Ben Jonson's opinion of Drummond's poems, that "they were all good . . . save that they smelled too much of the schooles and were not after the Fancie of the tyme," has an air of finality to it that has impressed generations of critics.[23] Drummond was a Petrarchan, and the new wave of poetry, led by John Donne and Jonson himself, was not Petrarchan. The fashion of the early seventeenth century was what we now call metaphysical.

This was, however, only the English "Fancie," for continental poets developed in another way, no "strong lines" or analytical concerns, but a preoccupation with style and ornament, with decoration almost for its own sake. This movement has been called the baroque, or mannerism, or marinism (after its chief practitioner, the Italian poet Giambattista Marino); it was, whatever Jonson said, very much a "Fancie of the tyme."[24] Jonson was an insular Englishman, well-trained in classical literature but not very familiar with French, and knowing less of Italian and Spanish.[25] Drummond on the other hand was a European, an internationalist by temperament. He was also probably the best read poet of his day, and although his own work was based in an eclectic way upon "the schooles" (the French Pléiade, the Italian Petrarchans), he was far from ignorant of current literary developments. We could, in fact, make a case for Drummond, in his fondness for Marino—then at the height of his fame—being as well aware of fashion as Jonson and Donne. But Drummond's taste was not for "strong lines," and his "Fancie" was not an English one.

The essence of Drummond's writing is in its appeal to the senses. His poetry delights the ear and pleases the eye; its phrases are decorative, its rhythms musical.

> On this colde World of Ours,
> Flowre of the Seasons, Season of the Flowrs,
> Sonne of the Sunne sweet Spring,
> Such hote and burning Dayes why doest thou bring?[26]

He likes the sound of words, and the sound they make together. He is a master of harmony, delicately varying cadence; he plays with rhythms and makes of his verse melodious patterns. There is a fluidity in his work that seems effortless (though we know it was worked for):

> Sound hoarse sad Lute, true Witnesse of my Woe,
> And strive no more to ease selfe-chosen Paine
> With Soule-enchanting Sounds, your Accents straine
> Unto these Teares uncessantly which flow.[27]

The songs and madrigals of the early poems are light and contrived, the sonnets weighty and measured, while the later religious verse becomes sonorous.

His poetry too was designed to catch the eye: it is marked by its decorative quality; it is colourful, fanciful, exotic. Drummond liked the unusual word and the obscure epithet; he collected them and displayed them like rare flowers. He enjoyed ornament for its own sake, and his work is full of the most elaborate toys. Adjectives such as "diamantine" and "sinople" appear, the sun "ensaffrons" the sea, God we find characterized as "the first and only Fair." His use of classical epithets and allusion is extensive. The sun is Phoebus or Apollo, the moon Cynthia or Phoebe, Venus the Acidalian queen, the Cyprian star or half a dozen other names, the rainbow is called Iris and the north wind Boreas. This was standard practice for poets working in the late Petrarchan convention, yet Drummond's employment of the epithet seems based not only on decorum but on a delight, both poetic and scholarly in rare and strange coinage.

> Phoebus arise,
> And paint the sable Skies
> With azure, white and Red:
> Rowse Memnons Mother from her Tythons Bed,
> That Shee thy Cariere may with Roses spred. . . .[28]

As a prose writer Drummond exploits the same sensual talents and indulges the same fondness for ornament. In his best piece, *A Cypresse Grove*, his rhetoric is elaborate yet masterful. Employing all the tricks of Elizabethan copious style, balance, antithesis, gradation, he constructs a complex set of variations on a theme, meditating on the commonplace of death and the vanity of the things of this world. As in his poetry, his technique depends not so much upon the logical development of argument, but on repetition and exploration of kindred topics, a kind of rhetorical fugue that precisely matches the solemn subject. The appeal is as much to the ear as to the mind:

> Now although Death were an extreme Paine, sith it comes in an Instant, what can it bee? why should we feare it? for while wee are, it commeth not, and it beeing come, wee are no more. Nay, though it were most painefull, long continuing, and terrible-uglie, why should wee feare it? Sith Feare is a foolish passion but where it may preserve; but it can not preserve us from Death,

yea, rather Feare maketh us to meete with that which wee would shunne, and banishing the Comfortes of present Contentmentes bringeth Death more neare unto us: That is ever terrible which is unknowne; so doe little Children feare to goe in the darke, and their Feare is increased with Tales.[29]

Both his prose and his poetry should be read then, or better heard, as sensual delights. Drummond has earned his reputation for sweetness and charm, and rather than depreciate these qualities, we should enjoy them.

His range as a writer is not large. The bulk of his poetry is in the Petrarchan tradition, which by Drummond's time had developed conventions of an extra-ordinary complexity and artificiality. His immediate models were not Petrarch himself, but a considerable number of contemporary and near-contemporary writers, Scottish, English, Italian, French and Spanish.[30] His poetry, in a sense, represents a distillation of the best work of the Petrarchan movement.

His first published piece, *Teares on the Death of Moeliades*—his formal epitaph for the untimely death of Prince Henry—is an accomplished exercise using the conventional motifs of the pastoral lament. The emphasis is on extravagant decoration and hyperbole, accepted and expected according to the usual decorum of the genre: Moeliades (Prince Henry), a paragon of virtue and valour, is dead, and all the world mourns, the rivers, the flowers all weep, the sun, the moon show grief, even the gods stop their business:

> Chaste Maides which haunt faire Aganippe Well,
> And you in Tempes sacred Shade who dwell,
> Let fall your Harpes, cease Tunes of Joy to sing,
> Discheveled make all Parnassus ring. . . .[31]

Safe in heaven, Henry's ghost looks down on earth.

Perhaps the most characteristic element in *Teares* is the couplet which serves as a refrain. It is musical, and it is exotic:

> Moeliades sweet courtly Nymphes deplore,
> From Thuly to Hydaspes pearlie shore.[32]

Probably before *Teares* was published in 1613, Drummond had begun writing love poetry; songs, sonnets and madrigals in the Petrarchan mode. His first attempts may have been made as early as 1609,

when he was twenty-three; written in Scots, they are prentice work
modelled on the Castalian school of the Scottish court:

> Quhen the great God gave first this breath to man
> Alas to keepe quhy gave he him a laue
> And threatnd pains to make him stand in aw. . . .[33]

And so on. King James was in England; his courtiers would henceforth
write as Englishmen. Drummond was friendly by now with Sir
William Alexander, whose sonnet sequence *Aurora* had been published
in 1604, and so identifying himself with the current change to English
usage, Drummond conscientiously, if not always successfully, endeav-
oured to erase Scotticisms from his verse.[34] Of course, except for some
English rhymes his pronunciation remained Scottish, and so read his
poems achieve simple and vigorous effects too often denied to them in
an English reading.

His *Poems* came out in a trial edition in 1614, and were corrected
and added to for the edition of 1616. Advertised (in imitation of his
favourite author Marino) as "Amorous, Funerall, Divine, Pastorall," and
divided into "Sonnets, Songs, Sextains, Madrigals," the poems should
be regarded as not so much a collection of specimen verse as a related
whole. In conventional Petrarchan fashion they celebrate the poet's
love of his mistress—Drummond called himself Damon, and his love
Auristella—her death, and his undying devotion. Drummond here
went a little further, and taking the later development of the conven-
tion, rounded out his work with "poems spiritual," a set of medita-
tional pieces on the vanity of life and the consolations of Christianity.
In their first form these last poems were titled "Urania;" afterwards
they became in a much more elaborate form *Flowres of Sion*. I thus
regard these two works, the *Poems* (1616) and *Flowres of Sion* (1923)
as two parts of a whole, designed as such and to be read as such.

They are both variations on a set of themes. The poet, as is usual in
the convention, adores his mistress. She is a remote and ethereal
figure, to be glimpsed in her pastoral Arcadia, a nymph by the river,
a favourite of nature and favoured by the gods. Her eyes outshine the
sun, her hair is more golden than the finest gold, her cheeks outblush
the dawn and her lips put to shame the deepest rose, in short, she is
perfection, while, he, as her lover, suffers the torments of hell, and
neglected by her cruelty his groans silence the cooing doves; he is on
fire, he swoons, he weeps. As Petrarch had celebrated his Laura
Drummond hymns his Auristella, and after her poetic death laments his

loss and gradually subdues his passion in a reflective melancholy. This mood naturally evolves into consideration of the transitoriness of our span on earth and the rewards of the life hereafter.

The experience is conventional more than autobiographical. In reality Drummond had his love, a Euphemia Cunningham, and she did die, and no doubt if his love for her was sincere he did regret her death. Yet to see his *Poems* as a "little history of love" is absurd: the feelings expressed by the poet are conventionally exaggerated, the experiences imaginary, and the poetic mistress herself is a fiction. The most telling proof of this is that Drummond completed his "poems funerall" at least a year before Miss Cunningham's death.[35]

One must avoid in reading Drummond's work the romantic compulsion to insist that the artist express *real* feeling, that is, one must not claim that only art that is written from and relates to a personal experience is valid. To make this mistake is to dismiss, or to misinterpret, most of Renaissance art: to judge Jonson as a one or two poem poet ("On my first Sonne," "My Picture left in Scotland") and Donne as a chameleon of emotion and a posturing fraud.

We should too in the matter of originality be careful not to impose modern articles of faith on seventeenth-century practice. Drummond was an exceptionally derivative poet; modern scholarship has conclusively demonstrated that he borrowed, translated, paraphrased and imitated a wide number of writers, using the considerable resources of his reading as a mine for both his poetry and his prose. The list of his sources and models is long: Fowler and Alexander, Spenser, Daniel and Sidney, Du Bellay and Du Bartas, Tasso, Guarini and Marino, Garcilaso and Granada. Every country from Scotland to Spain is represented; hardly an author of note (Shakespeare, Montaigne, Ronsard, Bembo) cannot be cited for some passage or other.[36] Yet here again our attitude should be one of caution. Imitation in Drummond's day was encouraged by most authorities, and extensive borrowing was practised by most poets. Drummond may at times have overstepped the mark, but there was nothing that he touched that did not receive his own modifying imprint. He took what he needed, and transformed what he took. The synthesis seems unified, distinguished by Drummond's own decorative instinct, a collage that becomes more than all its parts.

In his notebooks one can see how he worked. He wrote out excerpts from his reading, translating if necessary into English. He made notes of decorative epithets, explained to himself obscure references, took account of rhymes, alliterations and rhetorical devices. From Jonson's masque *Hymenaei*, for instance, he marked down the rhymes "wast, past, tast, cast, last," (as a reminder of English rather than Scots pronunciation?) and noted especially the epithet "the bright Idalian starre" (as Jonson explained in his notes, this was Venus).[37] The charge of excessive imitation cannot be entirely discounted, but it should be modified by an understanding of seventeenth-century practice.

There is an overriding fondness in Drummond's work for the melancholic humour, and he is happiest when he is sad. His *Poems* are at their best when they are most sombre, and one can mark a mood of increasing confidence in those of the second part, the "poems funerall." This mood is at its most assured in the *Flowres of Sion*, which indeed form a climax to the two works. Here Drummond's favourite subjects, love of solitude, *contemptus mundi* and contemplation of the Christian solution, are presented as the solemn music of meditation. The language is weighty and often florid; there is the same attention paid to the sound of words. In the sonnets Drummond sometimes indulges himself in Italianate elaborations; read in isolation they may seem extreme and even grotesque, yet in the context of the whole they make their own effect. The Magdalene's hair is described as

> These Lockes, of blushing deeds the faire attire,
> Smooth-frizled Waves, sad shelfes which shadow deepe,
> Soule-stinging Serpents in gilt curles which creepe,
> To touch thy sacred Feete doe now aspire.[38]

The wit here is in the language, rather than the conceit, but wit there is, not so very far removed from that of the contemporary metaphysicals.

The five madrigals in *Flowres* lighten the heavy tread. Two in particular seem especially delicate: "The Permanencie of Life" and "The World a Game." These are naked emblems, morals without pictures (but far superior to anything done by Whitney, Wither or Quarles).

> This world a Hunting is,
> The Pray poore Man, the Nimrod fierce is Death,
> His speedie Grei-hounds are,
> Lust, sicknesse, Envie, Care,
> Strife that neere falles amisse,
> With all those ills which haunt us while wee breath.

xxi

Now, if (by chance) wee flie
Of these the eager Chase,
Old Age with stealing Pace,
Castes up his Nets, and there wee panting die.[39]

In all, I believe that the *Flowres* are the best of Drummond's verse.
The justly admired sonnet "For the Baptiste," with its witty climax

Who listned to his voyce, obey'd his crye?
Onelie the Ecchoes which hee made relent,
Rung from their Marble Caves, repent, repent.[40]

or the equally fine "Content and Resolute" have a fine rhythmic weight
to them. The whole work has an architectural splendour, and with the
possible exception of the incomplete "Shadow of the Judgement,"
which concludes the set, should be seen and read as one. The variety of
forms, from the sonnets which act as foundation, to the madrigals
as ornament, to the expansive hymns which carry the eye upwards
towards God, should be seen as a complete design, a cathedral in
verse. Here, as in the *Poems*, we should not look for narrative (though
there is a formal progression based on the life of Christ and the
Christian response), but instead see the *Flowres* as variations on con-
ventional religious themes.

The remainder of Drummond's poetry does not amount to much.
Jonson praised his *Forth Feasting*—written to celebrate the return of
King James to Scotland—but probably for politic considerations.[42] Of
its kind, it is well done, a judicious mixture of hyperbole and courtly
advice.

No Guard so sure as Love unto a Crown[43] the Scottish river tells her
king—a conventional piece of wisdom which however seems to have
been chosen by James as the subject for a court debate. (In a letter to
Sir William Alexander, Drummond hastened to substantiate his
argument and refute the Machiavellian contrary that kings must rule
by fear.)[44] Here as later in his dealing with the monarchy Drummond
takes a conservative line. In his verse written to welcome King Charles
to the city of Edinburgh in 1633 ("The Entertainment") he again
reminds his monarch of his duty, quite sharply, this time:

True *Honour* shall reside within thy Court,
Sobrietie, and *Truth* there still resort,
Keepe promis'd faith thou shalt, Supercheries
Detest, and beagling Marmosets despise,

Thou, others to make rich, shalt not make poore
Thy selfe, but give that thou mayst still give more;
Thou shalt no Paranymph raise to high place,
For frizl'd locks, quaint pace, or painted face. . . .[45]

Of his posthumously published verse, some satires deserve to be distinguished from the rest. The lines "A Character of the Anti-Covenanter, or Malignant" show Drummond's other side: no more the Petrarchan lover or pastoral Damon; instead a harsh, satirical ironist of spleen. These and other pieces are close to the tradition of Scottish flyting. None is cruder or more virulent than the hitherto unpublished "To Kite," a lampoon of some unfortunate woman whose sexual appetites were excessive.[46]

Towards the end of his life Drummond turned to history and politics, and reflecting the troubled times, his writing is often bitter in tone and disillusioned in mood. Gone is the Stoical, neo-Platonic and Christian resignation of *A Cypresse Grove*, gone the reflective melancholy, gone the indulgent meditation, and in their place we find impassioned pleas for reasonableness and half-cynical demands for moderation.[47] His long and derivative *History of Scotland* is undistinguished as history, but it is notable for a number of Livian political speeches whose subject is toleration of religion and moderation in government. Written during the 1630's, these are clearly topical. The *History* was unpublished in his lifetime, as were his political pamphlets, and these too show the same concern for sanity in a time of civil disturbance, a time indeed when

"The best lack all conviction, while the worst
Are full of passionate intensity."

I find these pieces brave and dignified, echoing the more catholic and humanistic sentiments of an earlier age.

In his critical opinions as in his political life, Drummond was a conservative. He thought Petrarch the best and most exquisite poet on the subject of love; he admired Sidney and Alexander. Daniel he liked for sweetness in rhyming, Drayton for his *Poly-Olbion*, and Sylvester for his translations of Du Bartas. John Donne he thought second to none among the "Anacreonick Lyricks," that is, the non-Petrarchan love poets.[48]

He had a very firm idea of what poetry was, based on a theory of classical and Renaissance tradition: decorum in genre, subject and execution. He was out of sympathy with poetry that did not seem to conform with this tradition; the work of Donne probably, and Malherbe. His letter to Dr Arthur Johnston makes this clear. Poesy endures, he says, though

> In vaine have some men of late [Transformeres of
> evrye thing) consulted upon her reformation, and
> endevured to abstracte her to Metaphysicall Ideas,
> and Scholasticall Quiddityes, denuding her of
> her own Habites and those ornamentes with which shee
> hath amused the World some thousand yeeres.

Not an innovator himself, Drummond understood very well the traditions of poetry.

*   *   *

My intention in this edition is to present a comprehensive selection of Drummond's work. I have printed the whole of the *Poems* (with the exception of the unincorporated madrigals and epigrams and the divine poems of the *Urania*) in the belief that they form a cohesive whole. Seeing the *Flowres of Sion* (which grew from the sonnets of the *Urania*) as a natural conclusion to the *Poems*, and again as designed as a whole, I have printed all of these with the exception of the long and in-complete "Shadow of the Judgement." The occasional pieces, *Teares on the Death of Moeliades* and *Forth Feasting* are given in part, as are some lines from *The Entertainment*. I have only included what seemed to me the best of Drummond's posthumously published verse.

Of the prose, it seemed proper to print the whole of *A Cypresse Grove* (surely among the best of all seventeenth-century essays). To this I have added some selections from Drummond's *History* and political pamphlets, and his brief journal or "Memorialls." The "Conversations" with Jonson can be read elsewhere.

The texts of most of the poetry and *A Cypresse Grove* are based, with kind permission, upon those of the Scottish Text Society and the Manchester University Press. Other texts rely on the earliest printed edition, collated whenever possible with Drummond's fair copy in the Hawthornden MSS. A couple of poems are published here for the first time; again the source is the Hawthornden MSS. I have aimed in my annotations at providing the reader with an answer to all obvious obscurity, whether classical references, archaisms, or difficult words, though I have not thought it necessary to explain every classical epithet. The reader who wishes to look into the question of Drummond's sources is referred, in the first place, to L. E. Kastner's *S.T.S.* edition. I have not attempted to modernize Drummond's spelling or capitalization, beyond making "u" and "v" and "i" and "j" conform to current usage, and expanding whatever contractions appeared in the texts. Similarly, I have not tampered with Drummond's punctuation, believing that it is logical and consistent.

INTRODUCTION — NOTES

1. John Sage was co-editor, with Thomas Ruddiman, of the collected edition of Drummond's *Works* (Edinburgh, 1711).
2. *Drummond of Hawthornden: the Story of his Life and Writings* (London, 1873).
3. *A Critical Study of William Drummond of Hawthornden* (New York, 1952).
4. See my *The Library of Drummond of Hawthornden* (Edinburgh, 1971).
5. See L. E. Kastner, *The Poetical Works of William Drummond*, Scottish Text Society, 2 vols. (Edinburgh, 1913), Vol. I, for bibliographical information.
6. See *The Library*, pp. 11–13.
7. See Kastner, Vol. II, for an iconography.
8. Based on unpublished evidence in the Hawthornden MSS.
9. In a dedication accompanying the gift of some poems to George Preston of Craigmillar Drummond wrote "Read these verses bred under the calme shades of your landes and written to the notes of the solitarie Nightingal on the bankes of the Eske. . . ." Hawthornden MSS, N.L.S. MS 2061, f. 131r.
10. The full inscription is given by Masson, p. 289.
11. Hawthornden MSS, N.L.S. MS 2061, f. 146r.
12. See *The Library*, p. 22.
13. Drummond's correspondence is printed (clumsily) in the *Works* (1711). Other letters were printed from the Hawthornden MSS by David Laing in *Archaeologia Scotica* IV (Transactions of the Society of Antiquaries of Scotland, Edinburgh, 1857).
14. In 1620 Alexander wrote to Drummond to report on the latest progress: "I Received your last Letter, with the Psalm you sent, which I think very well done: I had done the same, long before it came, but he prefers his own to all else, tho' perchance, when you see it, you will think it the worse of the Three. No Man must meddle with that Subject, and therefore I advise you to take no more Pains therein. . . ." *Works* (1711), p. 151.
15. See *The Library*, pp. 143–4, pp. 228–31.
16. R. H. MacDonald, "Drummond of Hawthornden: the Season at Bourges, 1607," *Comparative Drama*, IV (1970), 89–109.

17. Hawthornden MSS, N.L.S. MS 2061, f. 74r, MS 2063, f. 65r, and elsewhere.
18. See his essay on impresas and anagrams, *Works* (1711), pp. 228–9.
19. Hawthornden MSS, N.L.S. MS 2060, f. 68r, f. 63r, f. 25v.
20. Hawthornden MSS, N.L.S. MS 2060, f. 16v.
21. Masson, pp. 156–61.
22. Hawthornden MSS, N.L.S. MS 2066, ff. 70–71.
23. *Works of Ben Jonson*, ed. C. H. Herford and Percy Simpson (Oxford, 1925), I, 135.
24. Drummond was not the only writer in English to be influenced: Crashaw also took Marino for a model.
25. After recording the opinions of Jonson on various Italian and French poets, Drummond remarks "all this was to no purpose, for he neither doeth understand French nor Italianne." Herford and Simpson, I, 134.
26. Madrigal vi, *Poems* (The First Part).
27. Sonnet xxviii, *Poems* (The First Part).
28. Song ii, *Poems* (The First Part).
29. *A Cypresse Grove*, in this edition p. 157.
30. See the "Notes on the Poems and Prose" for a summary of information on Drummond's sources.
31. *Teares on the Death of Moeliades*, ll. 97–100.
32. *Teares*, ll. 119–20.
33. From an unpublished sonnet, Hawthornden MSS, N.L.S. MS 2062, f. 156v.
34. See Kastner's notes.
35. See R. H. MacDonald, "Drummond of Hawthornden, Miss Euphemia Kyninghame, and the *Poems*," *MLR*, LX(1965), 494–9.
36. For a discussion of this question see my chapter on Drummond as a writer in *The Library*, pp. 22–31. My summary of the theory of imitation is accurate, I believe, although my tone is harsh and disapproving, and I think, unfair to Drummond's own merits.
37. Hawthornden MSS, N.L.S. MS 2060, f. 294v. Drummond found much esoteric information in the notes printed with the work of Jonson and Ronsard. He also used handy poetical references works like the *Epitheta* and the *Officina* of Ravisius Textor.
38. Sonnet xii, *Flowres of Sion*.
39. Madrigal iv, *Flowres of Sion*.
40. Sonnet xi, *Flowres of Sion*.
41. Sonnet xxiv, *Flowres of Sion*.
42. "Yett that he wished to please the King, that piece of Forth-Feasting had been his owne." Herford and Simpson, I, 135.
43. *Forth Feasting*, l. 246.
44. Hawthornden MSS, N.L.S. MS 2062, ff. 237–40.
45. Jove's speech, *The Entertainment*, in this edition p. 134.
46. See Satirical Verses, v.
47. For a discussion of Drummond's political opinions see Thomas I. Rae, "The Political Attitudes of William Drummond of Hawthornden," in *The Scottish Tradition: Essays presented to R. G. Cant*, ed. G. W. S. Barrow (Edinburgh, 1974), pp. 132–46.
48. See the "Character of Several Authors," in *Works* (1711), p. 226.

SELECT BIBLIOGRAPHY

The authoritative edition is *The Poetical Works of William Drummond of Hawthornden*, edited by L. E. Kastner (Scottish Text Society, 2 vols., Edinburgh, 1913). This includes the prose essay *A Cypresse Grove*. Drummond's *History of Scotland*, his political pamphlets and other prose pieces are not readily accessible, the most recent and in some cases the only edition being the *Works* (Edinburgh, 1711). Some additional poems from the Hawthornden MSS are printed in French Rowe Fogle, *A Critical Study of William Drummond of Hawthornden* (New York, 1952). A recent and sympathetic appreciation of Drummond's work can be found in R. D. S. Jack, *The Italian Influence on Scottish Literature* (London, 1972). The Victorian life by David Masson, *Drummond of Hawthornden: The Story of his Life and Writings* (London, 1873) is still useful. Additional biographical detail, together with a study of Drummond's intellectual and cultural background, can be found in the editor's *The Library of Drummond of Hawthornden* (Edinburgh, 1971). For a detailed discussion of Drummond as historian see Thomas I. Rae, "The Historical Writing of Drummond of Hawthornden," in *The Scottish Historical Review*, LIV (1975), 22–66.

POEMS

TEARES ON THE DEATH
OF MŒLIADES

O *Heavens!* then is it true that Thou art gone,
And left this woefull *Ile* her Losse to mone,
Mœliades? bright *Day-Starre* of the *West*,
A *Comet*, blazing Terrour to the *East*:
And neither that thy *Spright* so heavenlywise,   5
Nor *Bodie* (though of *Earth*) more pure than *Skies*,
Nor royall *Stemme*, nor thy sweet tender *Age*,
Of adamantine *Fates* could quench the *Rage?*
O fading *Hopes!* O short-while-lasting *Joy!*
Of Earth-borne Man, which one Houre can destroy!   10
Then even of *Vertues* Spoyles *Death* Trophees reares,
As if hee gloried most in many Teares.
Forc'd by grimme *Destines*, *Heavens* neglect our Cryes,
Starres seeme set only to acte *Tragœdies*:
And let them doe their *Worst*, since thou art gone,   15
Raise whom they list to Thrones, enthron'd dethrone,
Staine Princely *Bowres* with *Blood*, and even to *Gange*,
In *Cypresse* sad, glad *Hymens Torches* change.
Ah! thou hast left to live, and in the Time,
When scarce thou blossom'd in thy pleasant Prime,   20
So falles by Northerne Blast a virgine *Rose*,
At halfe that doth her bashfull Bosome close . . .

★   ★   ★

l. 5 *Spright*. Spirit.
l. 8 *adamantine*. Unalterable.
l. 17 *Gange*. The river Ganges, thus, the end of the world.
l. 18 *Cypresse . . . change*. Change wedding ornaments to funeral.

Chaste *Maides* which haunt faire *Aganippe Well*,
And you in *Tempes* sacred *Shade* who dwell,
Let fall your Harpes, cease Tunes of Joy to sing,
Discheveled make all *Parnassus* ring   100
With *Antheames* sad, thy Musicke *Phœbus* turne
In dolefull Plaints, whilst *Joy* it selfe doth mourne:
Dead is thy *Darling*, who decor'd thy Bayes,
Who oft was wont to cherish thy sweet Layes,
And to a *Trumpet* raise thine amorous *Stile*,   105
That floting *Delos* envie might this *Ile*.
You *Acidalian* Archers breake your Bowes,
Your Brandons quench, with Teares blot *Beauties* Snowes,
And bid your weeping *Mother* yet againe
A second *Adons* Death, nay, *Marses* plaine: 110
His *Eyes* once were your Darts, nay, even his *Name*
Where ever heard, did every *Heart* inflame:
Tagus did court his Love, with *golden Streames*,
Rhein with his *Townes*, faire *Seine*, with *all shee claimes*.
But *ah* (poore Lovers) *Death* did them betrey,   115
And (not suspected) made their *Hopes* his *Prey*!
Tagus bewailes his *Losse*, with *golden Streames*,
Rhein with his *Townes*, faire *Seine* with *all shee claimes*.
Mœliades sweet courtly *Nymphes* deplore,
From *Thuly* to *Hydaspes* pearlie Shore.   120
Delicious *Meads*, whose checkred *Plaine* foorth brings,
White, golden, azure Flowres, which once were Kings,
In mourning *Blacke*, their *shining Colours* dye,

---

ll. 97-8   *Chaste Maides . . . dwell.* The Muses and followers of Apollo, god of
              poetry.
l. 103   *Bayes.* Laurel leaves.
l. 106   *Delos.* Delos, which was supposed to float on the sea, was the birthplace
              of Apollo.
l. 107   *Acidalian Archers.* The bowmen of Venus, thus cupids.
l. 108   *Brandons.* Torches.
l. 110   *Adons Death.* Adonis, beloved of Venus, was killed by a boar.
              Marses. Mars, god of war.
l. 120   *Thuly.* Thule, the northernmost land (Iceland, or the Shetlands?)
              Hydaspes. A tributary of the river Indus and easternmost boundary of
              Alexander's conquests; thus, the end of the world.
l. 122   *White, golden, azure Flowres . . .* Narcissus, crocus, hyacinth: they were
              once the youths Narcissus, Crocus and Hyacinthus.

Bow downe their Heads, whilst sighing *Zephyres* flye.
Queene of the Fields, whose Blush makes blushe the
Morne,   125
Sweet *Rose*, a Princes Death in *Purple* mourne,
O *Hyacinthes*, for ay your *AI* keepe still,
Nay, with moe Markes of *Woe* your Leaves now fill:
And you, O *Flowre* of *Helens* Teares first borne,
Into those liquide Pearles againe you turne.   130
Your greene Lockes, *Forrests*, cut, in weeping *Myrrhes*,
The deadly *Cypresse*, and Inke-dropping *Firres*,
Your *Palmes* and *Mirtles* change; from Shadowes darke
Wing'd *Syrens* waile, and you sad *Ecchoes* marke
The lamentable Accents of their Mone,   135
And plaine that brave *Mœliades* is gone.
Stay *Skie* thy turning Course, and now become
A stately *Arche*, unto the *Earth* his Tombe:
Over which ay the watrie *Iris* keepe,
And sad *Electras* Sisters which still weepe.   140
Mœliades sweet courtly *Nymphes* deplore,
From *Thuly* to *Hydaspes* pearlie Shore.
    Deare *Ghost*, forgive these our untimely Teares,
By which our loving Minde, though weake, appeares,
Our Losse not Thine (when wee complaine) wee weepe,   145
For thee the glistring Walles of *Heaven* doe keepe,
Beyond the *Planets* Wheeles, above that Source
Of Spheares, that turnes the lower in its Course,
Where *Sunne* doth never set, nor ugly *Night*
Ever appeares in mourning Garments dight: 150
Where *Boreas* stormie Trumpet doth not sound,
Nor Cloudes in Lightnings bursting, Minds astound.
From *Cares* cold Climates farre, and hote *Desire*,
Where *Time* is banish'd, *Ages* ne're expire:
Amongst pure Sprights environed with Beames,   155

l. 127 *Hyacinthes* . . .   The hyacinth supposedly spelled out the letters
AI (alas!).
l. 129 *Flowre of Helens Teares.* The herb elecampane.
l. 139 *Iris.* Goddess of the rainbow.
l. 140 *Electras Sisters.*   The Pleiades, made a constellation after their death.
l. 151 *Boreas.* The north wind.
l. 155 *Sprights.* Spirits.

Thou think'st all things below to bee but Dreames,
And joy'st to looke downe to the azur'd Barres
Of *Heaven*, indented all with streaming *Starres*;
And in their turning *Temples* to behold,
In silver Robe the *Moone*, the *Sunne* in Gold,   160
Like young Eye-speaking *Lovers* in a Dance,
With Majestie by Turnes retire, advance,
Thou wondrest *Earth* to see hang like a Ball,
Clos'd in the gastly *Cloyster* of this *All*:
And that poore *Men* should prove so madly fond,   165
To tosse themselves for a small Foot of Ground.
Nay, that they even dare brave the *Powers* above,
From this base *Stage* of Change, that cannot move.
All worldly Pompe and Pride thou seest arise
Like Smoake, that scattreth in the emptie Skies.   170
Other *Hilles* and *Forrests*, other sumptuous *Towres*,
Amaz'd thou find'st, excelling our poore Bowres,
Courts voyde of Flatterie, of Malice *Mindes*,
Pleasure which lasts, not such as *Reason* blindes:
Farre sweeter Songs thou hear'st and Carrolings,   175
Whilst *Heavens* doe dance, and *Quire* of *Angells* sings,
Than moldie *Mindes* could faine, even our *Annoy*
(If it approach that Place) is chang'd in Joy.
    Rest blessed *Spright*, rest saciate with the Sight
Of him, whose Beames both dazell and delight,   180
Life of all Lives, *Cause* of each other Cause,
The *Spheare*, and *Center*, where the *Minde* doth pause:
Narcissus of himselfe, himselfe the *Well*,
Lover, and *Beautie*, that doth all excell.
Rest happie *Ghost*, and wonder in that *Glasse*,   185
Where seene is all that *shall be*, *is*, or *was*,
While *shall be*, *is*, or *was* doe passe away,
And nought remaine but an *Eternall Day*.
For ever rest, thy Praise *Fame* may enroule
In golden Annalles, whilst about the *Pole*   190
The slow *Boötes* turnes, or *Sunne* doth rise
With skarlet Scarfe, to cheare the mourning *Skies*:

l. 177 *moldie*. Earth-born.
l. 191 *Boötes*, Arcturus, the constellation.

6

The Virgines to thy Tombe may Garlands beare
Of Flowres, and on each Flowre let fall a Teare.
Mœliades sweet courtly *Nymphes* deplore,
From *Thuly* to *Hydaspes* pearlie Shore.

195

POEMS

THE FIRST PART

Sonnet i

In my first Yeeres, and *Prime* yet not at Hight,
When sweet Conceits my Wits did entertaine,
Ere *Beauties* Force I knew or false Delight,
Or to what Oare shee did her Captives chaine;
Led by a sacred Troupe of *Phœbus* Traine,   5
I first beganne to reade, then Love to write,
And so to praise a perfect Red and White,
But (God wot) wist not what was in my Braine:
Love smylde to see in what an awfull Guise
I turn'd those *Antiques* of the Age of Gold,   10
And that I might moe *Mysteries* behold,
Hee set so faire a *Volumne* to mine Eyes,
    That I [quires clos'd which (dead) dead Sighs but breath]
    Joye on this *living Booke* to reade my Death.

l. 5 *Phœbus Traine*. Followers of Phoebus or Apollo, god of poetry and music.
l. 7 *Red and White*. Female beauty.
l. 10 *Antiques of the Age of Gold*. Classical forms.
l. 11. *moe*. More.
l. 13 *quires*. Book leaves.

Sonnet ii

I know that all beneath the *Moone* decayes,
And what by Mortalles in this World is brought,
In *Times* great Periods shall returne to nought,
That fairest States have fatall Nights and Dayes:
I know how all the *Muses* heavenly Layes,   5

8

With Toyle of Spright which are so dearely bought,
As *idle Sounds* of few, or none are sought,
And that nought lighter is than airie Praise.
I know fraile *Beautie* like the purple Flowre,
To which one Morne oft Birth and Death affords,   10
That Love a Jarring is of Mindes Accords,
Where *Sense* and *Will* invassall *Reasons* Power:
    Know what I list, this all can not mee move,
    But that (*ô mee!*) I both must write, and love.

l. 6   *Toyle of Spright.* Work of Angel(s); inspiration.

Sonnet iii

Yee who so curiously doe paint your Thoughts,
Enlightning ev'rie Line in such a Guise,
That they seeme rather to have fallen from Skies,
Than of a humane Hand bee mortall Draughts;
In one Part *Sorrow* so tormented lies,   5
As if his Life at ev'ry Sigh would parte,
Love here blindfolded stands with Bow and Dart,
There *Hope* lookes pale, *Despaire* with rainie Eyes:
Of my rude Pincell looke not for such *Arte*,
My Wit I finde now lessened to devise   10
So high Conceptions to expresse my Smart,
And some thinke Love but fain'd, if too too wise:
    These troubled Words and Lines confus'd you finde,
    Are like unto their Modell *my sicke Minde.*

Sonnet iv

Faire is my Yoke, though grievous bee my Paines,
Sweet are my Wounds, although they deeply smart,
My Bit is Gold, though shortned bee the Raines,
My Bondage brave, though I may not depart:
Although I burne, the Fire which doth impart   5
Those Flames, so sweet reviving Force containes,

9

That (like *Arabias* Bird) my wasted Heart
Made quicke by Death, more lively still remaines.
I joye, though oft my waking Eyes spend Teares,
I never want Delight, even when I grone,   10
Best companied when most I am alone,
A Heaven of Hopes I have midst Hells of Feares:
   Thus every Way Contentment strange I finde,
   But most in Her rare Beautie, my rare Minde.

l. 7 *Arabias Bird*. The phoenix.

Sonnet v

How that vaste Heaven intitled *First* is rold,
If any other *Worlds* beyond it lie,
And *People* living in Eternitie,
Or *Essence* pure that doth this *All* uphold:
What Motion have those *fixed Sparkes* of Gold,   5
The *wandring Carbuncles* which shine from hie,
By Sprights, or Bodies, contrare-Wayes in Skie
If they bee turn'd, and mortall Things behold:
How *Sunne* postes Heaven about, how *Nights pale Queene*
With borrowed Beames lookes on this hanging *Round*,   10
What Cause faire *Iris* hath, and Monsters seene
In Aires large Fields of Light, and Seas profound,
   Did hold my wandring Thoughts; when thy sweet Eye
   Bade mee leave all, and only thinke on Thee.

l. 7 *Sprights*. Spirits.
l. 11 *Iris*. Goddess of the rainbow.

Sonnet vi

Vaunt not, faire *Heavens*, of your two glorious Lights,
Which though most bright, yet see not when they shine,
And shining, cannot shew their Beames divine
Both in one Place, but parte by Dayes and Nights,
Earth, vaunt not of those Treasures yee enshrine,   5
Held only deare because hidde from our Sights,

Your pure and burnish'd Gold, your Diamonds fine,
Snow-passing Ivorie that the Eye delights:
Nor *Seas* of those deare Wares are in you found,
Vaunt not, rich Pearle, red Corrall, which doe stirre   10
A fond Desire in Fooles to plunge your Ground;
Those all (more faire) are to bee had in Her:
    Pearle, Ivorie, Corrall, Diamond, Sunnes, Gold,
    Teeth, Necke, Lips, Heart, Eyes, Haire, are to behold.

Sonnet vii

That learned *Græcian* (who did so excell
In Knowledge passing Sense, that hee is nam'd
Of all the after-Worlds *Divine*) doth tell,
That at the Time when first our Soules are fram'd,
Ere in these Mansions blinde they come to dwell,   5
They live bright Rayes of that *Eternall Light*,
And others see, know, love, in Heavens great Hight,
Not toylde with ought to *Reason* doth rebell;
Most true it is, for straight at the first Sight
My Minde mee told, that in some other Place   10
It elsewhere saw the *Idea* of that Face,
And lov'd a Love of heavenly pure Delight.
    No Wonder now I feele so faire a Flame,
    Sith I Her lov'd ere on this *Earth* shee came.

l. 1   *That learned Græcian*. Plato.
l. 8   *Not toylde . . . rebell*. Not tied to the flesh.
l. 11   *the Idea*. The Neo-Platonic idea; see Notes.

Sonnet viii

Now while the *Night* her sable Vaile hath spred,
And silently her restie Coach doth rolle,
Rowsing with Her from TETHIS azure Bed
Those starrie *Nymphes* which dance about the Pole,

l. 2   *restie*. Restive.
l. 3   *Tethis azure Bed*. The sea.

While Cʏɴᴛʜɪᴀ, in purest Cipres cled,   5
The *Latmian* Shepheard in a Trance descries,
And whiles lookes pale from hight of all the Skies,
Whiles dyes her Beauties in a bashfull Red,
While *Sleepe* (in Triumph) closed hath all Eyes,
And Birds and Beastes a Silence sweet doe keepe,   10
And Pʀᴏᴛᴇᴜs monstrous People in the Deepe,
The Winds and Waves (husht up) to rest entise,
    I wake, muse, weepe, and who my Heart hath slaine
    See still before me to augment my Paine.

ll. 5–6 *Cynthia . . . descries.* Cynthia or Selene the moon-goddess loved Endym-
    ion, a shepherd of Mount Latmos.

Sonnet ix

Sleepe, Silence Child, sweet Father of soft Rest,
Prince whose Approach Peace to all Mortalls brings,
Indifferent Host to Shepheards and to Kings,
Sole Comforter of Minds with Griefe opprest.
Loe, by thy charming Rod all breathing things   5
Lie slumbring, with forgetfulnesse possest,
And yet o're me to spred thy drowsie Wings
Thou spares (alas) who cannot be thy Guest.
Since I am thine, O come, but with that Face
To inward Light which thou art wont to show,   10
With fained Solace ease a true felt Woe,
Or if *deafe God* thou doe denie that Grace,
    Come as thou wilt, and what thou wilt bequeath,
    I long to kisse the *Image of my Death*.

Sonnet x

Faire *Moone* who with thy Cold and Silver Shine
Makes sweet the Horrour of the dreadfull *Night*,
Delighting the weake Eye with Smiles divine,
Which Pʜᴇʙᴜs dazells with his too much Light.
Bright Queene of the *first Heaven*, if in thy Shrine   5

By turning oft, and Heavens eternall Might,
Thou hast not yet that *once sweet Fire* of thine
ENDEMION, forgot, and Lovers Plight?
If Cause like thine may Pitie breede in thee,
And Pitie somewhat els to it obtaine,   10
Since thou hast Power of Dreames as well as Hee
Who paints strange Figures in the slumbring Braine:
    Now while She sleepes in dolefull Guise her Show
    These Teares, and the blacke *Mappe* of all my Woe.

l. 8   *Endemion*. The shepherd loved by Selene; see sonnet viii.

Sonnet *xi*

Lampe of Heavens Christall Hall that brings the Hours,
Eye-dazaler who makes the uglie *Night*
At thine Approach flie to her slumbrie Bowrs,
And fills the World with Wonder and Delight:
Life of all Lifes, Death-giver by thy Flight   5
To Southerne Pole from these six Signes of ours,
Gold-smith of all the Starres, with Silver bright
Who *Moone* enamells, *Apelles* of the Flowrs.
Ah, from those watrie Plaines thy golden Head
Raise up, and bring the so long lingring *Morne*,   10
A Grave, nay Hell, I finde become this Bed,
This Bed so grievously where I am torne:
    But (woe is me) though thou now brought the Day,
    Day shall but serve more Sorrowe to display.

l. 6   *Six Signes*. The winter signs of the zodiac.
l. 8   *Apelles*. The classical painter; thus, the sun paints the flowers.

Song *i*

It was the time when to our Northerne Pole
The brightest Lampe of Heaven beginnes to rolle,
When Earth more wanton in new Robes appeareth,
And scorning Skies her Flowrs in Raine-bowes beareth,

13

On which the *Aire* moist *Saphires* doth bequeath,   5
Which quake to feele the kissing *Zephires* breath:
When *Birds* from shadie *Groves* their *Love* foorth warble,
And *Sea* like *Heaven, Heaven* lookes like smoothest *Marble,*
When *I,* in simple *Course,* free from all *Cares,*
Farre from the muddie *Worlds* captiving *Snares,*   10
By *Oras* flowrie *Bancks* alone did wander,
Ora that sports her like to old *Meander,*
A *Floud* more worthie *Fame* and lasting *Praise*
Than that which *Phaetons* Fall so high did raise:
Into whose mooving *Glasse* the *Milk-white Lillies*   15
Doe dresse their *Tresses* and the *Daffadillies.*
Where *Ora* with a *Wood* is crown'd about
And seemes forget the *Way* how to come out,
A *Place* there is, where a delicious *Fountaine*
Springs from the swelling *Paps* of a proud *Mountaine,*   20
Whose falling *Streames* the quiet *Caves* doe wound,
And make the *Ecchoes* shrill resound that *Sound.*
The *Lawrell* there the shining *Channell* graces,
The *Palme* her *Love* with long-stretch'd *Armes* embraces,
The *Poplar* spreds her *Branches* to the *Skie,*   25
And hides from sight that azure *Cannopie.*
The *Streames* the *Trees,* the *Trees* their leaves still nourish,
That *Place* grave *Winter* finds not without *Flourish.*
If living *Eyes* Elysian fields could see
This little *Arden* might *Elysium* bee.   30
Here *Diane* often used to repose *Her,*
And *Acidalias Queene* with *Mars* rejoyce her:
The *Nymphes* oft here doe bring their *Maunds* with *Flowres,*
And *Anadeames* weave for their *Paramours,*
The *Satyres* in those *Shades* are heard to languish,   35
And make the *Shepheards Partners* of their *Anguish,*
The *Shepheards* who in *Barkes* of tender *Trees*
Doe grave their *Loves, Disdaines,* and *Jelousies,*
Which *Phillis* when there by *Her Flockes* she feedeth

l. 11   *Oras.* The river Ore in Fife, scene of the poet's idyll.
l. 30   *Arden.* The English pastoral country.
l. 32   *Acidalias Queene.* Venus.
l. 33   *Maunds.* Baskets.
l. 34   *Anadeames.* Wreaths.

14

With Pitie whyles, sometime with laughter reedeth.   40
   Neare to this place when Sunne in midst of Day,
In highest top of Heaven his Coach did stay,
And (as advising) on his Carier glanced
The way did rest, the space he had advanced
His panting Steeds along those Fields of light,   45
Most princely looking from that gastly hight:
When most the Grashoppers are heard in Meadowes,
And loftie Pines have small, or els no Shadowes,
It was my hap, O wofull hap! to bide
Where thickest Shades me from all Rayes did hide   50
Into a shut-up-place, some Sylvans *Chamber,*
Whose Seeling spred was with the Lockes of Amber
Of new-bloom'd Sicamors, Floore wrought with Flowres,
More sweete and rich than those in Princes Bowres.
Here Adon *blush't, and* Clitia *all amazed*   55
Lookt pale, with Him who in the Fountaine gazed,
The Amaranthus *smyl'd, and that sweet Boy*
Which sometime was the God of Delos *joy:*
The brave Carnation, speckled Pinke here shined,
The Violet her fainting Head declined   60
Beneath a drowsie Chasbow, all of Gold
The Marigold her leaves did here unfold.
   Now while that ravish'd with delight and wonder,
Halfe in a trance I lay those Arches under,
The season, silence, place, did all entise   65
Eyes heavie lids to bring Night on their Skies,
Which softly having stollen themselves together
(Like Evening Clouds) me plac'd I wote not whether.
As Cowards leave the Fort which they should keepe
My senses one by one gave place to Sleepe,   70
Who followed with a Troupe of golden Slombers
Thrust from my quiet Braine all base Encombers,
And thrise me touching with his Rod of Gold,
A Heaven of Visions in my Temples roll'd,
To countervaile those Pleasures were bereft me,   75

ll. 55 *et seq. Adon blush't* . . . The anemone, the heliotrope, and various other
    flowers.
l. 61 *Chasbow.* The poppy.
l. 75 *countervaile.* Counterbalance.

15

Thus in his silent Prison clos'd he left me.
     Me thought through all the Neighbour Woods a noyce
Of Quiristers, more sweet than Lute or voyce,
(For those harmonious sounds to JOVE are given
By the swift touches of the nyne-string'd Heaven,   80
Such are, and nothing else) did wound mine Eare,
No Soule, that then became all Eare to heare:
And whilst I listning lay O gastly wonder!
I saw a pleasant Mirtle cleave asunder,
A Mirtle great with birth, from whose rent wombe   85
Three naked Nymphes more white than snow foorth come.
For Nymphes they seem'd, about their heavenly Faces
In Waves of Gold did flow their curling Tresses,
About each Arme, their Armes more white than milke,
Each weare a blushing Armelet of silke,   90
The Goddesses such were that by Scamander,
Appeared to the Phrygian Alexander,
Aglaia, and her Sisters such perchance
Be, when about some sacred Spring they dance.
But scarce the Grove their naked Beauties graced,   95
And on the amorous Verdure had not traced,
When to the Floud they ran, the Floud in Robes
Of curling Christall to brests Ivorie Globes
Who wrapt them all about, yet seem'd take pleasure
To showe warme Snowes throughout her liquid Azure.   100
     Looke howe Prometheus Man when heavenly Fire
First gave him Breath Dayes Brandon did admire,
And wondred of this Worlds Amphitheater,
So gaz'd I on those new guests of the Water.
All three were faire, yet one excell'd as farre   105
The rest, as Phebus doth the Cyprian Starre,
Or Diamonds small Gemmes, or Gemmes doe other,
Or Pearles that shining shell is call'd their Mother.
     Her haire more bright than are the Mornings Beames
Hang in a golden shower above the Streames,   110

l. 80   *Nyne-string'd Heaven.* The heavenly spheres (making heavenly music).
l. 93   *Aglaia.* Youngest of the three Graces.
l. 101   *Prometheus Man.* Prometheus created man from clay and gave him fire.
l. 102   *Dayes Brandon.* The torch of the day, thus the sun.
l. 106   *Cyprian Starre.* Venus.

And (*sweetly tous'd*) *her forehead sought to cover,*
Which seene did straight a Skie of Milke discover,
With two faire Browes, Loves *Bowes, which never bend*
But that a Golden Arrow foorth they send.
Beneath the which two burning Planets *glancing*   115
Flasht Flames of Love, for Love *there still is dancing.*
Her either Cheeke resembl'd a blushing Morne,
Or Roses Gueules *in field of Lillies borne:*
Betwixt the which a Wall so faire is raised,
That it is but abased even when praised.   120
Her Lips like Rowes of Corrall soft did swell,
And th' one like th' other only doth excell:
The Tyrian *Fish lookes pale, pale looke the Roses,*
The Rubies pale, when Mouthes sweet Cherrie closes.
Her Chinne like silver Phebe *did appeare*   125
Darke in the midst to make the rest more cleare:
Her Necke seem'd fram'd by curious Phidias *Master,*
Most smooth, most white, a piece of Alabaster.
Two foaming Billowes flow'd upon her Brest,
Which did their tops with Corrall red encrest: 130
There all about as Brookes them sport at leasure,
With Circling Branches veines did swell in Azure:
Within those Crookes are only found those Isles
Which Fortunate *the dreaming old World Stiles.*
The rest the Streames did hide, but as a Lillie   135
Suncke in a Christalls faire transparent Bellie.
       I, who yet humane weaknesse did not know
(For yet I had not felt that Archers Bow,
Ne could I thinke that from the coldest Water
The winged Youngling burning Flames could scatter)   140
On every part my vagabounding Sight
Did cast, and drowne mine Eyes in sweet Delight.
What wondrous Thing is this that Beautie's *named*
(Said I) I finde I heretofore have dreamed?
And never knowne in all my flying Dayes   145

l. 118   *Gueules.* Red.
l. 125   *silver Phebe.* The moon.
l. 127   *Phidias Master.* The instructor of the famous Greek sculptor.
ll. 133-4   *those Isles . . . Stiles.* The Blessed Isles; heaven.
l. 140   *winged Youngling.* Cupid.

17

Good unto this, that only merites Praise.
My Pleasures have beene Paines, my Comforts Crosses,
My Treasure Povertie, my Gaines but Losses.
O precious Sight! which none doth els descrie
Except the burning Sunne, and quivering I.   150
And yet O deare bought Sight! O would for ever
I might enjoy you, or had joy'd you never!
O happie Floud! if so yee might abide,
Yet ever glorie of this Moments Pride,
Adjure your Rillets all now to beholde Her,   155
And in their Christall Armes to come and fold Her:
And sith yee may not ay your Blisse embrace,
Draw thousand Pourtraits of Her on your Face,
Pourtraits which in my Heart be more apparent,
If like to yours my Brest but were transparent.   160
O that I were while she doth in you play,
A Daulphine to transport Her to the Sea,
To none of all those Gods I would Her rander
From Thule to Inde though I should with Her wander.
Oh! what is this? the more I fixe mine Eye,   165
Mine Eye the more new Wonders doth espie,
The more I spie, the more in uncouth fashion
My Soule is ravish'd in a pleasant Passion.
     But looke not Eyes, as more I would have said
A Sound of whirling Wheeles me all dismayde,   170
And with the Sound foorth from the timorous Bushes
With storme-like Course a sumptuous Chariot rushes,
A Chariot all of Gold, the Wheeles were Gold,
The Nailes, and Axetree Gold on which it roll'd:
The upmost Part, a Scarlet Vaile did cover,   175
More rich than Danaes Lap spred with her Lover:
In midst of it in a triumphing Chaire,
A Ladie sate miraculously faire,
Whose pensive Countenance, and Lookes of Honor,
Doe more allure the Mind that thinketh on Her,   180

l. 155   *Rillets.* Rivulets.
l. 163   *Rander.* Render.
l. 164   *Thule to Inde.* From the northernmost land to India.
l. 174   *Axetree.* Axle.
l. 176   *Danaes Lap.* Zeus appeared to Danae in a shower of gold.

Than the most wanton Face and amorous Eyes,
That Amathus or flowrie Paphos sees.
A Crue of Virgins made a Ring about Her,
The Diamond shee, they seeme the Gold without Her.
Such Thetis is when to the Billowes rore   185
With Mermaids nyce shee danceth on the Shore:
So in a sable Night the Sunnes bright Sister
Among the lesser twinckling Lights doth glister.
Faire Yoakes of Ermelines, whose Colour passe
The whitest Snowes on aged Grampius Face,   190
More swift than Venus Birds this Chariot guided
To the astonish'd Bancke where as it bided.
But long it did not bide, when poore those Streames
Aye me! it made, transporting those rich Gemmes,
And by that Burthen lighter, swiftly drived   195
Till (as me thought) it at a Towre arrived.
    Upon a Rocke of Christall shining cleare
Of Diamonds this Castle did appeare,
Whose rising Spires of Gold so high them reared
That Atlas-like it seem'd the Heaven they beared.   200
Amidst which Hights on Arches did arise
(Arches which guilt Flames brandish to the Skies)
Of sparking Topaces, Prowde, Gorgeous, Ample,
(Like to a litle Heaven) a sacred Temple:
Whose Walls no Windowes have, nay all the Wall   205
Is but one Window, Night there doth not fall
More when the Sunne to Westerne Worlds declineth,
Than in our Zenith when at Noone He shineth.
Two flaming Hills the Passage strait defend
Which to this radiant Building doth ascend,   210
Upon whose Arching tops on a Pilastre
A Port stands open, rais'd in Loves Disastre,
For none that narrow Bridge and Gate can passe,
Who have their Faces seene in Venus Glasse.
If those within, but to come foorth doe venter,   215
That stately Place againe they never enter.

l. 182 Amathus . . . Paphos. Cities of Cyprus, sacred to Venus.
l. 189 Ermelines. Ermines.
l. 211 Pilastre. Pillar.
l. 215 venter. Venture.

19

The Precinct strengthened with a Ditch appeares,
In which doth swell a Lake of Inkie Teares
Of madding Lovers, who abide there moning,
And thicken even the Aire with piteous Groning.   220
This Hold (to brave the Skies) the Destines fram'd,
The World the Fort of Chastitie it nam'd.
The Queene of the third Heaven once to appall it,
The God of Thrace here brought who could not thrall it,
For which he vow'd ne're Armes more to put on,   225
And on Riphean Hills was heard to grone.
Here Psyches Lover hurles his Darts at randon,
Which all for nought him serve as doth his Brandon.
        What bitter Anguish did invade my Minde,
When in that Place my Hope I saw confinde,   230
Where with high-towring Thoughts I onely reacht Her,
Which did burne up their Wings when they approacht Her?
Mee thought I set me by a Cypresse Shade,
And Night and Day the Hyacinthe there reade:
And that bewailing Nightingalles did borrow   235
Plaints of my Plaint, and Sorrowes of my Sorrow.
My Food was Wormewood, mine owne Teares my Drinke,
My Rest on Death, and sad Mishaps to thinke.
And for such Thoughts to have my Heart enlarged,
And ease mine Eyes with brinie Tribute charged,   240
Over a Brooke (me thought) my pining Face
I laid, which then (as griev'd at my Disgrace)
A Face Me shew'd againe so over-clouded,
That at the Sight mine Eyes afray'd them shrowded.
This is the guerdon Love, this is the Gaine   245
In end which to thy Servants doth remaine,
I would have said, when Feare made Sleepe to leave me,

l. 223 *Queene of the third Heaven.* Venus.
l. 224 *God of Thrace.* Mars.
l. 227 *Psyches Lover.* Cupid.
l. 228 *Brandon.* Torch.
l. 234 *the Hyacinthe there reade.* The hyacinth supposedly spelled out the letters
        AI (alas!).
l. 237 *Wormewood.* A bitter tasting plant.
l. 245 *guerdon.* Reward.

20

And of those fatall Shadowes did bereave me.
But ah alas! in stead to dreame of Love,
And Woes, mee made them in effect to prove,   250
For what into my troubled Braine was painted,
I waking found that Time, and Place presented.

Sonnet xii

Ah burning Thoughts now let me take some Rest,
And your tumultuous Broyles a while appease,
Is't not enough, *Starres, Fortune, Love* molest
Me all at once, but yee must to displease?
Let *Hope* (though false) yet lodge within my Brest,   5
My high Attempt (though dangerous) yet praise,
What though I trace not right Heavens steppie Wayes?
It doth suffice, my Fall shall make me blest.
I doe not doate on Dayes, nor feare not *Death*,
So that my Life be brave, what though not long?   10
Let me Renown'd live from the vulgare Throng,
And when yee list (Heavens) take this borrowed Breath.
    Men but like Visions are, *Time* all doth claime,
    He lives, who dies to winne a lasting Name.

l. 7 *steppie.* Steep.

Madrigall i

A DEDALE *of my Death,*
Now I resemble that subtile Worme on Earth
Which prone to its owne evill can take no rest.
For with strange Thoughts possest,
I feede on fading Leaves   5
Of Hope, *which me deceaves,*
And thousand Webs doth warpe within my Brest.
And thus in end unto my selfe I weave
A fast-shut Prison, no, but even a Grave.

l. 1 *Dedale.* Daedalus, thus an inventor or artificer.
l. 2 *that subtile Worme.* The silkworm.

21

Sextain i

The Heaven doth not containe so many Starres,
So many Leaves not prostrate lie in Woods,
When Autumne's old, and Boreas sounds his Warres,
So many Waves have not the Ocean Floods,
As my rent Mind hath Torments all the Night,   5
And Heart spends Sighes, when PHEBUS brings the Light.

Why should I beene a Partner of the Light?
Who crost in Birth by bad Aspects of Starres,
Have never since had happie Day nor Night,
Why was not I a Liver in the Woods,   10
Or Citizen of THETIS Christall Floods,
Than made a Man, for Love and Fortunes Warres?

I looke each Day when Death should ende the Warres,
Uncivill Warres, twixt Sense and Reasons Light,
My Paines I count to Mountaines, Meads, and Floods,   15
And of my Sorrow Partners makes the Starres,
All desolate I haunt the fearfull Woods
When I should give my selfe to Rest at Night.

With watchfull Eyes I ne're beholde the Night,
Mother of Peace, but ah to me of Warres,   20
And CYNTHIA Queene-like shining through the Woods,
When straight those Lamps come in my Thought, whose Light
My Judgement dazel'd, passing brightest Starres,
And then mine Eyes en-isle themselves with Floods.

Turne to their Springs againe first shall the Floods, 25
Cleare shall the Sunne the sad and gloomie Night,
To dance about the Pole cease shall the Starres,
The Elements renew their ancient Warres
Shall first, and bee depriv'd of Place and Light,
Ere I finde Rest in Citie, Fields, or Woods.   30

l. 3 *Boreas.* The north wind.
l. 6 *Phebus.* The sun.
l. 11 *Thetis.* A Nereid or water spirit.
l. 21 *Cynthia.* The moon.

Ende these my Dayes Endwellers of the Woods,
Take this my Life yee deepe and raging Floods,
Sunne never rise to cleare mee with thy Light,
Horror and Darknesse keepe a lasting Night,
Consume me Care with thy intestine Warres,   35
And stay your Influence o're me bright Starres.

In vaine the Starres, Endwellers of the Woods,
Care, Horror, Warres I call and raging Floods,
For all have sworne no Night shall dimme my Sight.

l. 31 *Endwellers*. Inhabitants.

Sonnet xiii

O sacred Blush impurpling Cheekes pure Skies,
With crimson Wings which spred thee like the *Morne*,
O bashfull Looke sent from those shining Eyes,
Which (though cast down on Earth) couldst Heaven adorne!
O Tongue in which most lushious Nectar lies,   5
That can at once both blesse and make forlorne,
Deare Corrall Lip which *Beautie* beautifies,
That trembling stood ere that her words were borne.
And you her Words, Words no, but Golden Chaines
Which did captive mine Eares, ensnare my Soule,   10
Wise Image of her Minde, Minde that containes
A Power all Power of *Senses* to controule:
    Yee all from Love disswade so sweetly mee,
    That I love more, if more may Love could bee.

Sonnet xiv

Nor *Arne*, nor *Mincius*, nor stately *Tyber*,
Sebethus, nor the Floud into whose Streames
He fell who burnt the World with borrow'd Beames,
Gold-rolling *Tagus*, *Munda*, famous *Iber*;

ll. 1–12 *Arne . . . range*. Rivers of the modern and classical worlds.
l. 3 *He*. Phaeton, driving the sun-chariot, fell into the Eridanus.

Sorgue, Rosne, Loire, Garron, nor prowd-banked Seine,　　　5
Peneus, Phasis, Xanthus, humble Ladon,
Nor Shee whose Nymphes excell her who lov'd Adon
Faire Tamesis, nor Ister large, nor Rheine,
Euphrates, Tigris, Indus, Hermus, Gange,
Pearlie Hydaspes, Serpent-like Meander,　　　10
The Golfe bereft sweet Hero her Leander,
Nile that farre farre his hidden Head doth range,
　　　Have ever had so rare a Cause of Praise,
　　　As Ora, where this Northerne Phenix stayes.

l. 14　Ora. the river Ore in Fife.
　　　this Northern Phenix. This rare creature, the sun of the north (the poet's mistress).

Sonnet xv

To heare my Plaints faire River Christalline
Thou in a silent Slumber seemes to stay,
Delicious Flowrs, Lillie and Columbine,
Yee bowe your Heades when I my Woes display.
Forrests, in you the Mirtle, Palme, and Bay,　　　5
Have had compassion listning to my Grones,
The Winds with Sighes have solemniz'd my Mones
Mong Leaves, which whisper'd what they could not say.
The Caves, the Rockes, the Hills the Sylvans Thrones
(As if even Pitie did in them appeare)　　　10
Have at my Sorrowes rent their ruethlesse Stones,
Each thing I finde hath sense except my Deare
　　　Who doth not thinke I love, or will not know
　　　My Griefe, perchance delighting in my Woe.

l. 9　Sylvans. Wood-spirits.

Sonnet xvi

Sweet Brooke, in whose cleare Christall I mine Eyes
Have oft seene great in Labour of their Teares,
Enamell'd Banke, whose shining Gravell beares

These sad Characters of my Miseries.
High Woods, whose mounting Tops menace the Spheares,   5
Wild Citizens, *Amphions* of the Trees,
You gloomie Groves at hottest Noones which freeze,
Elysian Shades which *Phebus* never cleares,
Vaste solitarie Mountaines, pleasant Plaines,
Embrodred Meads that *Ocean*-wayes you reach,   10
Hills, Dales, Springs, all that my sad Cry constraines
To take part of my Plaints, and learne Woes Speach,
    Will that remorselesse Faire e're Pitie show,
    Of Grace now answere if yee ought know? *No.*

l. 6   *Amphions of the Trees.* The birds, musicians of the woods; from Amphion
the lyrist.

Sonnet xvii

With flaming Hornes the *Bull* now brings the Yeare,
Melt doe the horride *Mountaines* Helmes of Snow,
The silver Flouds in pearlie Channells flow,
The late-bare Woods greene Anadeams doe weare.
The Nightingall forgetting Winters Woe,   5
Calls up the lazie *Morne* her Notes to heare,
Those Flowrs are spred which *Names of Princes beare,*
Some red, some azure, white, and golden grow.
Here lowes a Heifer, there *bea*-wailing strayes
A harmelesse Lambe, not farre a Stag rebounds,   10
The Sheepe-heards sing to grazing Flockes sweet Layes,
And all about the Ecchoing Aire resounds.
    Hills, Dales, Woods, Flouds, and every thing doth change,
    But *Shee* in *Rigour, I* in *Love* am strange.

l. 1   *the Bull.* The zodiacal sign.
l. 4   *Anadeams.* Wreaths.
l. 7   *Those Flowrs . . .* Anemone, hyacinth, narcissus, crocus(?).

Sonnet xviii

When *Nature* now had wonderfully wrought
All Auristellas Parts, except her Eyes,
To make those Twinnes two Lamps in *Beauties* Skies,
Shee Counsell of her *starrie Senate* sought.
Mars and *Apollo* first did Her advise   5
In Colour Blacke to wrappe those Comets bright,
That *Love* him so might soberly disguise,
And unperceived Wound at every Sight.
Chaste PHEBE spake for purest azure Dyes,
But JOVE and VENUS greene about the Light   10
To frame thought best, as bringing most Delight,
That to pin'd Hearts *Hope* might for ay arise:
    Nature (all said) a *Paradise* of Greene
    There plac'd, to make all love which have them seene.

l. 2 *Auristella*. The poet's mistress.
l. 9 *Phebe*. Artemis or Diana.
ll. 12–13 *Hope . . . Greene*. Green is the colour of hope.

Madrigall ii

*To the delightful Greene
Of you faire radiant Eine,
Let each Blacke yeeld beneath the starrie Arche.
Eyes, burnisht Heavens of Love,
Sinople Lampes of Jove,*   5
*Save that those Hearts which with your Flames yee parche
Two burning Sunnes you prove,
All other Eyes compar'd with you (deare Lights)
Bee Hells, or if not Hells yet dumpish Nights.
The Heavens (if we their Glasse*   10
*The Sea beleeve) bee greene, not perfect blew.
They all make faire what ever faire yet was,
And they bee faire because they looke like you.*

l. 2 *Eine*. Eyes.
l. 5 *Sinople*. Green.

Sonnet xix

In vaine I haunt the colde and silver Springs,
To quench the Fever burning in my Vaines,
In vaine (*Loves* Pilgrime) Mountaines, Dales, and Plaines,
I over-runne, vaine Helpe long Absence brings.
In vaine (my Friends) your Counsell me constraines   5
To flie, and place my Thoughts on other Things,
Ah! like the Bird that fired hath her Wings,
The more I move, the greater are my Paines.
Desire (alas) *Desire* a *Zeuxis* new,
From *Indies* borrowing Gold, from *Westerne* Skies   10
Most bright Cynoper, sets before mine Eyes
In every Place, her Haire, sweet Looke and Hew:
　　That flie, runne, rest I, all doth prove but vaine,
　　My Life lies in those Lookes which have me slaine.

l. 7   *the Bird.* The phoenix.
l. 9   *Zeuxis.* The Greek painter.
l. 11   *Cynoper.* Vermilion.

Sonnet xx

All other Beauties how so e're they shine
In Haires more bright than is the golden Ore,
Or Cheekes more faire than fairest *Eglantine*,
Or Hands like Hers who comes the Sunne before:
Match'd with that Heavenly Hue, and Shape divine,   5
With those deare Starres which my weake Thoughts adore,
Looke but like Shaddowes, or if they bee more,
It is in that that they are like to thine.
Who sees those Eyes, their Force and doth not prove,
Who gazeth on the Dimple of that Chinne,   10
And findes not *Venus* Sonne entrench'd therein,
Or hath not Sense, or knowes not what is Love.
　　To see thee had *Narcissus* had the Grace,
　　Hee sure had died with wondring on thy Face.

l. 3   *Eglantine.* The sweet-briar or wild rose.
l. 11   *Venus Sonne.* Cupid.

27

Sonnet xxi

My Teares may well *Numidian* Lions tame,
And Pitie breede into the hardest Hart
That ever *Pirrha* did to Maide impart,
When Shee them first of blushing Rockes did frame.
Ah Eyes which only serve to waile my Smart,   5
How long will you mine inward Woes proclaime?
Let it suffice you beare a weeping Part
All Night, at Day though yee doe not the same:
Cease idle Sighes to spend your Stormes in vaine,
And these calme secret Shades more to molest,   10
Containe you in the Prison of my Brest,
You not doe ease but aggravate my Paine,
　　Or (if burst foorth you must?) that Tempest move
　　In Sight of Her whome I so dearely love.

l. 3　*Pirrha.* Wife of Deucalion. She created women from stones.

Sonnet xxii

Nymphes, Sister *Nymphes* which haunt this christall Brooke,
And (happie) in these Floting Bowrs abide,
Where trembling Roofes of Trees from Sunne you hide,
Which make *Ideall Woods* in every Crooke,
Whether yee Garlands for your Lockes provide,   5
Or pearlie Letters seeke in sandie Booke,
Or count your Loves when *Thetis* was a Bride?
Lift up your golden Heads and on mee looke.
Read in mine Eyes mine agonizing Cares,
And what yee read recount to Her againe: 10
Faire Nymphes, say all these Streames are but my Teares,
And if Shee aske you how they sweet remaine,
　　Tell that the bittrest Teares which Eyes can powre,
　　When shed for Her doe cease more to be sowre.

28

Madrigall iii

Like the Idalian *Queene*
Her Haire about her Eyne,
With Necke and Brests ripe Apples to be seene,
At first Glance of the Morne
In Cyprus *Gardens gathering those faire Flowrs*   5
Which of her Bloud were borne,
I saw, but fainting saw, my Paramours.
The Graces *naked danc'd about the Place,*
The Winds *and* Trees *amaz'd*
With Silence on Her gaz'd,   10
The Flowrs did smile, like those upon her Face,
And as their Aspine Stalkes those Fingers band,
(That Shee might read my Case)
A Hyacinth *I wisht mee in her Hand.*

l. 1   *the Idalian Queene.* Venus.
l. 2   *Eyne.* Eyes.
l. 5   *those faire Flowrs.* Roses.
l. 7   *my Paramours.* My lover's (form).
l. 8   *The Graces.* The three goddesses of beauty and charm.
l. 12   *Aspine.* Quivering.
l. 14   *A Hyacinth . . .* The hyacinth supposedly spelled out the letters AI (alas!).

Sonnet xxiii

Then is Shee gone? O Foole and Coward I!
O good Occasion lost, ne're to bee found!
What fatall Chaines have my dull Senses bound
When best they may that they not *Fortune* trie?
Here is the flowrie Bed where Shee did lie,   5
With Roses here *Shee* stellified the Ground,
Shee fix'd her Eyes on this (yet smyling) Pond,
Nor Time, nor courteous Place seem'd ought denie.
Too long, too long (*Respect*) I doe embrace
Your Counsell, full of Threats and sharpe Disdaine;   10
Disdaine in her sweet Heart can have no Place,

l. 6   *stellified.* Made star-like, transformed.

29

And though come there, must straight retire againe:
    Hencefoorth *Respect* farewell, I oft heare tolde
    Who lives in Love can never bee too bolde.

Sonnet xxiv

In Minds pure Glasse when I my selfe behold,
And vively see how my best Dayes are spent,
What Clouds of Care above my Head are roll'd,
What comming Harmes, which I can not prevent:
My begunne Course I (wearied) doe repent,   5
And would embrace what *Reason* oft hath told,
But scarce thus thinke I, when Love hath controld
All the best Reasons *Reason* could invent.
Though sure I know my Labours End is Griefe,
The more I strive that I the more shall pine,   10
That only Death can be my last Reliefe:
Yet when I thinke upon that Face divine,
    Like one with Arrow shot in Laughters Place,
    Malgre my Heart I joye in my Disgrace.

l. 2 *vively*. Vividly.
l. 13 *Laughters Place*. The heart.
l. 14 *Malgre*. In spite of.

Sonnet xxv

Deare Quirister, who from those Shaddowes sends
(Ere that the blushing Dawne dare show her Light)
Such sad lamenting Straines, that *Night* attends
Become all Eare, *Starres* stay to heare thy Plight.
If one whose Griefe even Reach of Thought transcends,   5
Who ne're (not in a Dreame) did taste Delight,
May thee importune who like Case pretends,
And seemes to joy in Woe, in *Woes* Despight?
Tell me (so may thou *Fortune* milder trie,
And long long sing) for what thou thus complaines?   10

ll. 1–14. *Deare Quirister* . . . Chorister, the Nightingale.

30

Sith (*Winter* gone) the *Sunne* in dapled Skie
Now smiles on Meadowes, Mountaines, Woods and Plaines:
    The Bird, as if my questions did her move,
    With trembling Wings sobb'd foorth *I love, I love*.

Sonnet xxvi

Trust not sweet Soule those curled Waves of Gold
With gentle Tides which on your Temples flow,
Nor Temples spread with Flackes of Virgine Snow,
Nor Snow of Cheekes with *Tyrian* Graine enroll'd.
Trust not those shining Lights which wrought my Woe,   5
When first I did their burning Rayes beholde,
Nor Voyce, whose Sounds more strange Effects doe show
Than of the *Thracian* Harper have beene tolde:
Looke to this dying *Lillie*, fading *Rose*,
Darke *Hyacinthe*, of late whose blushing Beames   10
Made all the neighbouring Herbes and Grasse rejoyce,
And thinke how litle is twixt Lifes Extreames:
    The cruell Tyrant that did kill those Flowrs,
    Shall once (*aye mee*) not spare that Spring of yours.

l. 3   *Flackes*. Flecks.
l. 4   *Tyrian Graine*. Colour, purple.
l. 8   *Thracian Harper*. Orpheus.
l. 13   *The cruell Tyrant*. Time.

Sonnet xxvii

That I so slenderly set foorth my Minde,
Writing I wote not what in ragged Rimes,
And charg'd with Brasse into these golden Times
When others towre so high am left behinde:
I crave not PHEBUS leave his sacred Cell   5
To binde my Browes with fresh *Aonian* Bayes,
Let them have that who tuning sweetest Layes

l. 5   *Phebus*. Apollo, or the sun.
l. 6   *Aonian Bayes*. Laurel garlands for the poet. Aonia was sacred to the Muses

By *Tempe* sit, or *Aganippe* Well,
Nor yet to *Venus* Tree doe I aspire,
Sith *Shee* for whome I might affect that Praise,   10
My best Attempts with cruell Words gainsayes,
And I seeke not that Others me admire.
    Of weeping *Myrrhe* the Crowne is which I crave,
    With a sad *Cypresse* to adorne my Grave.

l. 8   *Tempe.* Vale sacred to Apollo.
       Aganippe Well. The Muses' fountain.
l. 9   *Venus Tree.* The myrtle, symbol of love and marriage.

Sonnet xxviii

Sound hoarse sad *Lute*, true Witnesse of my Woe,
And strive no more to ease selfe-chosen Paine
With Soule-enchanting Sounds, your Accents straine
Unto these Teares uncessantly which flow.
Shrill Treeble weepe, and you dull Basses show   5
Your Masters Sorrow *in a deadly Vaine*,
Let never joyfull Hand upon you goe,
Nor Consort keepe but when you doe complaine.
Flie *Phœbus* Rayes, nay, hate the irkesome Light,
Woods solitarie Shades for thee are best,   10
Or the blacke Horrours of the blackest Night,
When all the *World* (save Thou and I) doth rest:
    Then sound sad Lute, and beare a mourning Part,
    Thou *Hell* may'st moove, though not a Womans *Heart*.

l. 8   *Consort.* Musical accord.
l. 9   *Phœbus.* The sun.

Sonnet xxix

You restlesse Seas, appease your roaring Waves,
And you who raise hudge Mountaines in that Plaine
Aires Trumpeters, your blustring Stormes restraine,
And listen to the Plaints my Griefe doth cause.

Eternall *Lights*, though adamantine Lawes   5
Of Destinies to moove still you ordaine,
Turne hitherward your Eyes, your Axetree pause,
And wonder at the Torments I sustaine.
Earth (if thou bee not dull'd by my Disgrace,
And senseless made?) now aske those Powers above   10
Why they so crost a Wretch brought on thy Face?
Fram'd for Mis-hap, th' *Anachorite* of Love,
    And bid them if they would moe ÆTNAS burne,
      In *Rhodopee* or *Erimanthe* mee turne.

l. 5   *Adamantine.* Unbreakable.
l. 7   *Axetree.* Axle.
l. 12   *Anachorite.* Hermit.
l. 13   *moe.* More.
ll. 13–14   *Ætnas . . . turne.* If he were changed to cold and snowy mountains he
       would transform them to volcanos.

Sonnet xxx

What cruell *Starre* into this World mee brought?
What gloomie Day did dawne to give mee Light?
What unkinde Hand to nourse mee (Orphane) sought,
And would not leave mee in eternall Night?
What thing so deare as I hath Essence bought?   5
The Elements, drie, humid, heavie, light,
The smallest living things by *Nature* wrought,
Bee freed of Woe if they have small Delight.
Ah only I, abandon'd to *Despaire*,
Nail'd to my Torments, in pale *Horrours* Shade,   10
Like wandring Clouds see all my Comforts fled,
And Evill on Evill with Hours my Life impaire:
    The Heaven and *Fortune* which were wont to turne,
    Fixt in one Mansion staye to cause mee mourne.

Sonnet xxxi

Deare Eye which daign'st on this sad *Monument*
The *sable Scroule* of my Mis-haps to view,

Though with the mourning *Muses* Teares besprent,
And darkly drawne, which is not fain'd, but true,
If thou not dazell'd with a Heavenly Hue,   5
And comely Feature, didst not yet lament?
But happie liv'st unto thy selfe content,
O let not *Love* thee to his Lawes subdue.
Looke on the wofull Shipwracke of my Youth,
And let my Ruines for a *Phare* thee serve   10
To shunne this Rocke *Capharean* of Untrueth,
And serve no God who doth his Church-men sterve:
    His Kingdome is but Plaints, his Guerdon Teares,
    What hee gives more are Jealousies and Feares.

l. 3   *besprent.* Besprinkled.
l. 10 *Phare.* Lighthouse.
l. 11 *Rocke Capharean.* The rock which wrecked the Greek fleet returning from
       Troy.
l. 13 *Guerdon.* Reward

Sonnet xxxii

If crost with all Mis-haps bee my poore Life,
If one short Day I never spent in Mirth,
If my Spright with it selfe holds lasting Strife,
If Sorrowes Death is but new Sorrowes Birth?
If this vaine World bee but a sable Stage   5
Where slave-borne Man playes to the scoffing Starres,
If Youth bee toss'd with Love, with Weaknesse Age,
If Knowledge serve to holde our Thoughts in Warres?
If *Time* can close the hundreth Mouths of *Fame*,
And make what long since past, like that to bee,   10
If *Vertue* only bee an *idle Name*,
If I when I was borne was borne to die?
    Why seeke I to prolong these loathsome Dayes,
    The fairest *Rose* in shortest time decayes?

l. 3   *Spright.* Spirit.

Sonnet xxxiii

Let *Fortune* triumph now, and *Iö* sing,
Sith I must fall beneath this Load of Care,
Let Her what most I prize of ev'rie Thing
Now wicked Trophees in her Temple reare.
Shee who high Palmie Empires doth not spare,   5
And tramples in the Dust the prowdest King,
Let Her vaunt how my Blisse Shee did impaire,
To what low Ebbe Shee now my Flow doth bring.
Let Her count how (*a new Ixion*) Mee
Shee in her Wheele did turne, how high nor low   10
I never stood, but more to tortur'd bee:
Weepe Soule, weepe plaintfull Soule, thy Sorrowes know,
  Weepe, of thy Teares till a blacke River swell,
  Which may *Cocytus* be to this thy Hell.

l. 1   *Iö*. Exclamation of joy.
l. 9   *Ixion*. A murderer, would-be lover of Hera, punished on a wheel.
l. 14   *Cocytus*. A river of Hades.

Sonnet xxxiv

O cruell Beautie, Meekenesse inhumaine,
That Night and day contend with my Desire,
And seeke my Hope to kill, not quench my Fire,
By Death, not Baulme to ease my pleasant Paine.
Though yee my Thoughts tread downe which would aspire,   5
And bound my Blisse, doe not (*alas*) disdaine
That I your matchlesse Worth and Grace admire,
And for their Cause these Torments sharpe sustaine.
Let great *Empedocles* vaunt of his Death
Found in the midst of those *Sicylian* Flames,   10
And *Phaëton* that Heaven him reft of Breath,
And *Dædals* Sonne He nam'd the *Samian* Streames:

l. 9   *Empedocles*. The Greek philosopher. He supposedly tried to achieve divinity
       by throwing himself into the volcano Ætna.
l. 11 *Phaëton*. After mismanaging the sun-chariot, he was struck dead by Zeus.
l. 12 *Dædals Sonne*. Icarus flew too near the sun, then fell into the Icarean sea.

35

Their Haps I envie not, my Praise shall bee,
The fairest *Shee that liv'd* gave Death to mee.

Sonnet xxxv

The *Hyperborean* Hills, *Ceraunus* Snow,
Or *Arimaspus* (cruell) first thee bred,
The *Caspian* Tigers with their Milke thee fed,
And *Faunes* did humane Bloud on thee bestow.
Fierce *Orithyas* Lover in thy Bed   5
Thee lull'd asleepe, where he enrag'd doth blow,
Thou didst not drinke the Flouds which here doe flow,
But Teares, or those by icie *Tanais* Hed.
Sith thou disdaines my Love, neglects my Griefe,
Laughs at my Grones, and still affects my Death,   10
Of thee, nor Heaven I'll seeke no more Reliefe,
Nor longer entertaine this loathsome Breath,
    But yeeld unto my *Starre*, that thou mayst prove,
    What Losse thou hadst in losing such a Love.

ll. 1–8 *Hyperborean Hills . . . Tanais Hed.* Distant and savage lands.
l. 5 *Orithyas Lover.* Boreas, the north wind.

Song ii

Phoebus arise,
And paint the sable Skies
With azure, white, and Red:
Rowse Memnons *Mother from her* Tythons *Bed,*
That Shee thy Cariere may with Roses spred,   5
The Nightingalles thy Comming each where sing,
Make an eternall Spring,
Give Life to this darke World which lieth dead.
Spreade foorth thy golden Haire
In larger Lockes than thou wast wont before,   10

l. 4 *Memnons Mother.* Eos, goddess of the dawn, who married Tithonus.
l. 5 *Cariere.* Carriage.

36

And Emperour-like decore
With Diademe of Pearle thy Temples faire:
Chase hence the uglie Night
Which serves but to make deare thy glorious Light.
This is that happie Morne,   15
That Day long wished Day,
Of all my Life so darke,
(If cruell Starres have not my Ruine sworne,
And Fates not Hope betray?)
Which (only white) deserves   20
A Diamond for ever should it marke:
This is the Morne should bring unto this Grove
My Love, to heare, and recompense my love.
Faire King who all preserves,
But show thy blushing Beames,   25
And thou two sweeter Eyes
Shalt see than those which by Peneus Streames
Did once thy Heart surprise:
Nay, Sunnes, which shine as cleare
As thou when two thou did to Rome appeare.   30
Now Flora decke thy selfe in fairest Guise,
If that yee, Winds, would heare
A Voyce surpassing farre Amphions Lyre,
Your stormie chiding stay,
Let Zephyre only breath,   35
And with her Tresses play,
Kissing sometimes these purple Ports of Death.
The Windes all silent are,
And Phœbus in his Chaire
Ensaffroning Sea and Aire,   40
Makes vanish every Starre:
Night like a Drunkard reeles
Beyond the Hills to shunne his flaming Wheeles.
The Fields with Flowrs are deckt in every Hue,
The Clouds bespangle with bright Gold their Blew: 45
Here is the pleasant Place
And ev'ry thing, save Her, who all should grace.

l. 11   *decore.* Decorate.
l. 30   *As thou when two* . . . At one time in the Punic wars two suns were sup-
        posedly seen in the sky at Rome.

Who hath not seene into her saffron Bed
The Mornings Goddesse mildly Her repose,
Or Her of whose pure Bloud first sprang the Rose,
Lull'd in a Slumber by a Mirtle Shade.
Who hath not seene that sleeping White and Red   5
Makes *Phœbe* looke so pale, which Shee did close
In that *Iönian* Hill, to ease her Woes,
Which only lives by Nectare Kisses fed:
Come but and see my Ladie sweetly sleepe,
The sighing Rubies of those heavenly Lips,   10
The *Cupids* which Brests golden Apples keepe,
Those Eyes which shine in midst of their Ecclipse,
    And Hee them all shall see (perhaps) and prove
    Shee waking but perswades, now forceth Love.

l. 2   *The Mornings Goddesse.* Aurora, the dawn.
l. 3   *Her of whose pure Bloud.* Venus.
l. 5   *that sleeping White and Red.* The body of the beloved.
l. 6   *Phœbe.* The moon-goddess, see sonnet viii.

Of *Cithereas* Birds that milke-white paire
On yonder leavie *Mirtle* Tree which grone,
And waken with their kisses in the Aire
Enamour'd *Zephyres* murmuring one by one,
If thou but Sense hadst like *Pigmalions* Stone?   5
Or hadst not seene *Medusas* snakie haire,
Loves Lessons thou mightst learne? and learne sweete Faire,
To *Summers* Heat ere that thy *Spring* bee growne.
And if those kissing Lovers seeme but Cold,
Looke how that *Elme* this *Ivie* doth embrace,   10
And bindes, and claspes with many a wanton Fold,

l. 1   *Cithereas Birds.* Doves, sacred to Venus.
l. 5   *Pigmalions Stone.* A statue, first carved by Pigmalion, then given life by
     Venus.
l. 6   *Medusas snakie haire.* Medusa's hair turned men to stone.

And courting Sleepe o'reshadowes all the Place:
  Nay seemes to say, deare Tree we shall not parte,
  In Signe whereof loe in each Leafe a *Heart*.

Sonnet xxxviii

The *Sunne* is faire when hee with crimson Crowne,
And flaming Rubies leaves his Easterne Bed,
Faire is *Thaumantias* in her christall Gowne
When Clouds engemm'd hang azure, greene, and Red.
To Westerne Worlds when wearied Day goes downe,   5
And from Heavens Windowes each *Starre* showes her Hed,
Earths silent Daughter *Night* is faire, though browne,
Faire is the *Moone* though in *Loves* Liverie cled.
Faire *Chloris* is when Shee doth paint Aprile,
Faire are the *Meads*, the *Woods*, the *Flouds* are faire,   10
Faire looketh *Ceres* with her yellow Haire,
And *Apples* Queene when *Rose*-cheekt Shee doth smile.
  That Heaven, and Earth, and Seas are faire is true,
  Yet true that all not please so much as you.

l. 3   *Thaumantias*. Iris, goddess of the rainbow.
l. 9   *Chloris*. Flora, goddess of flowers.
l. 11 *Ceres*. Goddess of fruits.
l. 12 *Apples Queene*. Venus.

Madrigall iv

When as shee smiles I finde
More light before mine Eyes,
Nor when the Sunne from Inde
Brings to our World a flowrie Paradise:
But when shee gently weepes,   5
And powres foorth pearlie Showres,
On Cheekes faire blushing Flowres,
A sweet Melancholie my Senses keepes.
Both feede so my Disease,
So much both doe me please,   10

That oft I doubt, which more my Heart doth burne,
Like Love to see her smile, or Pitie mourne.

Sonnet xxxix

Slide soft faire FORTH, and make a christall Plaine,
Cut your white Lockes, and on your foamie Face
Let not a Wrinckle bee, when you embrace
The Boat that *Earths Perfections* doth containe.
Windes wonder, and through wondring holde your Peace,　　5
Or if that yee your Hearts cannot restraine
From sending Sighes, *mov'd by a Lovers Case*,
Sigh, and in her faire Haire your selves enchaine:
Or take these Sighes which Absence makes arise
From mine oppressed Brest and wave the Sailes,　　10
Or some sweet Breath new brought from *Paradise*:
Flouds seeme to smile, *Love* o're the Winds preveails,
　　And yet hudge Waves arise, the Cause is this,
　　The *Ocean* strives with FORTH the Boate to kisse.

ll. 11–14　*Forth*. The river Forth, lying between the poet and his mistress.

Sonnet xl

Ah! who can see those Fruites of *Paradise*,
Celestiall Cherries which so sweetly swell
That *Sweetnesse* selfe confinde there seemes to dwell,
And all those sweetest Parts about despise?
Ah! who can see and feele no Flame surprise　　5
His hardened Heart? for mee (*alas*) too well
I know their Force, and how they doe excell,
Now burne I through Desire, now doe I freeze:
I die (deare Life) unlesse to mee bee given
As many Kisses as the *Spring* hath Flowrs,　　10
Or as the silver Drops of *Iris* Showrs,
Or as the Starres in all-embracing Heaven,
　　And if displeas'd yee of the Match complaine,
　　Yee shall have leave to take them backe againe.

40

Sonnet xli

Is't not enough (aye mee) mee thus to see
Like some Heaven-banish'd Ghost still wailing goe?
A *Shadow* which your Rayes doe only show,
To vexe mee more, unlesse yee bid mee die?
What could yee worse allotte unto your Foe?   5
But die will I, so yee will not denie
That Grace to mee which mortall Foes even trie,
To chuse what sort of Death should ende my Woe.
One Time I found when as yee did mee kisse,
Yee gave my panting Soule so sweet a Touch,   10
That halfe I sown'd in midst of all my Blisse,
I doe but crave my Deaths Wound may bee such:
    For though by Griefe I die not and Annoy,
    Is't not enough to die through too much Joy?

l. 11 *sown'd.* Swooned.

Madrigall v

Sweete Rose whence is this Hue
Which doth all Hues excell?
Whence this most fragrant Smell?
And whence this Forme and gracing Grace in you?
In flowrie Paestums *Field (perhaps) yee grew,*   5
Or Hyblas *Hills you bred,*
Or odoriferous Ennas *Plaines you fed,*
Or Tmolus, *or where Bore yong* Adon *slew,*
Or hath the Queene of Love you dy'd of new
In that deare Bloud, which makes you looke so red?   10
    No, none of those, but Cause more high you blist,
    My Ladies Brest you bare, and Lips you kist.

ll. 5–8 *Paestums Field . . . Adon slew.* Classical and exotic rose countries.

41

Sonnet xlii

Shee whose faire flowrs no *Autumne* makes decay,
Whose Hue celestiall, earthly Hues doth staine,
Into a pleasant odoriferous Plaine
Did walke alone, to brave the Pride of *Maye*:
And whilst through chekred Lists shee made her Way,   5
Which smil'd about her Sight to entertaine,
Loe (unawares) where *Love* did hid remaine
Shee spide, and sought to make of him her Prey:
For which of golden Lockes a fairest Haire
(To binde the Boy) shee tooke, But hee afraid   10
At her Approach sprang swiftly in the Aire,
And mounting farre from Reach look'd backe and said,
    Why shouldst thou (Sweet) me seeke in Chaines to binde,
    Sith in thine Eyes I dayly am confinde.

l. 5   *chekred Lists.* Flower borders.

Madrigall vi

On this colde World of Ours,
Flowre of the Seasons, Season of the Flowrs,
Sonne of the Sunne sweet Spring,
Such hote and burning Dayes why doest thou bring?
Is this for that those high Eternall Pow'rs   5
Flash downe that Fire this All environing?
Or that now Phœbus *keepes his Sisters Spheare?*
Or doth some Phaëton
Enflame the Sea and Aire?
Or rather is it (Usher of the Yeare)   10
For that last Day amongst thy Flowrs alone
Unmask'd thou saw'st my Faire?
    And whilst thou on her gaz'd shee did thee burne,
    And in thy Brother Summer *doth thee turne.*

l. 7   *Phœbus.* The sun, which now shines long hours into the moon's usual time.
l. 8   *Phaëton.* Phaeton drove the sun-chariot.

42

Sonnet xliii

Deare Wood, and you sweet solitarie Place,
Where from the vulgare I estranged live,
Contented more with what your Shades mee give,
Than if I had what *Thetis* doth embrace:
What snakie Eye growne jealous of my Peace, 5
Now from your silent Horrours would mee drive?
When Sunne progressing in his glorious Race
Beyond the *Twinnes*, doth neare our Pole arrive.
What sweet Delight a quiet Life affords,
And what it is to bee of Bondage free, 10
Farre from the madding Worldlings hoarse Discords,
Sweet flowrie Place I first did learne of thee:
    Ah! if I were mine owne, your deare Resorts
    I would not change with *Princes stately Courts*.

l. 4 *what Thetis doth embrace.* All that the seas embrace.
l. 8 *the Twinnes.* Gemini, the zodiacal sign, thus summer.

Sextain ii

Sith gone is my Delight and only Pleasure,
The last of all my Hopes, the chearfull Sunne
That clear'd my Lifes darke Day, Natures sweet Treasure,
More deare to mee than all beneath the Moone,
What resteth now, but that upon this Mountaine 5
I weepe, till Heaven transforme mee in a Fountaine?

Fresh, faire, delicious, christall, pearlie Fountaine,
On whose smoothe Face to looke shee oft tooke Pleasure,
Tell mee (so may thy Streames long cheare this Mountaine,
So Serpent ne're thee staine, nor scorch the Sunne, 10
So may with gentle Beames thee kisse the Moone)
Doest thou not mourne to want so faire a Treasure?

l. 5 *resteth.* Remains to be done.

43

While shee her glass'd in thee, rich TAGUS Treasure
Thou envie needed not, nor yet the Fountaine
In which that Hunter saw the naked Moone,   15
Absence hath robb'd thee of thy Wealth and Pleasure,
And I remaine like Marigold of Sunne
Depriv'd, that dies by Shadow of some Mountaine.

Nymphes of the Forrests, Nymphes who on this Mountaine
Are wont to dance, shewing your Beauties Treasure   20
To Goate-feete Sylvans, and the wondring Sunne,
When as you gather Flowres about this Fountaine,
Bid Her Farewell who placed here her Pleasure,
And sing her Praises to the Starres and Moone.

Among the lesser Lights as is the Moone,   25
Blushing through Scarfe of Clouds on LATMOS Mountaine,
Or when her silver Lockes shee lookes for Pleasure
In Thetis Streames, prowde of so gay a Treasure,
Such was my Faire when Shee sate by this Fountaine
With other Nymphes, to shunne the amorous Sunne.   30

As is our Earth in Absence of the Sunne,
Or when of Sunne deprived is the Moone,
As is without a verdant Shade a Fountaine,
Or wanting Grasse, a Mead, a Vale, a Mountaine,
Such is my State, bereft of my deare Treasure,   35
To know whose only Worth was all my Pleasure.

Ne're thinke of Pleasure Heart, Eyes shunne the Sunne,
Teares be your Treasure, which the wandring Moone
Shall see you shed by Mountaine, Vale, and Fountaine.

l. 13   glass'd. Looked at the reflection of.
        Tagus Treasure. Gold.
l. 15   that Hunter. Actaeon surprised Diana bathing.
l. 17   Marigold of Sunne. An emblematic figure: the marigold opened with the
        sun and followed its path.
l. 21   Sylvans. Wood-spirits.

44

Sonnet xliv

Thou Window, once which served for a Spheare
To that deare Planet of my Heart, whose Light
Made often blush the glorious Queene of Night,
While *Shee* in thee more beautious did appeare,
What mourning Weedes (alas) now do'st thou weare?   5
How loathsome to mine Eyes is thy sad Sight?
How poorely look'st thou, with what heavie cheare,
Since that Sunne set, which made thee shine so bright?
Unhappie now thee close, for as of late
To wondring Eyes thou wast a Paradise,   10
Bereft of Her who made thee fortunate,
A Gulfe thou art, whence Cloudes of Sighes arise:
   But unto none so noysome as to mee,
   Who hourly see my murth'red Joyes in thee.

Sonnet xlv

Are these the flowrie Bankes? is this the *Mead*
Where *Shee* was wont to passe the pleasant hours?
Did here her Eyes exhale mine Eyes salt Showrs,
When on her Lap I laide my wearie Head?
Is this the goodly *Elme* did us o'respread,   5
Whose tender Rine cut out in curious Flowrs
By that white Hand, containes those Flames of Ours?
Is this the rusling *Spring* us Musicke made?
Deflourish'd *Mead* where is your heavenly Hue?
Banke, where that *Arras* did you late adorne,   10
How looke yee *Elme* all withered and forlorne?
Onely sweet *Spring* nought altered seemes in you:
   But while here chang'd each other thing appeares,
   To sowre your Streames take of mine Eyes these Teares.

l. 6 *Rine.* Bark.
l. 10 *Arras.* Tapestry; thus, his mistress' presence.

Sonnet xlvi

Alexis, here *shee* stay'd among these Pines
(*Sweet Hermitresse*) *shee* did alone repaire,
Here did *shee* spreade the Treasure of her Haire,
More rich than that brought from the *Colchian* Mines.
Shee set Her by these musket Eglantines,   5
The happie Place the Print seemes yet to beare,
Her Voyce did sweeten here thy sugred Lines,
To which Winds, Trees, Beasts, Birds did lend their Eare.
Mee here *shee* first perceiv'd, and here a Morne
Of bright *Carnations* did o'respreade her Face,   10
Here did *shee* sigh, here first my Hopes were borne,
And I first got a Pledge of promis'd Grace:
    But (*ah*) what serv'd it to bee happie so?
    Sith passed Pleasures double but new Woe.

l. 1   *Alexis.* The poet's friend, identified with Sir William Alexander.
l. 5   *musket Eglantines.* Strong-smelling roses.

Sonnet xlvii

O Night, cleare Night, O darke and gloomie Day!
O wofull Waking! O Soule-pleasing Sleepe!
O sweet Conceits which in my Braines did creepe!
Yet sowre Conceits which went so soone away.
A Sleepe I had more than poore Words can say,   5
For clos'd in Armes (mee thought) I did thee keepe,
A sorie Wretch plung'd in Mis-fortunes deepe
Am I not wak'd? when Light doth Lies bewray.
O that that Night had ever still bene blacke!
O that that Day had never yet begunne!   10
And you mine Eyes would yee no time saw Sunne!
To have your *Sunne* in such a *Zodiacke*:
    Loe, what is good of Life is but a Dreame,
    When Sorrow is a never-ebbing Streame.

l. 8   *bewray.* Expose.

46

Sonnet xlviii

Haire, precious Haire which *Midas* Hand did straine,
Part of the Wreathe of Gold that crownes those Browes
Which *Winters* whitest White in Whitenesse staine,
And Lillie, by *Eridans* Banke that growes.
Haire (fatall Present) which first caus'd my Woes,   5
When loose yee hang like *Danaës* golden Raine,
Sweet Nettes, which sweetly doe all Hearts enchaine,
Strings, deadly Strings, with which *Love* bends his Bowes.
How are yee hither come? tell me, O Haire,
Deare Armelet, for what thus were yee given?   10
I know a Badge of Bondage I you weare,
Yet Haire for you, ô that I were a *Heaven!*
    Like *Berenices Locke* that yee might shine
    (But brighter farre) about this Arme of mine.

l. 1   *Midas Hand*. All that Midas touched turned to gold.
l. 6   *Danaës golden Raine*. Zeus appeared to Danae in a shower of gold.
l. 13   *Berenices Locke*. Her hair became a constellation.

Madrigall vii

Unhappy Light,
Doe not approach to bring the wofull Day,
When I must bid for ay
Farewell to Her, and live in endlesse Plight.
Faire Moone, *with gentle Beames*   5
The Sight who never marres,
Long cleare Heavens sable Vault, and you bright Starres
Your golden Lockes long glasse in Earths pure Streames,
Let Phœbus *never rise*
To dimme your watchfull Eyes: 10
    Prolong (alas) prolong my short Delight,
    And if yee can, make an eternall Night.

Sonnet xlix

With Griefe in Heart, and Teares in sowning Eyes,
When I to Her had giv'n a sad Fare-well,
Close sealed with a Kisse, and Dew which fell
On my else-moystned Face from *Beauties* Skies.
So strange Amazement did my Minde surprise,   5
That at each Pace I fainting turn'd againe,
Like One whome a *Torpedo* stupifies,
Not feeling *Honours* Bit, nor *Reasons* Raine.
But when fierce Starres to parte mee did constraine,
With backe-cast Lookes I envi'd both and bless'd   10
The happie Walles and Place did Her containe,
Till that Sights Shafts their flying Object miss'd,
  So wailing parted *Ganamede* the faire,
  When Eagles Talents bare him through the Aire.

l. 1   *sowning.* Swooning.
l. 7   *Torpedo.* An electric fish.
l. 9   *fierce Starres.* Fate.
l. 13 *Ganamede.* The beautiful youth abducted by Zeus.

Madrigall viii

I feare not hencefoorth Death,
Sith after this Departure yet I breath,
Let Rocks, and Seas, and Wind,
Their highest Treasons show,
Let Skie and Earth combinde   5
Strive (if they can) to ende my Life and Woe:
Sith Griefe can not, mee nothing can o'rethrow,
  Or if that ought can cause my fatall Lot,
  It will bee when I heare I am forgot.

Sonnet l

How many times *Nights silent Queene* her Face
Hath hid, how oft with Starres in silver Maske
In Heavens great Hall shee hath begunne her Taske,

48

And chear'd the waking Eye in lower Place:
How oft the *Sunne* hath made by Heavens swift Race   5
The happie Lover to forsake the Brest
Of his deare Ladie, wishing in the West
His golden Coach to runne had larger Space:
I ever count, and number, since alas
I bade Farewell to my Hearts dearest Guest,   10
The Miles I compasse, and in Minde I chase
The Flouds and Mountaines holde mee from my Rest:
    But (woe is mee) long count and count may I,
    Ere I see Her whose Absence makes mee die.

Sonnet li

So grievous is my Paine, so painefull *Life*,
That oft I finde mee in the Armes of *Death*,
But (Breath halfe gone) that Tyrant called *Death*
Who others killes, restoreth mee to *Life*:
For while I thinke how Woe shall ende with *Life*,   5
And that I quiet Peace shall joye by *Death*,
That Thought even doth o'repowre the Paines of *Death*,
And call mee home againe to lothed *Life*:
Thus doth mine evill transcend both *Life* and *Death*,
While no *Death* is so bad as is my *Life*,   10
Nor no *Life* such which doth not ende by *Death*,
And *Protean* Changes turne my *Death* and *Life*:
    O happie those who in their Birth finde *Death*,
    Sith but to languish Heaven affordeth *Life*.

l. 12   *Protean Changes*. Proteus, the old man of the sea, was a shape-changer.

Sonnet lii

Fame, who with golden Pennes abroad dost range
Where *Phœbus* leaves the Night, and brings the Day,
Fame, in one Place who (restlesse) dost not stay
Till thou hast flowne from *Atlas* unto *Gange*:

l. 1   *Pennes*. Feathers, thus wings.
l. 4   *Atlas unto Gange*. From one end of the known world to the other.

Fame, Enemie to *Time* that still doth change,   5
And in his changing Course would make decay
What here below he findeth in his Way,
Even making *Vertue* to her selfe looke strange.
Daughter of Heaven; Now all thy Trumpets sound,
Raise up thy Head unto the highest Skie,   10
With Wonder blaze the Gifts in Her are found,
And when *shee* from this mortall Globe shall flie,
    In thy wide Mouth, keepe long long keepe her Name,
    So thou by Her, shee by thee live shall *Fame.*

Madrigall ix

The Ivorie, Corrall, Gold,
Of Brest, of Lips, of Haire,
So lively Sleepe *doth show to inward Sight,*
That wake I thinke I hold
No Shadow, but my Faire: 5
My selfe so to deceave
With long-shut Eyes I shunne the irkesome Light.
Such Pleasure thus I have
Delighting in false Gleames,
If Death Sleepes *Brother bee?*   10
    And Soules reliev'd of Sense have so sweete Dreames?
    That I would wish mee thus to dreame and die.

Sonnet liii

I curse the Night, yet doth from Day mee hide,
The *Pandionian* Birds I tyre with Mones,
The *Ecchoes* even are weari'd with my Grones.
Since Absence did mee from my Blisse divide.
Each Dreame, each Toy, my Reason doth affright,   5
And when Remembrance reades the curious Scroule
Of pass'd Contentments caused by her Sight,

---

l. 2 *Pandionian Birds.* Nightingales.

Then bitter Anguish doth invade my Soule.
While thus I live ecclipsed of her Light
(O *mee!*) what better am I than the Mole?   10
Or those whose *Zenith* is the only Pole,
Whose Hemispheare is hid with so long Night?
    Save that in Earth he rests, they hope for Sunne,
    I pine, and finde mine endlesse Night begunne.

Sonnet liv

Of Death some tell, some of the cruell Paine
Which that bad Crafts-man in his Worke did trie,
When (a new Monster) Flames once did constraine
A humane Corps to yeeld a brutish Crie.
Some tell of those in burning Beds who lie,   5
For that they durst in the *Phlegræan* Plaine
The mightie Rulers of the Skie defie,
And siege those christall Towres which all containe.
An other countes of *Phlegethons* hote Floods
The Soules which drinke, *Ixions* endlesse Smart,   10
And his to whom a Vulture eates the Heart,
One telles of Specters in enchanted Woods:
    Of all those Paines he who the worst would prove,
    Let him bee absent, and but pine in Love.

l. 2   *that bad Crafts-man.* The inventor Perillus was burned alive inside his own
      construction, a brazen bull.
l. 6   *Phlegræan Plaine.* A burning plain, home of the giants who defied the gods.
l. 9   *Phlegethons hote Floods.* The flaming river of Hades.
l. 10 *Ixions endlesse Smart.* Ixion was tied to a wheel.
l. 11 *And his . . .* Both Prometheus and Tityus were punished with vultures
      continually tearing at their livers.

Madrigall x

Tritons, which bounding dive
Through Neptunes *liquide Plaine,*
When as yee shall arrive

With tilting Tides where silver Ora *playes,*
And to your King his watrie Tribute payes, 5
Tell how I dying live,
And burne in midst of all the coldest Maine.

l. 4   *Ora.* The river Ore in Fife.

Sonnet lv

Place mee where angry *Titan* burnes the *More,*
And thirstie *Africke* firie Monsters brings,
Or where the new-borne *Phœnix* spreades her Wings,
And Troupes of wondring Birds her Flight adore.
Place mee by *Gange,* or *Indes* empampred Shore, 5
Where smyling Heavens on Earth cause double Springs,
Place mee where *Neptunes* Quire of *Syrens* sings,
Or where (made hoarse through Cold) hee leaves to roare.
Mee place where *Fortune* doth her Darlings crowne,
A *Wonder,* or a *Sparke* in *Envies* Eye, 10
Or late outragious *Fates* upon mee frowne,
And *Pittie* wailing see disastred *Mee,*
    Affections Print my Minde so deepe doth prove,
    I may forget my Selfe, but not my Love.

l. 1   *Place mee* . . . Where the sun burns the Moor.
l. 3   *where . . . Phoenix* . . . In Arabia.
l. 5   *empampred.* Luxurious.
l. 7   *where Neptunes Quire* . . . At sea.
l. 8   *Or where* . . . At the poles.
       leaves. Ceases.

POEMS

THE SECOND PART

Sonnet i

Of mortall Glorie ô soone darkned Raye!
O posting Joyes of Man! more swift than Winde,
O fond Desires! which wing'd with Fancies straye,
O traitrous Hopes! which doe our Judgements blinde:
Loe, in a Flash that Light is gone away,   5
Which dazell did each Eye, Delight each Minde,
And with that *Sunne* (from whence it came) combinde,
Now makes more radiant Heavens eternall Day.
Let *Beautie* now be blubbred Cheekes with Teares,
Let widow'd *Musicke* only roare, and plaine,   10
Poore *Vertue* get thee Wings, and mount the Spheares,
And let thine only Name on Earth remaine.
    Death hath thy Temple raz'd, *Loves* Empire foylde,
    The World of Honour, Worth, and Sweetnesse spoylde.

l. 2 *posting.* Speeding.

Sonnet ii

Those Eyes, those sparkling Saphires of Delight,
Which thousand thousand Hearts did set on fire,
Which made that Eye of Heaven that brings the Light
(Oft jealous) staye amaz'd them to admire.
That living Snow, those crimson Roses bright,   5
Those Pearles, those Rubies, which did breede Desire,
Those Lockes of Gold, that Purple faire of *Tyre*,

l. 7 *Purple faire of Tyre.* Cheeks.

53

Are wrapt (*aye mee!*) up in eternall Night.
What hast thou more to vaunt of, wretched World?
Sith *shee* (who cursed thee made blest) is gone?   10
Thine ever-burning Lamps, Rounds ever whorld,
Can unto thee not modell such a one:
    For if they would such Beautie bring on Earth,
    They should be forc'd againe to make Her breath.

Sonnet iii

O *Fate!* conspir'd to powre your Worst on mee,
O rigorous Rigour, which doth all confound!
With cruell Hands yee have cut downe the Tree,
And Fruit and Flowre dispersed on the Ground.
A litle Space of Earth my Love doth bound,   5
That Beautie which did raise it to the Skie,
Turn'd in neglected Dust, now low doth lie,
Deafe to my Plaints, and senslesse of my Wound.
Ah! did I live for this, *ah!* did I love?
For this and was it shee did so excell?   10
That ere shee well Lifes sweet-sowre Joyes did prove,
Shee should (too deare a Guest) with *Horrour* dwell?
    Weake Influence of Heaven! what faire yee frame,
    Falles in the Prime, and passeth like a Dreame.

Sonnet iv

O woefull Life! Life, no, but living Death,
Fraile Boat of Christall in a rockie Sea,
A Sport expos'd to *Fortunes* stormie Breath,
Which kept with Paine, with Terrour doth decay:
The false Delights, true Woes thou dost bequeath,   5
Mine all-appalled Minde doe so affraye,
That I those envie who are laid in Earth,
And pittie them that runne thy dreadfull Waye.
When did mine Eyes behold one chearefull Morne?
When had my tossed Soule one Night of rest?   10
When did not hatefull Starres my Projects scorne?

O! now I finde for Mortalls what is best:
  Even, sith our voyage shamefull is, and short,
  Soone to strike Saile, and perish in the Port.

Sonnet v

Mine Eyes, dissolve your Globes in brinie Streames,
And with a Cloud of Sorrow dimme your Sight,
The Sunnes bright *Sunne* is set, of late whose Beames
Gave Luster to your Day, Day to your Night.
My Voyce now deafen Earth with Anatheames,   5
Roare foorth a Challenge in the Worlds Despight,
Tell that disguised Griefe is her Delight,
That Life a Slumber is of fearfull Dreames.
And woefull Minde abhorre to thinke of Joy,
My Senses all now comfortlesse you hide,   10
Accept no Object but of blacke Annoy,
Teares, Plaints, Sighs, mourning Weeds, Graves gaping wide,
  I have nought left to wish, my Hopes are dead,
  And all with Her beneath a Marble laide.

l. 5 *Anatheames*. Curses.

Sonnet vi

Sweet Soule, which in the Aprill of thy Yeares
So to enrich the Heaven mad'st poore this Round,
And now with golden Rayes of Glorie crown'd
Most blest abid'st above the Spheare of Spheares;
If heavenly Lawes (*alas*) have not thee bound   5
From looking to this Globe that all upbeares?
If Rueth and Pittie there above bee found?
O daigne to lend a Looke unto those Teares.
Doe not disdaine (deare Ghost) this sacrifice,
And though I raise not Pillars to thy Praise   10
Mine Offerings take, let this for mee suffice,

l. 7 *Rueth*. Compassion.

My Heart *a living Piramide* I raise:
    And whilst Kings Tombes with Lawrels flourish greene,
    Thine shall with Mirtles, and these Flowrs bee seene.

l. 14   *Mirtles.* Sacred to Venus, goddess of love.

Madrigall i

This Life which seemes so faire,
Is like a Bubble blowen up in the Aire,
By sporting Childrens Breath,
Who chase it every where,
And strive who can most Motion it bequeath: 5
And though it sometime seeme of its owne Might
(Like to an Eye of gold) to be fix'd there,
And firme to hover in that emptie Hight,
That only is because it is so light,
But in that Pompe it doth not long appeare;   10
    For even when most admir'd, it in a Thought
    As swell'd from nothing, doth dissolve in nought.

Sonnet vii

O! it is not to mee bright Lampe of Day,
That in the East thou shew'st thy rosie Face,
O! it is not to mee thou leav'st that Sea,
And in these azure Lists beginst thy Race.
Thou shin'st not to the Dead in any Place,   5
And I (dead) from this World am gone away,
Or if I seeme (a Shadow) yet to stay,
It is a while but to bemone my Case.
My Mirth is lost, my Comforts are dismay'd,
And unto sad Mis-haps their Place doe yeeld;   10
My Knowledge doth resemble a bloudie field,
Where I my Hopes, and Helps see prostrate layd.
    So painefull is Lifes Course which I have runne,
    That I doe wish it never had begunne.

56

Song i

Sad Damon *beeing come*
To that for-ever lamentable Tombe,
Which those eternall Powers that all controule
Unto his living Soule
A melancholie Prison had prescriv'd: 5
Of Hue, of Heate, of Motion quite depriv'd
In Armes wake, trembling, cold,
A Marble, hee the Marble did infold:
And having made it warme with many a Showre,
Which dimmed Eyes did powre,   10
When Griefe had given him leave, and Sighes them stay'd,
Thus with a sad alas *at last he said.*
    Who would have thought to mee
The Place where thou didst lie could grievous bee?
And that (deare Body) long thee having sought   15
(O mee!) who would have thought?
Thee once to finde it should my Soule confound,
And give my Heart than Death a deeper Wound?
Thou didst disdaine my Teares,
But grieve not that this ruethfull Stone them beares,   20
Mine Eyes serve only now for thee to weepe,
And let their Course them keepe,
Although thou never wouldst them Comfort show,
Doe not repine, they have Part of thy Woe.
    Ah *Wretch! too late I finde,*   25
How Vertues *glorious Titles prove but Winde;*
For if shee any could release from Death,
Thou yet enjoy'd hadst Breath;
For if shee ere appear'd to mortall Eine,
It was in thy faire Shape that shee was seene.   30
But ô! if I was made
For thee, with thee why too am I not dead?
Why doe outragious Fates *which dimm'd thy Sight,*
Let mee see hatefull Light?
They without mee made Death *thee to surprise*   35

l. 1   *Damon.* The poet, identified with Drummond himself.
l. 7   *wake.* Weak.
l. 29   *Eine*   Eyes.

57

Tyrants (perhaps) *that they might kill mee twise.*
    O Griefe! and could one Day
Have Force such Excellence to take away?
Could a swift-flying Moment (ah) deface
Those matchlesse Gifts, that Grace   40
Which Art *and* Nature *had in thee combinde,*
To make thy Body paragone thy Minde?
Have all past like a Cloud,
And doth eternall Silence now them shroud?
Is what so much admir'd was nought but Dust,   45
Of which a Stone hath trust?
O Change! ô cruell Change! thou to our Sight
Shewes Destines *Rigour equall doth their Might.*
    When thou from Earth didst passe
(Sweet Nymph) Perfections Mirrour broken was,   50
And this of late so glorious World of ours,
Like Meadow without Flowrs,
Or Ring of a rich Gemme made blind, appear'd,
Or Night, by Starre nor Cynthia *neither clear'd.*
Love when hee saw thee die,   55
Entomb'd him in the Lidde of either Eye,
And left his Torch within thy sacred Urne,
There for a Lampe to burne:
Worth, Honour, Pleasure, with thy Life expir'd,
Death since (growne sweet) beginnes to bee desir'd.   60
    Whilst thou to us wast given,
The Earth her Venus *had as well as Heaven:*
Nay and her Sunne, *which burnt as many Hearts,*
As hee doth Easterne Parts;
Bright Sunne, which forc'd to leave these Hemispheares,   65
Benighted set into a Sea of Teares.
Ah Death! who shall thee flie?
Sith the most worthie bee o'rethrowne by thee?
Thou spar'st the Ravens, and Nightingalles dost kill,
And triumphes at thy will: 70
But give thou canst not such an other Blow,
Because like Her Earth can none other show.

l. 53   *made blind.* Robbed.
l. 54   *Cynthia.* The moon.

58

    O bitter-Sweets of Love!
How better is 't at all you not to prove?
Than when wee doe your Pleasure most possesse,   75
To find them then made lesse?
O! that the Cause which doth consume our Joy
Remembrance of it too, would too destroy!
What doth this Life bestow
But Flowrs on Thornes which grow?   80
Which though they sometime blandishing delighte,
Yet afterwards us smite?
And if the rising Sunne them faire doth see,
That Planet setting, too beholdes them die.
    This World is made a Hell,   85
Depriv'd of all that in it did excell.
O Pan, Pan, Winter is fallen in our May,
Turn'd is in Night our Day;
Forsake thy Pipe, a Scepter take to thee,
The Lockes disgarland, thou blacke Jove *shalt bee.*   90
The Flockes doe leave the Meads,
And loathing three-leaf'd Grasse, hold up their Heads.
The Streames not glide now with a gentle Rore,
Nor Birds sing as before,
Hilles stand with Clouds like Mourners, vail'd in Blacke,   95
And Owles on Caban Roofes fore-tell our Wracke.
    That Zephyre *everie Yeere*
So soone was heard to sigh in Forrests heere,
It was for Her: that wrapt in Gownes of Greene,
Meads were so earelie seene,   100
That in the saddest Months oft sung the Mearles,
It was for Her: for her Trees dropt foorth Pearles.
That prowde, and statelie Courts,
Did envie those our Shades, and calme Resorts,
It was for Her: and she is gone, ô Woe!   105
Woods cut, againe doe grow,
Budde doth the Rose, and Dazie, Winter done,
But wee once dead no more doe see the Sunne.

l. 74   *prove.* Experience.
l. 96   *Caban.* Cabin.
       Wracke. Punishment.
l. 101   *Mearles.* Blackbirds.

Whose Name shall now make ring
The Ecchoes? of whom shall the Nymphettes sing?　110
Whose heavenlie Voyce, whose Soule-invading Straines,
Shall fill with Joy the Plaines?
What Haire, what Eyes, can make the Morne in East
Weepe, that a fairer riseth in the West?
Faire Sunne, poste still away,　115
No Musicke heere is found thy Course to stay.
Sweet Hybla Swarmes with Wormewood fill your Bowrs,
Gone is the Flowre of Flowrs,
Blush no more Rose, nor Lillie pale remaine,
Dead is that Beautie which yours late did staine.　120
　　　Aye mee! to waile my Plight
Why have not I as many Eyes as Night?
Or as that Shepheard which Joves Love did keepe?
That I still still may weepe:
But though I had, my Teares unto my Crosse　125
Were not yet equall, nor Griefe to my Losse,
Yet of you brinie Showrs,
Which I heere powre, may spring as many Flowrs,
As came of those which fell from Helens Eyes,
And when yee doe arise,　130
May everie Leafe in sable Letters beare
The dolefull Cause for which yee spring up heere.

l. 117　Sweet Hybla. Famous for honey.
　　　Wormewood. A bitter plant.
l. 123　Joves Love. Iö, guarded by the hundred-eyed Argus.
ll. 128-9　Flowrs . . . which fell from Helens Eyes. The herb elecampane.

Madrigall ii

Deare Night, the Ease of Care,
Untroubled Seate of Peace,
Times eldest Childe, which oft the Blinde doe see,
On this our Hemispheare,
What makes thee now so sadly darke to bee?　5
Comm'st thou in funerall Pompe her Grave to grace?
Or doe those Starres which should thy Horrour cleare,

In Joves *high Hall advise,*
In what Part of the Skies,
With them, or Cynthia *shee shall appeare?*   10
Or (ah alas!) *because those matchless Eyes*
    Which shone so faire, below thou dost not finde,
    Striv'st thou to make all other Eyes looke blinde?

l. 10 *Cynthia.* The moon.

Sonnet viii

My Lute, bee as thou wast when thou didst grow
With thy greene Mother in some shadie Grove,
When immelodious *Windes* but made thee move,
And *Birds* on thee their Ramage did bestow.
Sith that deare Voyce which did thy Sounds approve,   5
Which us'd in such harmonious Straines to flow,
Is reft from Earth *to tune those Spheares above,*
What art thou but a Harbenger of Woe?
Thy pleasing Notes, be pleasing Notes no more,
But orphane Wailings to the fainting Eare,   10
Each Stoppe a Sigh, each Sound drawes foorth a Teare,
Bee therefore silent as in Woods before,
    Or if that any Hand to touch thee daigne,
    Like widow'd Turtle, still her Losse complaine.

l. 4 *Ramage.* Birdsong.
l. 8 *Harbenger.* Host.
l. 14 *Turtle.* Dove.

Sonnet ix

Sweet *Spring*, thou turn'st with all thy goodlie Traine,
Thy Head with Flames, thy Mantle bright with Flowrs,
The *Zephyres* curle the greene Lockes of the Plaine,
The Cloudes for Joy in Pearles weepe downe their Showrs.
Thou turn'st (sweet Youth) but *ah* my pleasant Howres,   5
And happie Dayes, with thee come not againe,

The sad Memorialls only of my Paine
Doe with thee turne, which turne my Sweets in Sowres.
Thou art the same which still thou wast before,
Delicious, wanton, amiable, faire,   10
But *shee*, whose Breath embaulm'd thy wholesome Aire,
Is gone: nor Gold, nor Gemmes Her can restore.
    Neglected *Vertue*, Seasons goe and come,
    While thine forgot lie closed in a Tombe.

Sonnet x

What doth it serve to see Sunnes burning Face?
And Skies enamell'd with both the *Indies* Gold?
Or Moone at Night in jettie Charriot roll'd?
And all the Glorie of that starrie Place?
What doth it serve Earths Beautie to behold?   5
The Mountaines Pride, the Meadowes flowrie Grace,
The statelie Comelinesse of Forrests old,
The Sport of Flouds which would themselves embrace?
What doth it serve to heare the *Sylvans* Songs,
The wanton Mearle, the Nightingalles sad Straines,   10
Which in darke Shades seeme to deplore my Wrongs?
For what doth serve all that this World containes,
    Sith shee for whome those once to mee were deare,
    No Part of them can have now with mee heere?

l. 9   *Sylvans*. Wood-spirits.
l. 10   *Mearle*. Blackbird.

Madrigall iii

The Beautie, and the Life,
Of Lifes, and Beauties fairest Paragon,
(O Teares! ô Griefe!) hang at a feeble Thread,
To which pale Atropos had set her Knife,
The Soule with many a Grone   5
Had left each outward Part,

l. 4   *Atropos*. The Fate who cuts the thread of life.

And now did take his last Leave of the Heart,
Nought else did want, save Death, *even to be dead:*
When the afflicted Band about her Bed
    (*Seeing so faire him come in Lips, Cheekes, Eyes*)   10
    Cried, ah! *and can* Death *enter Paradise?*

Sonnet xi

Ah *Napkin,* ominous Present of my Deare,
Gift miserable, which doth now remaine
The only Guerdon of my helplesse Paine,
When I thee got thou shew'd my State too cleare:
I never since have ceased to complaine,   5
Since, I the Badge of *Griefe* did ever weare,
Joy on my Face durst never since appeare,
Care was the Food which did mee entertaine.
Now (since made mine) deare *Napkin* doe not grieve
That I this Tribute pay thee from mine Eine,   10
And that (these posting Houres I am to live)
I laundre thy faire Figures in this Brine:
    No, I must yet even begge of thee the Grace,
    That thou wouldst daigne in Grave to shrowde my Face.

l. 3 *Guerdon.* Reward.
l. 10 *Eine.* Eyes.
l. 11 *Posting.* Fleeting.

Madrigall iv

Poore Turtle, thou bemones
The Losse of thy deare Love,
And I for mine send foorth these smoaking Grones,
Unhappie widow'd Dove,
While all about doe sing,   5
I at the Roote, Thou on the Branche above,
Even wearie with our Mones the gaudie Spring.

l. 1 *Turtle.* Dove.
l. 3 *smoaking.* Vaporous, intense.

Yet these our Plaints wee doe not spend in vaine,
Sith sighing Zephyres answere us againe.

Sonnet xii

As in a duskie and tempestuous Night,
A Starre is wont to spreade her Lockes of Gold,
And while her pleasant Rayes abroad are roll'd,
Some spitefull Cloude doth robbe us of her Sight:
(Faire Soule) in this blacke Age so shin'd thou bright,   5
And made all Eyes with Wonder thee beholde,
Till uglie *Death* depriving us of Light,
In his grimme mistie Armes thee did enfolde.
Who more shall vaunt true Beautie heere to see?
What Hope doth more in any Heart remaine,   10
That such Perfections shall his *Reason* raine?
If Beautie with thee borne too died with thee?
    World, plaine no more of *Love*, nor count his Harmes,
    With his pale Trophees *Death* hath hung his Armes.

Sonnet xiii

Sith it hath pleas'd that First and *onlie Faire*
To take that Beautie to himselfe againe,
Which in *this World of Sense* not to remaine,
But to amaze, was sent, and home repaire,
The Love which to that Beautie I did beare   5
(Made pure of mortall Spots which did it staine,
And endlesse, which even *Death* cannot impaire)
I place on him who will it not disdaine.
No shining Eyes, no Lockes of curling Gold,
No blushing Roses on a virgine Face,   10
No outward Show, no, nor no inward Grace,
Shall Force hereafter have my Thoughts to hold:
    Love heere on Earth hudge Stormes of Care doe tosse,
    But plac'd above, exempted is from Losse.

l. 1   *that First and onlie Faire*. God.

Madrigall v

My *Thoughts* hold mortall *Strife*,
I doe detest my *Life*,
And with lamenting *Cries*
(*Peace* to my *Soule* to bring)
Oft calles that *Prince* which here doth *Monarchise*,   5
But Hee grimme-grinning *King*,
Who Catives scornes, and doth the *Blest* surprise,
    Late having deckt with Beauties *Rose* his *Tombe*,
    Disdaines to croppe a *Weede*, and will not come.

l. 7   *Catives.* Caitiffs: wretches, slaves.

Song ii

It Autumne *was, and on our* Hemispheare
Faire Ericyne *began bright to appeare,*
Night *West-ward did her gemmie* World decline,
And hide her Lights, *that greater* Light *might shine:*
The crested Bird *had given* Alarum *twise*   5
To lazie Mortalls, *to unlocke their* Eyes,
The Owle *had left to plaine, and from each* Thorne
The wing'd Musicians *did salute the* Morne,
Who (while shee glass'd her Lockes *in* Ganges Streames)
Set open wide the christall Port *of* Dreames: 10
When I, whose Eyes *no drowsie* Night *could close,*
In Sleepes *soft* Armes *did quietly repose,*
And, for that Heavens *to die mee did denie,*
Deaths *Image kissed, and as dead did lie.*
I lay as dead, but scarce charm'd were my Cares,   15
And slaked scarce my Sighes, *scarce dried my* Teares,
Sleepe *scarce the uglie* Figures *of the* Day
Had with his sable Pincell *put away,*
And left mee in a still and calmie Mood,
When by my Bed *(me thought) a* Virgine *stood,*   20

l. 2   *Ericyne.* Venus.
l. 5   *the crested Bird.* The cock.
l. 18   *Pincell.* Pencil.

65

A *Virgine* in the *Blooming* of her *Prime*,
If such rare *Beautie* measur'd bee by *Time*?
Her *Head* a *Garland* ware of *Opalls* bright,
About Her flow'd a *Gowne* as pure as *Light*,
Deare amber *Lockes* gave *Umbrage* to her *Face*,   25
Where Modestie high Majestie did grace,
Her *Eyes* such *Beames* sent foorth, that but with *Paine*
Here, weaker *Sights* their sparckling could sustaine:
No *Deitie* faign'd which haunts the silent *Woods*
Is like to Her, nor Syrene of the *Floods*:   30
Such is the golden *Planet* of the *Yeare*,
When blushing in the East hee doth appeare.
Her *Grace* did *Beautie*, *Voyce* yet *Grace* did passe,
Which thus through *Pearles* and *Rubies* broken was.

         How long wilt thou (said shee) estrang'd from *Joy*,   35
Paint *Shadowes* to thy selfe of false *Annoy*?
How long thy *Minde* with horride *Shapes* affrighte,
And in imaginarie *Evills* delighte?
Esteeme that *Losse*, which (well when view'd) is *Gaine*,
Or if a *Losse*, yet not a *Losse* to plaine?   40
O leave thy tyred *Soule* more to molest,
And thinke that *Woe* when shortest then is best.
If shee for whom thou deafnest thus the *Skie*
Bee dead? what then? was shee not borne to die?
Was shee not mortall borne? if thou dost grieve   45
That *Times* should bee, in which shee should not live,
Ere e're shee was, weepe that *Dayes Wheele* was roll'd,
Weepe that shee liv'd not in the *Age* of *Gold*:
For that shee was not then, thou may'st deplore
As duely as that now shee is no more.   50
If onely shee had died, thou sure hadst *Cause*
To blame the *Destines* and *Heavens* irone *Lawes*:
But looke how many *Millions* Her advance,
What numbers with Her enter in this *Dance*,
With those which are to come: shall *Heavens* them staye,   55
And *Alls* faire *Order* breake, thee to obaye?
Even as thy *Birth*, *Death* which thee doth appall,

l. 25 *Umbrage.* Shade.
l. 53 *advance.* Go before.

66

A Piece is of the Life of this great All.
Strong Cities die, die doe high palmie Raignes,
And (weakling) thou thus to bee handled plaines. 60
    If shee bee dead? then shee of lothsome Dayes
Hath past the Line, whose Length but Losse bewrayes;
Then shee hath left this filthie Stage of Care,
Where Pleasure seldome, Woe doth still repaire:
For all the Pleasures which it doth containe, 65
Not contervaile the smallest Minutes Paine.
And tell mee, Thou who dost so much admire
This little Vapour, Smoake, this Sparke, or Fire,
Which Life *is call'd, what doth it thee bequeath,*
But some few Yeeres which Birth drawes out to Death? 70
Which if thou paragone, with Lusters runne,
And them whose Carriere is but now begunne,
In Dayes great Vaste they shall farre lesse appeare,
Than with the Sea when matched is a Teare.
But why wouldst thou Here longer wish to bee? 75
One Yeere doth serve all Natures *Pompe to see,*
Nay, even one Day, and Night: This Moone, that Sunne,
Those lesser Fires about this Round which runne,
Bee but the same which under Saturnes *Raigne*
Did the serpenting Seasons *enterchaine.* 80
How oft doth Life grow lesse by living long?
And what excelleth but what dieth yong?
For Age which all abhorre (yet would embrace)
Whiles makes the Minde as wrinckled as the Face:
And when that Destinies *conspire with Worth,* 85
That Yeeres not glorie Wrong, Life soone goes forth.
Leave then Laments, and thinke thou didst not live,
Lawes to that first eternall Cause to give,
But to obey those Lawes which hee hath given,
And bow unto the just Decrees of Heaven, 90
Which can not erre, what ever foggie Mists
Doe blinde Men in these sublunarie Lists.

l. 62   *bewrayes.* Exposes.
l. 66   *contervaile.* Counterbalance.
l. 71   *paragone.* Surpass.
      Lusters. Periods of five years.
l. 92   *in these sublunarie Lists.* On earth.

But what if shee for whom thou spend'st those Grones,
And wastest Lifes deare Torch in ruethfull Mones,
Shee for whose sake thou hat'st the joyfull Light,   95
Court'st solitarie Shades, and irkesome Night,
Doth live? ô! (if thou canst) through Teares a Space
Lift thy dimm'd Lights, and looke upon this Face,
Looke if those Eyes which (foole) thou didst adore,
Shine not more bright than they were wont before?   100
Looke if those Roses Death could ought impaire,
Those Roses to thee once which seem'd so faire?
And if these Lockes have lost ought of that Gold,
Which earst they had when thou them didst behold?
I live, and happie live, but thou art dead,   105
And still shalt bee, till thou be like mee made.
Alas! whilst wee are wrapt in Gownes of Earth,
And blinde, heere sucke the Aire of Woe beneath,
Each thing in Senses Ballances wee wie,
And but with Toyle, and Paine the Trueth descrie   110
    Above this vaste and admirable Frame,
This Temple visible, which World wee name,
Within whose Walles so many Lamps doe burne,
So many Arches opposite doe turne,
Where Elementall Brethren nurse their Strife,   115
And by intestine Warres maintaine their Life,
There is a World, a World of perfect Blisse,
Pure, immateriall, bright, more farre from this,
Than that high Circle which the rest enspheares
Is from this dull ignoble Vale of Teares,   120
A World, where all is found, that heere is found,
But further discrepant than Heaven and Ground:
It hath an Earth, as hath this World of yours,
With Creatures peopled, stor'd with Trees, and Flowrs,
It hath a Sea, like Saphire Girdle cast,   125
Which decketh of harmonious Shores the Waste,
It hath pure Fire, it hath delicious Aire,
Moone, Sunne, and Starres, Heavens wonderfully faire:
But there Flowrs doe not fade, Trees grow not olde,
The Creatures doe not die through Heat nor Colde,   130

l. 109   wie. Weigh.

68

Sea there not tossed is, nor Aire made blacke,
Fire doth not nurse it selfe on others Wracke;
There Heavens bee not constrain'd about to range,
For this World hath no neede of any Change:
The Minutes grow not Houres, Houres rise not Dayes,   135
Dayes make no Months, but ever-blooming Mayes.
   Heere I remaine, and hitherward doe tend
All who their Spanne of Dayes in Vertue spend:
What ever Pleasure this low Place containes,
It is a Glance but of what high remaines.   140
Those who (perchance) thinke there can nothing bee
Without this wide Expansion which they see,
And that nought else mounts Starres Circumference,
For that nought else is subject to their Sense,
Feele such a Case, as one whom some Abisme   145
Of the Deepe Ocean kept had all his Time:
Who borne and nourish'd there, can scarcely dreame
That ought can live without that brinie Streame,
Can not beleeve that there be Temples, Towres,
Which goe beyond his Caves and dampish Bowres,   150
Or there bee other People, Manners, Lawes,
Than them hee finds within the roaring Waves,
That sweeter Flowrs doe spring than grow on Rockes,
Or Beasts bee which excell the skalie Flockes,
That other Elements bee to bee found,   155
Than is the Water, and this Ball of Ground.
But thinke that Man from those Abismes were brought,
And saw what curious Nature here hath wrought,
Did see the Meads, the tall and shadie Woods,
The Hilles did see, the cleare and ambling Floods,   160
The diverse Shapes of Beasts which Kinds foorth bring,
The feathred Troupes, that flie and sweetly sing:
Did see the Palaces, the Cities faire,
The Forme of humane Life, the Fire, the Aire,
The brightnesse of the Sunne that dimmes his Sight,   165
The Moone, the gastly Splendors of the Night:
What uncouth Rapture would his Minde surprise?
How would hee his (late-deare) Resort despise?

l. 132 *Wracke.* Disaster.

How would hee muse how foolish hee had beene
To thinke nought bee, but what hee there had seene? 170
Why did wee get this high and vaste Desire,
Unto immortall things still to aspire?
Why doth our Minde extend it beyond Time,
And to that highest Happinesse even clime?
If wee be nought but what to Sense wee seeme, 175
And Dust, as most of Worldlings us esteeme?
Wee bee not made for Earth, though here wee come,
More than the Embryon for the Mothers Wombe:
It weepes to bee made free, and wee complaine
To leave this loathsome Jayle of Care and Paine. 180
    But thou who vulgare Foot-steps dost not trace,
Learne to raise up thy Minde unto this Place,
And what Earth-creeping Mortalles most affect,
If not at all to scorne, yet to neglect:
O chase not Shadowes vaine, which when obtain'd, 185
Were better lost, than with such Travell gain'd.
Thinke that, on Earth which Humanes Greatnesse call,
Is but a glorious Title to live thrall:
That Scepters, Diadems, and Chaires of State,
Not in themselves, but to small Mindes are great: 190
How those who loftiest mount, doe hardest light,
And deepest Falls bee from the highest Hight;
How Fame an Eccho is, how all Renowne
Like to a blasted Rose, ere Night falles downe:
And though it something were, thinke how this Round 195
Is but a litle Point, which doth it bound.
O leave that Love which reacheth but to Dust,
And in that Love eternall only trust,
And Beautie, which when once it is possest,
Can only fill the Soule, and make it blest. 200
Pale Envie, jealous Emulations, Feares,
Sighs, Plaints, Remorse, here have no Place, nor Teares,
False Joyes, vaine Hopes, here bee not, Hate nor Wrath,
What ends all Love, here most augments it, Death.
If such Force had the dimme Glance of an Eye, 205
Which some few Dayes thereafter was to die,

l. 186 *Travell.* Travail, toil.

That it could make thee leave all other things,
And like the *Taper-flie* there burne thy *Wings?*
And if a *Voyce,* of late which could but waile,
Such *Power* had, as through *Eares* thy *Soule* to steale?   210
If once thou on that only *Faire* couldst gaze,
What *Flames* of *Love* would hee within thee raise?
In what a *mazing Maze* would it thee bring,
To heare but once that *Quire celestiall* sing?
The fairest *Shapes* on which thy *Love* did sease,   215
Which earst did breede *Delight,* then would displease,
Then *Discords* hoarse were *Earths* entising *Sounds,*
All *Musicke* but a *Noyse* which *Sense* confounds.
This great and burning *Glasse* that cleares all *Eyes,*
And musters with such *Glorie* in the *Skies,*   220
That silver *Starre* which with its sober *Light,*
Makes *Day* oft envie the eye-pleasing *Night,*
Those golden *Letters* which so brightly shine
In *Heavens* great *Volume* gorgeously divine,
The *Wonders* all in *Sea,* in *Earth,* in *Aire,*   225
Bee but darke *Pictures* of that *Soveraigne Faire,*
Bee *Tongues,* which still thus crie into your *Eare,*
(Could yee amidst *Worlds* Cataracts them heare)
From fading things (*fond Wights*) lift your *Desire,*
And in our *Beautie,* his us made admire,   230
If wee seeme faire? ô thinke how faire is *Hee,*
Of whose faire *Fairnesse, Shadowes, Steps,* we bee.
No *Shadow* can compare it with the *Face,*
No *Step* with that deare *Foot* which did it trace;
Your *Soules* immortall are, then place them hence,   235
And doe not drowne them in the *Must* of *Sense:*
Doe not, ô doe not by false *Pleasures Might*
Deprive them of that true, and sole *Delight.*
That *Happinesse* yee seeke is not below,
Earths sweetest *Joy* is but disguised *Woe.*   240
        Heere did shee pause, and with a milde Aspect

l. 208   *Taper-flie.* Candle-fly, thus, a moth.
l. 213   *Mazing.* Bewildering.
l. 220   *musters.* Shows.
l. 229   *fond Wights.* Foolish creatures.
l. 236   *Must.* New wine.

71

Did towards mee those lamping Twinnes direct:
The wonted Rayes I knew, and thrice essay'd
To answere make, thrice faultring Tongue it stay'd.
And while upon that Face I fed my Sight,   245
Mee thought shee vanish'd up in Titans Light,
Who guilding with his Rayes each Hill and Plaine,
Seem'd to have brought the Gold-smiths World againe.

l. 242   *lamping Twinnes.* Flashing eyes.
l. 248   *Gold-smiths World.* Golden Age.

MADRIGALS AND EPIGRAMMES

i

THE STATUE OF MEDUSA

Of that *Medusa* strange,
Who those that did her see in Rockes did change,
None Image carv'd is this;
Medusas selfe it is,
For whilst at Heat of Day,   5
To quench her Thirst Shee by this Spring did stay,
Her curling Snakes beholding in this Glasse,
Life did Her leave, and thus transform'd Shee was.

l. 3   *None.* No.

ii

THE TROJANE HORSE

A Horse I am, whom Bit,
Raine, Rod, nor Spurre, not feare;
When I my Riders beare,
Within my Wombe, not on my Backe they sit:
No Streames I drinke, nor care for Grasse, nor Corne,   5
Arte mee a Monster wrought,
All *Natures* Workes to scorne:
A Mother, I was without Mother borne,
In End all arm'd my Father I forth brought:
What thousand Ships, and Champions of Renowne,   10
Could not doe free, I captive raz'd a Towne.

73

iii

THE POURTRAIT OF MARS AND VENUS

Faire *Paphos* wanton Queene,
Not drawne in White and Red,
Is truely heere, as when in *Vulcans* Bed
She was of all Heavens laughing *Senate* seene:
Gaze on her Haire, and Eine,   5
Her Browes, the Bowes of *Love*,
Her backe with Lillies spred:
And yee should see her turne, and sweetly move,
But that Shee neither so will doe, nor darre,
For feare to wake the angrie God of Warre.   10

l. 1 *Paphos*. City of Cyprus, sacred to Venus.
l. 2 *White and Red*. The painter's colours for the female form.
l. 5 *Eine*. Eyes.

iv

ICARUS

Whilst with audacious Wings
I sprang those airie Wayes,
And fill'd (a Monster new) with Dread and Feares,
The feathred People, and their Eagle Kings:
Dazel'd with *Phœbus* Rayes,   5
And charmed with the Musicke of the Spheares,
When Pennes could move no more, and Force did faile,
I measur'd by a Fall these loftie Bounds;
Yet doth Renowne my Losses countervaile,
For still the Shore my brave Attempt resounds: 10
A Sea, an Element doth beare my Name,
Who hath so vaste a *Tombe* in Place, or Fame?

l. 7   *Pennes*. Feathers, wings.
l. 9   *countervaile*. Counterbalance.
l. 10 *resounds*. Proclaims.
l. 11 *A Sea . . .* Icarean Sea.

CHERRIES

My Wanton, weepe no more
The losing of your Cherries,
Those, and farre sweeter Berries,
Your Sister in good store
Hath, spred on Lips, and Face: 5
Be glad, kisse but with me, and hold your peace.

vi

LOVE SUFFERETH NO PARASOL

Those Eyes, deare Eyes, bee Spheares,
Where two bright Sunnes are roll'd,
That faire Hand to behold,
Of whitest Snowe appeares:
Then while yee coylie stand,   5
To hide from mee those Eyes,
Sweet, I would you advise
To choose some other Fanne than that white Hand:
For if yee doe, for Trueth most true this know,
That Sunnes ere long must needes consume warme Snow.   10

vii

OF PHILLIS

In Peticote of Greene,
Her Haire about her Eine,
Phillis beneath an Oake
Sate milking her faire Flocke:
Among that strained Moysture (rare Delight!)   5
Her Hand seem'd Milke in Milke, it was so white.

viii

KISSES DESIRED

Though I with strange Desire
To kisse those rosie Lips am set on Fire,
Yet will I cease to crave
Sweet Touches in such store,
As hee who long before 5
From *Lesbia* them in thousands did receave;
Heart mine, but once mee kisse,
And I by that sweet Blisse
Even sweare to cease you to importune more,
Poore one no Number is: 10
Another Word of mee yee shall not heare,
After one Kisse, but still one Kisse, my Deare.

l. 5 *hee who long before.* Catullus.

ix

NARCISSUS

Flouds cannot quench my Flames, *ah!* in this Well
I burne, not drowne, for what I cannot tell.

x

A KISSE

Harke happie Lovers, harke,
This first and last of Joyes,
This Sweetner of Annoyes,
This Nectare of the Gods,
Yee call a Kisse, is with it selfe at ods: 5
And halfe so sweet is not
In equall Measure got,
At Light of Sunne, as it is in the Darke,
Harke, happie Lovers, harke.

OF A BEE

As an audacious Knight
Come with some Foe to fight,
His Sword doth brandish, makes his Armour ring:
So this prowde Bee (at home (perhaps) a King)
Did buzzing flie about,   5
And (Tyrant) after thy faire Lip did sting:
O Champion strange as stout!
Who hast by *Nature* found,
Sharpe Armes, and Trumpet shrill, to sound, and wound.

xii

OF THAT SAME

O doe not kill that Bee
That thus hath wounded thee,
(Sweet) it was no Despight,
But Hue did him deceave:
For when thy Lips did close,   5
Hee deemed them a Rose,
What wouldst thou further crave?
Hee wanting Wit, and blinded with Delight,
Would faine have kiss'd, but Mad with Joy did bite.

xiii

TO THAUMANTIA

Come, let us live, and love,
And kisse, *Thaumantia* mine,
I shall the Elme bee, bee to mee the Vine,
Come let us teach new Billing to the Dove:
Nay, to augment our Blisse,   5
Let Soules even other kisse,
Let *Love* a Worke-man bee,
Undoe, distemper, and his Cunning prove,

77

Of Kisses three make one, of one make three:
Though Moone, Sunne, Starres, bee Bodies farre more
bright,   10
Let them not vaunt they match us in Delight.

xiv

CLORUS TO A GROVE

Old Oake, and you thicke Grove,
I ever shall you love,
With these sweet-smelling Briers,
For Briers, Oake, Grove, yee crowned my Desires,
When underneath your Shade   5
I left my Woe, and *Flore* her Maidenhead.

xv

THE HAPPINESS OF A FLEA

How Happier is that Flea
Which in thy Brest doth playe,
Than that pied Butterflie
Which courtes the Flame, and in the same doth die?
That hath a light Delight   5
(Poore Foole) contented only with a Sight,
When this doth sporte, and swell with dearest Food,
And if hee die, hee Knight-like dies in Blood.

xvi

OF THAT SAME

Poore Flea, then thou didst die,
Yet by so faire a Hand,
That thus to die was *Destine* to command:
Thou die didst, yet didst trie
A Lovers last Delight,   5
To vault on virgine Plaines, Her kisse, and bite:

78

Thou diedst, yet hast thy Tombe
Betweene those Pappes, ô deare and stately Roome!
Flea, happier farre, more blest,
Than *Phœnix* burning in his spicie Nest.   10

l. 10   *Phoenix*. The phoenix was re-born on its nest of fire.

xvii

CHANGE OF LOVE

Once did I weepe, and grone,
Drinke Teares, draw loathed Breath,
And all for Love of one
Who did affect my Death:
But now (Thankes to *Disdaine*)   5
I live reliev'd of Paine,
For Sighs, I singing goe,
I burne not as before, no, no, no, no.

xviii

THIRSIS IN DISPRAISE OF BEAUTIE

That which so much the doating World doth prise,
Fond Ladies only Care, and sole Delight,
Soone-fading *Beautie*, which of Hues doth rise,
Is but an abject Let of *Natures* Might;
Most woefull Wretch, whom shining Haire and Eyes,   5
Leade to *Loves* Dungeon, traitor'd by a Sight,
    Most woefull: for hee might with greater Ease
    Hells Portalls enter, and pale *Death* appease.

As in delicious Meads beneath the Flowres,
And the most wholsome Herbes that *May* can show,   10
In christall Curles the speckled Serpent lowres,
As in the Apple (which most faire doth grow)
The rotten Worme is clos'd, which it devoures,

l. 4   *Let*. Hindrance.

79

As in gilt Cups with *Gnossian* Wine which flow,
Oft Poyson pompously doth hide its Sowres: 15
    So Lewdnesse, Falshood, Mischiefe, them advance,
    Clad with the pleasant Rayes of *Beauties* Glance.

Good thence is chas'd, where *Beautie* doth appeare,
Milde Lowlinesse with Pittie from it flie,
Where *Beautie* raignes as in their proper Spheare,   20
Ingratitude, Disdaine, Pride, all descrie,
The Flowre, and Fruit which *Vertues* Tree should beare,
With her bad Shadowe *Beautie* maketh die:
    Beautie a Monster is, a Monster hurld
    From angrie Heaven, to scourge this lower World.   25

As Fruits which are unripe, and sowre of Taste,
To bee confect'd more fit than sweet wee prove,
For Sweet in Spight of Care themselves will waste,
When they long kept, the Appetite doe move:
So in the Sweetnesse of his *Nectare, Love*   30
The foule confects, and seasons for his Feaste:
    Sowre is farre better which wee sweet may make,
    Than sweet which sweeter Sweetnesse will not take.

Foule may my Ladie bee, and may her Nose
(A *Tanarife*) give Umbrage to her Chinne;   35
May her gay Mouth (which shee no Time may close)
So wide be, that the Moone may turne therein,
May Eyes, and Teeth, bee made conforme to those,
Eyes set by Chance, and white, Teeth blacke and thinne:
    May all what seene is, and is hidde from Sight,   40
    Like unto these rare Parts bee framed right.

I shall not feare thus though shee straye alone,
That others Her pursue, entice, admire,
And though shee sometime counterfaite a Grone,
I shall not thinke her Heart feeles uncouth Fire,   45

l. 27 *confect'd.* Cooked, prepared.
l. 35 *Tanarife.* Tenerife, a mountain.
     Umbrage. Shade.

I shall not stile Her ruethlesse to my Mone,
Nor prowde, disdainfull, wayward to *Desire*:
    Her Thoughts with mine will hold an equall Line,
    I shall bee hers, and shee shall all bee mine.

xix

DESIRED DEATH

Deare Life while as I touch
These Corrall Ports of blisse,
Which still themselves do kisse,
And sweetly me invite to do as much,
All panting in my Lips,   5
My Life my Heart doth leave,
No sense my Senses have,
And inward Powers doe find a strange Ecclipse,
This Death so heavenly well
Doth so me please, that I   10
Would never longer seeke in sense to dwell,
If that even thus I only could but die.

xx

Trees happier farre then I,
Which have the Grace to heave your Heads so hie,
And over-looke those Plaines:
Grow till your Branches kisse that lofty Skie
Which her (sweet Her) containes.   5
There make her know mine endlesse Love, and Paines,
And how these Teares which from mine Eyes doe fall,
Helpt you to rise so Tall:
Her tell, as once I for her sake lov'd Breath,
So for her sake I now court lingring Death.   10

BEAUTIES FRAILTYE

Looke how the maying Rose
At sulphures azure fumes,
In a short space her crimsin blush doth lose,
And all amaz'd a pallid whit assumes:
So Tyme our best consumes,   5
Makes youth and Beautie passe,
And what was pryde turnes horrour in our Glasse.

xxii

Astrea in this Time
Now doth not live, but is fled up to Heaven;
Or if shee live, it is not without Crime
That she doth use her Power,
And shee is no more Virgine, but a Whoure,   5
Whoure prostitute for Gold;
For shee doth never holde her Ballance even,
And when her Sword is roll'd,
    The Bad, Injurious, False, shee not o'rethrowes,
    But on the Innocent lets fall her Blowes.   10

l. 1 *Astrea.* Goddess of justice.
l. 8 *roll'd.* Swung.

xxiii

EPITAPH

The Bawd of Justice, he who Lawes controll'd,
And made them fawne, and frowne as he got gold,
That *Proteus* of our State, whose Hart and Mouth
Were farther distant than is North from South,
That Cormorant who made himselfe so grosse   5
On Peoples Ruine, and the Princes Losse,
Is gone to . and though he here did evill,
He meanes below to proove an honest Devill.

l. 3 *Proteus.* Shape-changer.

FORTH FEASTING

A PANEGYRICKE TO THE
KINGS MOST EXCELLENT MAJESTY

What blustring Noise now interrupts my Sleepe?
What echoing Shouts thus cleave my chrystal Deep?
And call mee hence from out my watrie Court?
What Melodie, what Sounds of Joy and Sport,
Bee these heere hurl'd from ev'rie neighbour Spring?   5
With what lowd Rumours doe the Mountaines ring?
Which in unusuall Pompe on tip-toes stand,
And (full of Wonder) over-looke the Land?
Whence come these glittring Throngs, these Meteors bright,
This golden People set unto my Sight?   10
Whence doth this Praise, Applause, and Love, arise?
What Load-starre east-ward draweth thus all Eyes?
Am I awake? or have some Dreames conspir'd
To mocke my Sense with Shadowes much desir'd?
Stare I that living Face, see I those Lookes,   15
Which with Delight wont to amaze my Brookes?
Doe I behold that Worth, that Man divine,
This Ages Glorie, by these Bankes of mine?
Then is it true what long I wish'd in vaine?
That my much-loving Prince is come againe?   20

*   *   *

Swell prowd my Billowes, faint not to declare
Your Joyes, as ample as their Causes are:
For Murmures hoarse sound like *Arions* Harpe,
Now delicatlie flat, now sweetlie sharpe.

l. 12 *Load-starre.* Guiding star, the pole-star.
l. 43 *Arions Harpe.* Arion, the famous poet and musician.

83

And you my Nymphes, rise from your moyst Repaire,   45
Strow all your Springs and Grotts with Lillies faire:
Some swiftest-footed get her hence and pray
Our Floods and Lakes, come keepe this Holie-day;
What e're beneath *Albanias* Hills doe runne,
Which see the rising or the setting Sunne,   50
Which drinke sterne *Grampius* Mists, or *Ochells* Snows:
Stone-rowling *Taye*, *Tine* Tortoyse-like that flows,
The pearlie *Don*, the *Deas*, the fertile *Spay*,
Wild *Neverne* which doth see our longest Day,
Nesse smoaking-Sulphure, *Leave* with Mountaines crown'd,   55
Strange *Loumond* for his floting Isles renown'd:
The irish *Rian*, *Ken*, the silver *Aire*,
The snakie *Dun*, the *Ore* with rushie Haire,
The Chrystall-streaming *Nid*, lowd-bellowing *Clyd*,
Tweed which no more our Kingdomes shall devide: 60
Rancke-swelling *Annan*, *Lid* with curled Streames,
The *Eskes*, the *Solway* where they loose their Names,
To ev'rie one proclaime our Joyes, and Feasts,
Our Triumphes; bid all come, and bee our Guests:
And as they meet in *Neptunes* azure Hall,   65
Bid Them bid *Sea-Gods* keepe this Festivall.

*   *   *

By just Discent Thou from moe Kings dost shine,   205
Then manie can name Men in all their Line:
What most They toyle to find, and finding hold
Thou skornest, orient Gemmes, and flattring Gold:
Esteeming Treasure surer in Mens Brests,
Than when immur'd with Marble, closd in Chests;   210
No stormie Passions doe disturbe thy Mind,
No Mists of greatnesse ever could Thee blind:
Who yet hath beene so meeke? Thou life didst give
To Them who did repine to see Thee live;

l. 46   *Strow*. Strew.
l. 49   *Albanias*. Scotland's.
l. 54   *Neverne*. The river Naver in Sutherland.
l. 55   *Leave*. Leven.
l. 59   *Nid*. The Nith.
l. 61   *Lid*. Liddel Water.

What Prince by Goodnesse hath such Kingdomes gain'd? 215
Who hath so long his Peoples Peace maintain'd?

★   ★   ★

Thou a true Victor art, sent from above
What Others straine by Force to gaine by Love, 240
World-wandring *Fame* this Prayse to Thee imparts,
To bee the onlie Monarch of all Hearts.
They many feare who are of many fear'd,
And Kingdomes got by Wrongs by Wrongs are tear'd,
Such Thrones as Blood doth raise Blood throweth downe, 245
No Guard so sure as Love unto a Crowne.
    Eye of our westerne World, *Mars*-daunting King,
With whose Renowne the Earths seven Climats ring,
Thy Deedes not only claime these Diademes,
To which *Thame*, *Liffy*, *Taye*, subject their Streames: 250
But to thy Vertues rare, and Gifts, is due,
All that the Planet of the Yeere doth view;
Sure if the World above did want a Prince,
The World above to it would take thee hence.

★   ★   ★

    O *Vertues* Patterne, Glorie of our Times,
Sent of past Dayes to expiate the Crimes,
Great King, but better farre than thou art greate,
Whome State not honours, but who honours State,
By Wonder borne, by Wonder first enstall'd,
By Wonder after to new Kingdomes call'd, 290
Young kept by Wonder neare home-bred Alarmes,
Old sav'd by Wonder from pale Traitours Harmes,
To bee for this Thy Raigne which Wonders brings,
A King of Wonder, Wonder unto Kings.
If *Pict*, *Dane*, *Norman*, Thy smooth Yoke had seene, 295
Pict, *Dane*, and *Norman*, had thy Subjects beene:
If *Brutus* knew the Blisse Thy Rule doth give,
Even *Brutus* joye would under Thee to live:
For Thou Thy People dost so dearlie love,
That they a Father, more than Prince, Thee prove. 300
    O Dayes to bee desyr'd! Age happie thrice!

85

If yee your Heaven-sent-Good could duelie prize,
But yee (halfe-palsie-sicke) thinke never right
Of what yee hold, till it bee from your Sight,
Prize onlie Summers sweet and musked Breath,   305
When armed Winters threaten you with Death,
In pallid Sicknesse doe esteeme of Health,
And by sad Povertie discerne of Wealth:
I see ane Age when after manie Yeares,
And Revolutions of the slow-pac'd Spheares,   310
These Dayes shall bee to other farre esteem'd,
And like *Augustus* palmie Raigne bee deem'd.

* * *

The wanton *wood-Nymphes* of the verdant Spring,
Blew, Golden, Purple, Flowres shall to Thee bring,   370
Pomonas Fruits the *Paniskes*, *Thetis* Gyrles
Thy *Thulys* Amber, with the Ocean Pearles;
The *Tritons*, Heards-men of the glassie Field,
Shall give Thee what farre-distant Shores can yeeld,
The *Serean* Fleeces, *Erythrean* Gemmes,   375
Vaste *Platas* Silver, Gold of *Peru* Streames,
Antarticke Parrots, *Æthiopian* Plumes,
Sabæan Odours, Myrrhe, and sweet Perfumes:
And I my selfe, wrapt in a watchet Gowne,
Of Reedes and Lillies on mine Head a Crowne,   380
Shall Incense to Thee burne, greene Altars raise,
And yearly sing due *Pæans* to Thy Praise.
  Ah why should *Isis* only see Thee shine?
Is not thy FORTH, as well as *Isis* Thine?
Though *Isis* vaunt shee hath more Wealth in store,   385
Let it suffice Thy FORTH doth love Thee more:
Though Shee for Beautie may compare with *Seine*,

l. 371 *Pomonas Fruits.* Apples.
   Paniskes. Followers of Pan.
   Thetis Gyrles. Sea-nymphes.
l. 372 *Thy.* Thee?
   Thulys Amber. Northern amber.
l. 375 *Serean Fleeces.* Silks.
l. 378 *Sabæan Odours.* Arabian perfumes.
l. 379 *watchet.* Light-blue.

For Swannes and Sea-*Nymphes* with imperiall *Rhene*,
Yet in the Title may bee claim'd in Thee,
Nor Shee, nor all the World, can match with mee.   390
Now when (by *Honour* drawne) thou shalt away
To Her alreadie jelous of thy Stay,
When in Her amourous Armes Shee doth Thee fold,
And dries thy Dewie Haires with Hers of Gold,
Much questioning of Thy Fare, much of Thy Sport,   395
Much of Thine Absence, Long, how e're so short,
And chides (perhaps) Thy Comming to the North,
Loathe not to thinke on Thy much-loving FORTH:
O love these Bounds, whereof Thy royall Stemme
More then an hundreth wore a Diademe.   400
So ever Gold and Bayes Thy Browes adorne,
So never Time may see Thy Race out-worne,
So of Thine Owne still mayst Thou bee desir'd,
Of Strangers fear'd, redoubted, and admir'd;
So MEMORIE the Praise, so precious *Houres*   405
May character Thy Name in starrie Flowres;
So may Thy high Exployts at last make even,
With Earth thy Empyre, Glorie with the Heaven.

l. 388   *imperiall Rhene.* The Rhine in the Holy Roman Empire.

FLOWRES OF SION

OR

SPIRITUALL POEMES

Sonnet i

THE INSTABILITIE OF MORTALL GLORIE

Triumphant Arches, Statues crown'd with Bayes,
Proude Obeliskes, Tombes of the vastest frame,
Colosses, brasen *Atlases* of Fame,
Phanes vainelie builded to vaine Idoles praise;
States, which unsatiate Mindes in blood doe raise,   5
From the Crosse-starres unto the Articke Teame,
Alas! and what wee write to keepe our Name,
Like Spiders Caules are made the sport of Dayes:
All onely constant is in constant Change,
What done is, is undone, and when undone,   10
Into some other figure doeth it range;
Thus moves the restlesse World beneath the Moone:
    Wherefore (my Minde) above Time, Motion, Place,
    Thee raise, and Steppes, not reach'd by Nature trace.

l. 4 *Phanes.* Temples.
l. 6 *Crosse-starres.* The stars visible in the southern hemisphere; the constellation
     crux?
l. 8 *Caules.* Webs.

Sonnet ii

HUMANE FRAILTIE

A Good that never satisfies the Minde,
A Beautie fading like the Aprile flowres,

88

A Sweete with floodes of Gall that runnes combind,
A Pleasure passing ere in thought made ours,
A Honour that more fickle is than winde,   5
A Glorie at Opinions frowne that lowres,
A Treasurie which Bankrout Time devoures,
A Knowledge than grave Ignorance more blind:
A vaine Delight our equalles to command,
A Stile of greatnesse, in effect a Dreame,   10
A fabulous Thought of holding Sea and Land,
A servile Lot, deckt with a pompous Name,
  Are the strange endes wee toyle for heere below,
  Till wisest Death make us our errores know.

Madrigall i

THE PERMANENCIE OF LIFE

Life a right shadow is,
For if it long appeare,
Then is it spent, and Deathes long Night drawes neare;
Shadowes are moving, light,
And is there ought so moving as is this?   5
When it is most in Sight,
It steales away, and none can tell how, where,
So neere our Cradles to our Coffines are.

Sonnet iii

NO TRUST IN TYME

Looke how the Flowre, which lingringlie doth fade,
The Mornings Darling late, the Summers Queene,
Spoyl'd of that Juice, which kept it fresh and greene,
As high as it did raise, bowes low the head:
Right so my Life (Contentments beeing dead,   5
Or in their Contraries but onelie seene)
With swifter speede declines than earst it spred,
And (blasted) scarce now showes what it hath beene.
As doth the Pilgrime therefore whom the Night

By darknesse would imprison on his way,   10
Thinke on thy Home (my Soule) and thinke aright,
Of what yet restes thee of Lifes wasting Day:
    Thy Sunne postes Westward, passed is thy Morne,
    And twice it is not given thee to bee borne.

l. 12   *restes*. Remains.

Sonnet iv

WORLDES JOYES ARE TOYES

The wearie Mariner so fast not flies
An howling Tempest, Harbour to attaine,
Nor Sheepheard hastes, when frayes of Wolves arise,
So fast to Fold to save his bleeting Traine:
As I (wing'd with Contempt and just Disdaine)   5
Now flie the World, and what it most doth prize,
And Sanctuarie seeke, free to remaine
From wounds of abject Times, and Envies eyes.
Once did this World to mee seeme sweete and faire,
While Senses light Mindes prospective keept blind,   10
Now like imagin'd Landskip in the Aire,
And weeping Raine-bowes, her best Joyes I finde:
    Or if ought heere is had that praise should have,
    It is a Life obscure, and silent Grave.

l. 3   *frayes*. Terrors.
l. 11 *Landskip*. Landscape.

Sonnet v

NATURE MUST YEELDE TO GRACE

Too long I followed have on fond Desire,
And too long painted on deluding Streames,
Too long refreshment sought in burning Fire,
Runne after Joyes which to my Soule were Blames;
Ah! when I had what most I did admire,   5
And prov'd of Lifes delightes the last extreames,

I found all but a Rose hedg'd with a Bryer,
A nought, a thought, a show of golden Dreames.
Hence-foorth on Thee (mine onelie Good) I thinke,
For onelie Thou canst grant what I doe crave,   10
Thy Nailes my Pennes shall bee, thy Blood mine Inke,
Thy winding-sheete my Paper, Studie Grave:
    And till that Soule from Bodie parted bee,
    No hope I have, but onelie onelie Thee.

Sonnet vi

THE BOOKE OF THE WORLD

Of this faire Volumne which wee World doe name,
If wee the sheetes and leaves could turne with care,
Of Him who it correctes, and did it frame,
Wee cleare might read the Art and Wisedome rare?
Finde out his Power which wildest Pow'rs doth tame,   5
His Providence extending everie-where,
His Justice which proud Rebels doeth not spare,
In everie Page, no, Period of the same:
But sillie wee (like foolish Children) rest
Well pleas'd with colour'd Velame, Leaves of Gold,   10
Faire dangling Ribbones, leaving what is best,
On the great Writers sense nee'r taking hold;
    Or if by chance our Mindes doe muse on ought,
    It is some Picture on the Margine wrought.

Sonnet vii

THE MISERABLE ESTATE OF THE WORLD BEFORE
THE INCARNATION OF GOD

The Griefe was common, common were the Cryes,
Teares, Sobbes, and Groanes of that afflicted Traine,
Which of Gods chosen did the Summe containe,
And Earth rebounded with them, pierc'd were Skies;
All good had left the World, each Vice did raigne,   5
In the most hideous shapes Hell could devise,

91

And all degrees, and each Estate did staine,
Nor further had to goe, whom to surprise:
The World beneath the Prince of Darknesse lay,
In everie Phane who had himselfe install'd,   10
Was sacrifiz'd unto, by Prayers call'd,
Responses gave, which (Fooles) they did obey:
 When (pittying Man) God of a Virgines wombe
 Was borne, and those false Deities strooke dombe.

l. 10 *Phane.* Temple.

Sonnet viii

THE ANGELS FOR THE NATIVITIE OF OUR LORD

Runne (Sheepheards) run where *Bethleme* blest appeares,
Wee bring the best of newes, bee not dismay'd,
A Saviour there is borne, more olde than yeares,
Amidst Heavens rolling hights this Earth who stay'd;
In a poore Cotage Inn'd, a Virgine Maide   5
A weakling did him beare, who all upbeares,
There is hee poorelie swadl'd, in Manger lai'd,
To whom too narrow Swadlings are our Spheares:
Runne (Sheepheards) runne, and solemnize his Birth,
This is that Night, no, Day growne great with Blisse,   10
In which the power of *Sathan* broken is,
In Heaven bee glorie, Peace unto the Earth.
 Thus singing through the Aire the Angels swame,
 And Cope of Starres re-echoed the same.

Sonnet ix

FOR THE NATIVITIE OF OUR LORD

O than the fairest Day, thrice fairer Night!
Night to best Dayes in which a Sunne doth rise,
Of which that golden Eye, which cleares the Skies,
Is but a sparkling Ray, a Shadow light:
And blessed yee (in sillie Pastors sight)   5

92

Milde Creatures, in whose warme Cribe now lyes
That Heaven-sent Yongling, holie-Maide-borne Wight,
Midst, end, beginning of our Prophesies:
Blest Cotage that hath Flowres in Winter spred,
Though withered blessed Grasse, that hath the grace   10
To decke, and bee a Carpet to that Place.
Thus sang, unto the Soundes of oaten Reed,
    Before the Babe, the Sheepheards bow'd on knees,
    And Springs ranne Nectar, Honey dropt from Trees.

Sonnet x

AMAZEMENT AT THE INCARNATION OF GOD

To spread the azure Canopie of Heaven,
And make it twinkle with those spangs of Gold,
To stay this weightie masse of Earth so even,
That it should all, and nought should it up-hold;
To give strange motions to the Planets seven,   5
Or Jove to make so meeke, or Mars so bold,
To temper what is moist, drie, hote, and cold,
Of all their Jarres that sweete accords are given:
LORD, to thy Wisedome nought is, nor thy Might;
But that thou shouldst (thy Glorie laid aside)   10
Come meanelie in mortalitie to bide,
And die for those deserv'd eternall plight,
    A wonder is so farre above our wit,
    That Angels stand amaz'd to muse on it.

l. 2   *spangs.* Ornaments.
l. 7   *what is moist . . . cold.* The four elements.

Sonnet xi

FOR THE BAPTISTE

The last and greatest Herauld of Heavens King,
Girt with rough Skinnes, hyes to the Desarts wilde,
Among that savage brood the Woods foorth bring,

93

Which hee than Man more harmlesse found and milde:
His food was Blossomes, and what yong doth spring,   5
With Honey that from virgine Hives distil'd;
Parcht Bodie, hollow Eyes, some uncouth thing
Made him appeare, long since from Earth exilde.
There burst hee foorth; All yee, whose Hopes relye
On GOD, with mee amidst these Desarts mourne,   10
Repent, repent, and from olde errours turne.
Who listned to his voyce, obey'd his crye?
    Onelie the Ecchoes which hee made relent,
    Rung from their Marble Caves, repent, repent.

Sonnet xii

FOR THE MAGDALENE

These Eyes (deare Lord) once Brandons of Desire,
Fraile Scoutes betraying what they had to keepe,
Which their owne heart, then others set on fire,
Their traitrous blacke before thee heere out-weepe:
These Lockes, of blushing deedes the faire attire,   5
Smooth-frizled Waves, sad Shelfes which shadow deepe,
Soule-stinging Serpents in gilt curles which creepe,
To touch thy sacred Feete doe now aspire.
In Seas of Care behold a sinking Barke,
By windes of sharpe Remorse unto thee driven,   10
O let mee not expos'd be Ruines marke,
My faults confest (LORD) say they are forgiven.
    Thus sigh'd to JESUS the Bethanian faire,
    His teare-wet Feete still drying with her Haire.

l. 1 *Brandons.* Torches.

Sonnet xiii

FOR THE PRODIGALL

I Countries chang'd, new pleasures out to finde,
But *Ah!* for pleasure new I found new paine,

Enchanting pleasure so did Reason blind,
That Fathers love, and wordes I scorn'd as vaine:
For Tables rich, for bed, for frequent traine   5
Of carefull servants to observe my Minde,
These Heardes I keepe my fellowes are assign'd,
My Bed a Rocke is, Hearbes my Life sustaine.
Now while I famine feele, feare worser harmes,
Father and Lord I turne, thy Love (yet great)   10
My faults will pardon, pitty mine estate.
This, where an aged Oake had spread its Armes,
    Thought the lost Child, while as the Heardes hee led,
    Not farre off on the ackornes wilde them fed.

Sonnet xiv

FOR THE PASSION

If that the World doth in a maze remaine,
To heare in what a sad deploring mood,
The Pelican powres from her brest her Blood,
To bring to life her younglinges backe again?
How should wee wonder of that soveraigne Good,   5
Who from that Serpents sting (that had us slaine)
To save our lives, shed his Lifes purple flood,
And turn'd in endlesse Joy our endlesse Paine?
Ungratefull Soule, that charm'd with false Delight,
Hast long long wandr'd in Sinnes flowrie Path,   10
And didst not thinke at all, or thoughtst not right
On this thy Pelicanes great Love and Death,
    Heere pause, and let (though Earth it scorne) Heaven see
    Thee powre forth teares to him powr'd Blood for thee.

l. 3   *The Pelican* . . . An emblem of Christ: the pelican was supposed to feed her
       young with her own blood.

Hymne i

AN HYMNE OF THE PASSION

If, when farre in the East yee doe behold
  Foorth from his Christall Bed the Sunne to rise,
  With rosie Robes and Crowne of flaming Gold?
If gazing on that Empresse of the Skies,
  That takes so many Formes, and those faire Brands, 5
  Which blaze in Heavens high Vault, Nights watchfull eyes?
If Seeing how the Seas tumultuous Bands
  Of bellowing Billowes have their course confin'd,
  How unsustain'd the Earth still steadfast stands:
Poore mortall Wights, yee e're found in your Minde 10
  A thought, that some great King did sit above,
  Who had such Lawes and Rites to them assign'd;
A King who fix'd the Poles made Spheares to move,
  All Wisedome, purenesse, Excellence, and Might,
  All Goodnesse, Greatnesse, Justice, Beauty, Love? 15
With feare and wonder hither turne your Sight,
  See, see (alas) Him now, not in that State
  Thought could fore-cast Him into Reasons light.
Now Eyes with teares, now Hearts with griefe make great,
  Bemoane this cruell Death and dreary case, 20
  If ever plaints just Woe could aggravate?
From Sinne and Hell to save us, humaine Race,
  See this great King naill'd to an abject Tree,
  An object of reproach and sad disgrace.
O unheard Pitty, Love in strange degree! 25
  Hee his owne Life doth give, his Blood doth shed,
  For Wormelings base such Excellence to see.
Poore Wightes, behold His Visage pale as Lead,
  His Head bow'd to His Brest, Lockes sadlie rent,
  Like a cropt Rose that languishing doth fade. 30
Weake Nature weepe, astonish'd World lament,
  Lament, yee Windes, you Heaven that all containes,
  And thou (my Soule) let nought thy Griefe relent.
Those Hands, those sacred Hands which hold the raines
  Of this great All, and kept from mutuall warres 35
  The Elements, beare rent for thee their Veines:

Those feete which once must trade on golden Starres,
　　For thee with nailes would bee pierc'd through and torne,
　　For thee Heavens King from Heaven himselfe debarres.
This great heart-quaking Dolour waile and mourne,　　　　40
　　Yee that long since Him saw by might of Faith,
　　Yee now that are, and yee yet to bee borne.
Not to behold his great Creators Death,
　　The Sunne from sinfull eyes hath vail'd his light,
　　And faintly journeyes up Heavens saphire Path.　　　　45
And, cutting from her Browes her Tresses bright,
　　The Moone doth keepe her Lords sad Obsequies,
　　Impearling with her Teares this Robe of Night.
All staggering and lazie lowre the Skies,
　　The Earth and elemental Stages quake,　　　　50
　　The long since dead from bursted Graves arise.
And can things wanting sense yet sorrow take,
　　And beare a Part with him who all them wrought?
　　And Man (though borne with cries) shall pitty lacke?
Thinke what had beene your state, had hee not brought　　55
　　To these sharpe Pangs himselfe, and priz'd so hie
　　Your Soules, that with his Life them life Hee bought.
What Woes doe you attend, if still yee lie
　　Plung'd in your wonted ordures, wretched Brood,
　　Shall for your sake againe GOD ever die?　　　　60
O leave deluding shewes, embrace true good,
　　Hee on you calles, forgoe Sinnes shamefull trade,
　　With Prayers now seeke Heaven, and not with Blood.
Let not the Lambes more from their Dames bee had,
　　Nor Altars blush for Sinne; live every thing,　　　　65
　　That long time long'd-for sacrifice is made.
All that is from you crav'd by this great King
　　Is to beleeve, a pure Heart Incense is,
　　What gift (alas) can wee him meaner bring?
Haste sinne-sicke Soules, this season doe not misse,　　70
　　Now while remorselesse time doth grant you space,
　　And GOD invites you to your only Blisse.
Hee who you calles will not denie you Grace,

l. 37　*trade.* Tread.
l. 59　*ordures.* Filth.

But low-deepe burie faults, so yee repent,
  His armes (loe) stretched are you to embrace.
When Dayes are done, and Lifes small sparke is spent,
  So yee accept what freely here is given,
  Like brood of Angels, deathlesse, all-content,
Yee shall for ever live with him in Heaven.

Sonnet xv

TO THE ANGELS FOR THE PASSION

Come forth, come forth yee blest triumphing Bands,
Faire Citizens of that immortall Towne,
Come see that King which all this All commands,
Now (overcharg'd with Love) die for his owne;
Looke on those Nailes which pierce his Feete and Hands,   5
What a sharp Diademe his Browes doth crowne?
Behold his pallid Face, his Eyes which sowne,
And what a Throng of Theeves him mocking stands.
Come forth yee empyrean Troupes, come forth,
Preserve this sacred Blood that Earth adornes,   10
Those liquid Roses gather off his Thornes,
O! to bee lost they bee of too much worth:
     1   2   3   1
    For streams, Juice, Balm they are, when quench,
      2   3
      kils, charms
    1   2   3   1   2   3
  Of God, Death, Hel, the wrath, the life, the harmes.

l. 7   *sowne.* Swoon.
l. 9   *empyrean Troupes.* Angels.

Madrigall ii

FAITH ABOVE REASON

Soule, which to Hell wast thrall,
Hee, Hee for thine offence,
Did suffer Death, who could not die at all.

O soveraigne Excellence,
O Life of all that lives, 5
Eternall Bounty which each good thing gives,
How could Death mount so hie?
No wit this hight can reach,
Faith only doth us teach,
For us Hee died, at all who could not dye. 10

Sonnet xvi

UPON THE SEPULCHER OF OUR LORD

Life to give life deprived is of *Life,*
And Death displai'd hath ensigne against *Death;*
So violent the Rigour was of *Death,*
That nought could daunt it but the Life of *Life:*
No Power had Pow'r to thrall Lifes pow'r to *Death,* 5
But willingly Life hath abandon'd *Life,*
Love gave the wound which wrought this work of *Death,*
His Bow and Shafts were of the Tree of *Life.*
Now quakes the Author of eternall *Death,*
To finde that they whom earst he reft of *Life* 10
Shall fill his Roome above the listes of *Death:*
Now all rejoyce in Death who hope for *Life.*
    Dead JESUS lies, who Death hath kill'd by *Death,*
    His Tombe no Tombe is, but new Source of *Life.*

Hymne ii

AN HYMNE OF THE RESURRECTION

Rise from those fragrant Climes thee now embrace,
Unto this world of ours O haste thy Race,
Faire Sunne, and though contrary-wayes all yeare
Thou hold thy course, now with the highest Spheare
Joyne thy swift Wheeles, to hasten time that lowres, 5
And lazie Minutes turne in perfect Houres;
The Night and Death too long a league have made,
To stow the world in Horrors ugly shade.

99

Shake from thy Lockes a Day with saffron Rayes
So faire, that it out shine all other dayes;   10
And yet doe not presume (great Eye of light)
To be that which this Day shall make so bright:
See, an eternall Sunne hastes to arise,
Not from the Easterne blushing Seas or Skies,
Or any stranger Worlds Heavens Concaves have,   15
But from the Darknesse of an hollow Grave:
And this is that all-powerfull Sunne above,
That crownd thy Browes with Rayes, first made thee move.
Lights Trumpetters, yee neede not from your Bowres
Proclaime this Day, this the angelike Powres   20
Have done for you; But now an opall hew
Bepaintes Heavens Christall, to the longing view
Earths late hid Colours glance, Light doth adorne
The Worlde, and (weeping Joy) foorth comes the Morne;
And with her, as from a Lethargicke Transe   25
Breath (com'd againe) that Bodie doth advance,
Which two sad Nights in rocke lay coffin'd dead,
And with an iron Guard invironed,
Life out of Death, Light out of Darknesse springs,
From a base Jaile foorth comes the King of kings;   30
What late was mortall, thrall'd to every woe,
That lackeyes life, or upon sence doth grow,
Immortall is, of an eternall Stampe,
Farre brighter beaming than the morning Lampe.
So from a blacke Ecclipse out-peeres the Sunne: 35
Such [when a huge of Dayes have on her runne,
In a farre forest in the pearly East,
And shee her selfe hath burnt and spicie Nest]
The lonlie Bird with youthfull Pennes and Combe,
Doth soare from out her Cradle and her Tombe: 40
So a Small seede that in the Earth lies hidde
And dies, reviving burstes her cloddie Side,
Adorn'd with yellow Lockes, of new is borne,

l. 32   *lackeyes.* Waits upon.
l. 36   *a huge of Dayes.* A vast number: the phoenix was re-born every 500, 600 or
         1,000 years.
l. 39   *The lonlie Bird.* The phoenix.
         Pennes. Feathers, wings.

And doth become a *Mother* great with *Corne;*
Of *Graines* brings hundreths with it, which when old   45
Enrich the *Furrowes* with a Sea of *Gold.*
     Haile holy Victor, greatest Victor haile,
That *Hell* dost ransacke, against *Death* prevaile,
O how thou long'd for comes! with *Jubeling* cries,
The all-triumphing *Palladines* of *Skies*   50
Salute thy rising; *Earth* would *Joyes* no more
Beare, if thou rising didst them not restore:
A *silly Tombe* should not his flesh enclose,
Who did *Heavens* trembling *Tarasses* dispose;
No *Monument* should such a *Jewell* hold,   55
No *Rocke*, though *Rubye, Diamond,* and *Gold.*
Thou onely pittie didst us, humane *Race,*
Bestowing on us of thy free given *Grace*
More than wee forfaited and loosed first,
In Edens *Rebell* when wee were accurst.   60
Then *Earth* our portion was, *Earths Joyes* but given,
Earth and *Earths Blisse* thou hast exchang'd with *Heaven.*
O what a hight of good upon us streames
From the great splendor of thy *Bounties Beames!*
When wee deserv'd shame, horrour, flames of wrath,   65
Thou bled our wounds, and suffer didst our *Death;*
But *Fathers Justice* pleas'd, *Hell, Death* o'rcome,
In triumph now thou risest from thy *Tombe,*
With *Glories* which past *Sorrowes contervaile,*
Haile holy Victor, greatest Victor haile   70
     Hence humble sense, and hence yee *Guides* of sense,
Wee now reach *Heaven*, your weake intelligence
And searching *Pow'rs,* were in a flash made dim,
To learne from all eternitie, that him
The *Father* bred, then that hee heere did come   75
(His *Bearers* Parent) in a *Virgins Wombe;*
But then when sold, betray'd, scourg'd, crown'd with *Thorne,*
Naill'd to a Tree, all breathlesse, bloodlesse, torne,

l. 49   *Jubeling.* Rejoicing.
l. 50   *Palladines of Skies.* The champions of heaven, thus, the angels.
l. 53   *silly.* Lowly.
l. 54   *Tarasses.* Terraces.
l. 69   *contervaile.* Counterbalance.

Entomb'd, him rising from a Grave to finde,
Confounds your Cunning, turnes like Moles you blinde.   80
Death, thou that heretofore still barren wast,
Nay, didst each other Birth eate up and waste,
Imperious, hatefull, pittilesse, unjust,
Unpartiall Equaller of all with dust,
Sterne Executioner of heavenly doome,   85
Made fruitfull, now Lifes Mother art become,
A sweete releife of cares, the Soule molest,
An Harbinger to Glory, Peace and Rest,
Put off thy mourning Weedes, yeeld all thy Gall
To daylie sinning Life, proud of thy fall,   90
Assemble thy Captives; bid all hast to rise,
And everie Corse in Earth-quakes where it lies,
Sound from each flowrie Grave, and rockie Jaile,
Haile holy Victor, greatest Victor haile.

    The World, that wanning late and faint did lie,   95
Applauding to our joyes thy Victorie,
To a yong Prime essayes to turne againe,
And as ere soyl'd with Sinne yet to remaine,
Her chilling Agues shee beginnes to misse,
All Blisse returning with the LORD of Blisse.   100
With greater light Heavens Temples opened shine,
Mornes smiling rise, Evens blushing doe decline,
Cloudes dappled glister, boisterous Windes are calme,
Soft Zephires doe the Fields with sighes embalme,
In ammell blew the Sea hath husht his Roares,   105
And with enamour'd Curles doth kisse the Shoares.
All-bearing Earth, like a new-married Queene,
Her Beauties hightenes, in a Gowne of Greene
Perfumes the Aire, Her Meades are wrought with Flowres,
In colours various, figures, smelling, powres;   110
Trees wanton in the Groves with leavie Lockes,
Her Hilles empampred stand, the Vales, the Rockes
Ring Peales of joy, her Floods her christall Brookes
(The Meadowes tongues) with many maz-like Crookes,

l. 95   Wanning. Becoming pale.
l. 105   ammell. Enamel.
l. 112   Empampred. Luxurious.

And whispering murmures, sound unto the Maine,   115
That Worlds pure Age returned is againe.
The honny People leave their golden Bowres,
And innocently pray on budding Flowres;
In gloomy Shades, pearcht on the tender Sprayes,
The painted Singers fill the Aire with Layes: 120
Seas, Floods, Earth, Aire, all diverslie doe sound,
Yet all their diverse Notes have but one ground,
Re-ecchoed here downe from Heavens azure Vaile,
Haile holy Victor, greatest Victor haile.
O Day! on which Deathes Adamantine Chaine   125
The LORD did breake, ransacking Satans Raigne,
And in triumphing Pompe his Trophees rear'd,
Bee thou blest ever, hence-foorth still endear'd
With Name of his owne Day; the Law to Grace,
Types to their Substance yeelde, to Thee give place   130
The olde New-Moones, with all festivall Dayes,
And what above the rest deserveth praise
The reverent Saboth; what could else they bee,
Than golden Heraulds, telling what by thee
Wee should enjoy? Shades past, now shine thou cleare,   135
And hence-foorth bee thou Empresse of the Yeare;
This Glorie of thy Sisters sex to winne,
From worke on thee, as other Dayes from sinne,
That Man-kind shall forbeare, in everie place
The Prince of Planets warmeth in his race;   140
And farre beyond his Pathes in frozen Climes:
And may thou bee so blest to out-date Times,
That when Heavens Quire shall blaze in accents lowd,
The manie mercies of their soveraigne Good,
How hee on thee did sinne, Death, Hell destroy,   145
It may bee aye the Antheme of their Joy.

l. 125   *Adamantine.* Unbreakable.
l. 137   *sex.* Six.

Hymne iii

AN HYMNE OF THE ASCENSION

Bright *Portalles of the Skie,*
 Emboss'd with sparkling Starres,
 Doores of Eternitie,
 With diamantine barres,
 Your Arras rich up-hold,   5
 Loose all your bolts and Springs,
 Ope wyde your Leaves of gold;
That in your Roofes may come the King of kings.
Scarff'd in a rosie Cloud,
 Hee doth ascend the Aire,   10
 Straight doth the Moone him shrowd
 With her resplendant Haire;
 The next enchristall'd Light
 Submits to him its Beames,
 And hee doth trace the hight   15
Of that faire Lamp which flames of beautie streames.
Hee towers those golden Bounds
 Hee did to Sunne bequeath,
 The higher wandring Rounds
 Are found his Feete beneath;   20
 The milkie-way comes neare,
 Heavens Axell seemes to bend,
 Above each turning Spheare
That roab'd in Glorie Heavens King may ascend.
O Well-spring of this All,   25
 Thy Fathers Image vive,
 Word, that from nought did call
 What is, doth reason, live;
 The Soules eternall Foode,
 Earths Joy, Delight of Heaven;   30
 All Truth, Love, Beautie, Good,
To Thee, to Thee bee praises ever given.
What was dismarshall'd late

l. 4 *diamantine.* Made of diamonds.
l. 9 *Scarff'd.* Clothed.
l. 26 *vive.* Bright.

In this thy noble Frame,
And lost the prime estate,   35
Hath re-obtain'd the same,
Is now most perfect seene;
Streames which diverted were
(And troubled strayed uncleene)
From their first Source, by Thee home turned are.   40
By Thee that blemish old,
Of Edens leprous Prince,
Which on his Race tooke hold,
And him exyl'd from thence,
Now put away is farre;   45
With Sword, in irefull guise,
No Cherub more shall barre
Poore man the Entries into Paradise.
By Thee those Spirits pure,
First Children of the Light,   50
Now fixed stand and sure,
In their eternall Right;
Now humane Companies
Renew their ruin'd Wall,
Fall'n man as thou makst rise,   55
Thou giv'st to Angels that they shall not fall.
By Thee that Prince of Sinne,
That doth with mischiefe swell,
Hath lost what hee did winne,
And shall endungeon'd dwell;   60
His spoyles are made thy pray,
His Phanes are sackt and torne,
His Altars raz'd away,
And what ador'd was late, now lyes a Scorne.
These Mansions pure and cleare,   65
Which are not made by hands,
Which once by him joy'd were,
And his (then not stain'd) Bands
(Now forefait'd, dispossest,
And head-long from them throwne)   70
Shall Adams Heires make blest,
By Thee their great Redeemer made their owne.

l. 62 Phanes. Temples.

O Well-spring of this All,
    Thy Fathers Image vive,
    Word, that from nought did call,   75
    What is, doth Reason, live;
    Whose worke is, but to will,
    Gods coeternall Sonne,
    Great Banisher of ill,
    By none but Thee could these great Deedes bee done.   80
Now each etheriall Gate,
    To him hath opened bin;
    And glories King in state,
    His Pallace enters in;
    Now com'd is this high Prest,   85
    In the most holie Place,
    Not without Blood addrest,
    With Glorie Heaven the Earth to crowne with Grace.
Starres which all Eyes were late,
    And did with wonder burne,   90
    His Name to celebrate,
    In flaming Tongues them turne;
    Their orbye Christales move
    More active than before,
    And entheate from above,   95
    Their Soveraigne Prince laude, glorifie, adore.
The Quires of happie Soules,
    Wakt with that Musicke sweete,
    Whose Descant Care controules,
    Their Lord in Triumph meete;   100
    The spotlesse Sprightes of light,
    His Trophees doe extole,
    And archt in Squadrons bright,
    Greet their great victor in his Capitole.
O Glorie of the Heaven,   105
    O sole Delight of Earth,
    To Thee all power bee given,
    Gods uncreated Birth;
    Of Man-kind lover true,

l. 85   *Prest.* Priest.
l. 95   *entheate.* Divinely inspired.

Indeerer of his wrong,
Who dost the world renew,
Still bee thou our Salvation and our Song.
From Top of Olivet *such notes did rise,*
When mans Redeemer did transcend the Skies.

110

l. 110   *Indeerer* . . . Who makes dear to us the wrong done to him.

Sonnet xvii

MANS KNOWLEDGE, IGNORANCE IN THE MISTERIES OF GOD

Beneath a sable vaile, and Shadowes deepe,
Of Unaccessible and dimming light,
In Silence ebane Clouds more blacke than Night,
The *Worlds great King* his secrets hidde doth keepe:
Through those Thicke Mistes when any Mortall Wight   5
Aspires, with halting pace, and Eyes that weepe,
To pore, and in his Misteries to creepe,
With Thunders hee and Lightnings blastes their Sight.
O Sunne invisible, that dost abide
Within thy bright abysmes, most faire, most darke,   10
Where with thy proper Rayes thou dost thee hide;
O ever-shining, never full seene marke,
    To guide mee in Lifes Night, thy light mee show,
    The more I search of thee, The lesse I know.

l. 3   *ebane.* Ebony.
l. 11   *proper.* Own.

Sonnet xviii

CONTEMPLATION OF INVISIBLE EXCELLENCIES ABOVE, BY THE VISIBLE BELOW

If with such passing Beautie, choise Delights,
The Architect of this great Round did frame
This Pallace visible (short listes of Fame,
And sillie Mansion but of dying Wights)

l. 4   *sillie.* Lowly.

107

How many Wonders, what amazing Lights   5
Must that triumphing Seat of Glorie clame,
That doth transcend all this great Alls vaste hights,
Of whose bright Sunne ours heere is but a Beame?
O blest abod! O happie dwelling-place!
Where visiblie th' Invisible doth raigne,
Blest People which doe see true Beauties Face,
With whose farre Dawnings scarce he Earth doth daigne:
    All Joy is but Annoy, all Concord Strife,
    Match'd with your endlesse Blisse and happie life.

Madrigall iii

THE DIFFERENCE BETWEENE EARTHLIE AND HEAVENLIE LOVE

Love which is heere a Care,
That Wit and Will doth marre,
Uncertaine Truce, and a most certaine Warre;
A shrill tempestuous Winde,
Which doth disturbe the minde,   5
And like wilde Waves our designes all commove:
Among those Powres above,
Which see their Makers Face,
It a contentment is, a quiet Peace,
A Pleasure voide of Griefe, a constant Rest,
Eternall Joy, which nothing can molest.

Sonnet xix

EARTH AND ALL ON IT CHANGEABLE

That space, where raging Waves doe now divide
From the great Continent our happie Isle,
Was some-time Land, and where tall Shippes doe glide,
Once with deare Arte the crooked Plough did tyle:
Once those faire Bounds stretcht out so farre and wide,   5

l. 4 *tyle.* Toil.

Where Townes, no, Shires enwall'd, endeare each mile,
Were all ignoble Sea, and marish vile
Where *Proteus* Flockes danc'd measures to the Tyde.
So Age transforming all still forward runnes,
No wonder though the Earth doth change her face,   10
New Manners, Pleasures new, turne with new Sunnes,
Lockes now like Gold grow to an hoarie grace;
    Nay, Mindes rare shape doth change, that lyes despis'd
    Which was so deare of late and highlie pris'd.

l. 7 *marish*. Marsh.
l. 8 *Proteus Flockes*. Waves.

Madrigall iv

THE WORLD A GAME

This world a Hunting is,
The Pray poore Man, the Nimrod *fierce is Death,*
His speedie Grei-hounds are,
Lust, sicknesse, Envie, Care,
Strife that neere falles amisse,   5
With all those ills which haunt us while wee breath.
Now, if (by chance) wee flie
Of these the eager Chase,
Old Age with stealing Pace,
Castes up his Nets, and there wee panting die.

The World a Game. The world is a quarry, the world is hunted.
l. 2 *Nimrod*. "The mighty hunter" (Gen. X. 9).

Sonnet xx

THE COURT OF TRUE HONOUR

Why (worldlings) do ye trust fraile honours dreams?
And leane to guilted Glories which decay?
Why doe yee toyle to registrate your Names
On icie Pillars, which soone melt away?
True Honour is not heere, that place it clames,   5

Where blacke-brow'd Night doth not exile the Day,
Nor no farre-shining Lamp dives in the Sea,
But an eternall Sunne spreades lasting Beames:
There it attendeth you, where spotlesse Bands
Of Spirits, stand gazing on their Soveraigne Blisse,   10
Where yeeres not hold it in their canckring hands,
But who once noble, ever noble is.
    Looke home, lest hee your weakned Wit make thrall,
    Who *Edens* foolish Gardner earst made fall.

Sonnet xxi

AGAINST HYPOCRISIE

As are those Apples, pleasant to the Eye,
But full of Smoke within, which use to grow
Neere that strange Lake, where God powr'd from the Skie
Huge showres of Flames, worse flames to over-throw:
Such are their workes that with a glaring Show   5
Of humble Holinesse, in Vertues dye,
Would colour Mischiefe, while within they glow
With coales of Sinne, though none the Smoake descrie.
Ill is that Angell which earst fell from Heaven,
But not more ill than hee, nor in worse case,   10
Who hides a traitrous Minde with smiling face,
And with a Doves white feathers maskes a Raven:
    Each Sinne some colour hath it to adorne,
    Hypocrisie All-mighty GOD doth scorne.

l. 1   *those Apples.* Apples of Sodom.
l. 3   *that strange Lake.* The Dead Sea.
l. 9   *that Angell.* Lucifer.

Madrigall v

CHANGE SHOULD BREEDE CHANGE

New doth the Sunne appeare,
The Mountaines Snowes decay,
Crown'd with fraile Flowres foorth comes the Babye yeare.

My Soule, Time postes away,
And thou yet in that Frost   5
Which Flowre and fruit hath lost,
As if all heere immortall were, dost stay:
For shame thy Powers awake,
Looke to that Heaven which never Night makes blacke,   10
And there, at that immortall Sunnes bright Rayes,
Decke thee with Flowers which feare not rage of Dayes.

Sonnet xxii

THE PRAISE OF A SOLITARIE LIFE

Thrice happie hee, who by some shadie Grove,
Farre from the clamorous World, doth live his owne,
Though solitarie, who is not alone,
But doth converse with that Eternall Love:
O! how more sweete is Birds harmonious Moane,   5
Or the hoarse Sobbings of the widow'd Dove;
Than those smooth whisperings neere a Princes Throne,
Which Good make doubtfull, doe the evill approve?
O! how more sweet is Zephires wholesome Breath,
And Sighes embalm'd, which new-borne Flowrs unfold,   10
Than that applause vaine Honour doth bequeath?
How sweete are Streames to poison drunke in Gold?
    The World is full of Horrours, Troubles, Slights,
    Woods harmelesse Shades have only true Delightes.

Sonnet xxiii

TO A NIGHTINGALE

Sweet Bird, that sing'st away the early Howres,
Of Winters past or comming void of Care,
Well pleased with Delights which Present are,
Faire Seasones, budding Sprayes, sweet-smelling Flowers:
To Rocks, to Springs, to Rils, from leavy Bowres   5
Thou thy Creators Goodnesse dost declare,
And what deare Gifts on thee hee did not spare,

A Staine to humane sence in sinne that lowres.
What Soule can be so sicke, which by thy Songs
(Attir'd in sweetnesse) sweetly is not driven 10
Quite to forget Earths turmoiles, spights, and wrongs,
And lift a reverend Eye and Thought to Heaven?
    Sweet Artlesse Songstarre, thou my Minde dost raise
    To Ayres of Spheares, yes, and to Angels Layes.

Sonnet xxiv

CONTENT AND RESOLUTE

As when it hapneth that some lovely Towne
Unto a barbarous Besieger falles,
Who there by Sword and Flame himselfe enstalles,
And (Cruell) it in Teares and Blood doth drowne;
Her Beauty spoyl'd, her Citizens made Thralles, 5
His spight yet so cannot her all throw downe,
But that some Statue, Arch, Phan of renowne,
Yet lurkes unmaym'd within her weeping walles:
So after all the Spoile, Disgrace, and Wrake,
That Time, the World, and Death could bring combind, 10
Amidst that Masse of Ruines they did make,
Safe and all scarre-lesse yet remaines my Minde:
    From this so high transcending Rapture springes,
    That I, all else defac'd, not envie Kinges.

l. 7 *Phan.* Temple.

Sonnet xxv

DEATHES LAST-WILL

More oft than once, Death whisper'd in mine Eare,
Grave what thou heares in Diamond and Gold,
I am that Monarch whom all Monarches feare,
Who hath in Dust their farre-stretch'd Pride uproll'd.
All all is mine beneath Moones silver Spheare, 5
And nought, save Vertue, Can my power with-hold:

This (not believ'd) Experience true Thee told,
By Danger late when I to Thee came neare.
As Bugbeare then my Visage I did show,
That of my Horrours thou right Use mightst make,   10
And a more sacred Path of living take:
Now still walke armed for my ruthlesse Blow,
    Trust flattering Life no more, Redeeme Time past,
    And Live each Day as if it were thy Last.

Sonnet xxvi

THE BLESSEDNESSE OF FAITHFULL SOULES BY DEATH

Let us each day enure our selves to dye,
If this (and not our Feares) be truely Death;
Above the Circles both of Hope and Faith
With faire immortall pinniones to flie?
If this be Death our best Part to untie   5
(By running the Jaile) from Lust and Wrath,
And every drowsie languor heere beneath,
It turning deniz'd Citizen of Skie?
To have, more knowledge than all Bookes containe,
All Pleasures even surmounting wishing Powre,
The fellowship of Gods immortall Traine,
And these that Time nor force shall er'e devoure?
    If this be Death? what Joy, what golden care
    Of Life, can with Deaths ouglinesse compare?

l. 6   *Jaile.* The body.
l. 8   *deniz'd.* Naturalized.
    Citizen of Skie. Spirit.

Hymne iv

AN HYMNE OF TRUE HAPPINESSE

Amidst the azure cleare
    Of Jordans *sacred Streames,*
    Jordan *of* Libanon *the of-spring deare;*

When *Zephires* Flowers unclose,
And *Sunne* shines with new Beames,   5
With grave and stately Grace a Nimphe arose.
Upon her Head she ware
  Of *Amaranthes* a Crowne,
Her left hand Palmes, her right a Brandon bare,
Unvail'd Skinnes whitenesse lay,   10
Gold haires in Curles hang downe,
Eyes sparkled Joy, more bright than Starre of Day.
The Flood a Throne her rear'd
  Of Waves, most like that Heaven
Where beaming Starres in Glorie turne ensphear'd;   15
The Aire stood calme and cleare,
No Sigh by Windes was given,
Birdes left to sing, Heards feed, her voyce to heare.
World-wandring sorrie Wights,
  Whom nothing can content   20
Within those varying listes of Dayes and Nights,
Whose life (ere knowne amisse)
In glittering Griefes is spent,
Come learne (said shee) what is your choisest Blisse.
From *Toyle* and pressing Cares   25
  How yee may respit finde,
A Sanctuarie from Soule-thralling Snares,
A Port to harboure sure
In spight of waves and winde,
Which shall when Times Houre-glasse is runne endure.   30
Not happie is that Life
  Which yee as happie hold,
No, but a Sea of feares, a field of Strife,
Charg'd on a Throne to sit
With Diadems of Gold,   35
Preserv'd by Force, and still observ'd by Wit:
Huge Treasures to enjoy,
  Of all her Gemmes spoyle *Inde*,
All *Seres* silke in Garments to imploy,

l. 8 *Amaranthes.* Never-fading flowers.
l. 9 *Brandon.* Torch.
l. 39 *Seres.* China(?) a supposed source of silk.

Deliciously to feed,   40
  The Phenix plumes to finde
  To rest upon, or decke your purple Bed.
Fraile Beautie to abuse,
  And (wanton Sybarites)
  On past or present touch of sense to muse;   45
  Never to heare of Noise
  But what the Eare delites,
  Sweet musicks Charmes, or charming Flatterers voice.
Nor can it Blisse you bring,
  Hidde Natures Depthes to know,   50
  Why Matter changeth, whence each Forme doth spring;
  Nor that your Fame should range,
  And after-Worlds it blow
  From Tänäis to Nile, from Nile to Gange.
All these have not the Powre   55
  To free the Minde from feares,
  Nor hideous horror can allay one howre,
  When Death in steele doth glance,
  In Sicknesse lurke or yeares,
  And wakes the Soule from out her mortall Trance.   60
No, but blest Life is this,
  With chaste and pure desire,
  To turne unto the Load-starre of all Blisse,
  On GOD the Minde to rest,
  Burnt up with sacred Fire,   65
  Possessing him, to bee by him possest.
When to the baulmie East
  Sunne doth his light impart,
  Or When he diveth in the lowlie West,
  And ravisheth the Day,   70
  With spotlesse Hands and Hart
  Him chearefully to praise and to him pray.
To heed each action so,
  As ever in his sight,
  More fearing doing ill than passive woe;   75
  Not to seeme other thing

l. 54 *From Tanais to Nile* . . . From one end of the world to the other.
l. 63 *Load-starre.* The guiding star, the pole-star.

Than what yee are aright,
Never to doe what may Repentance bring:
Not to bee blowne with Pride,
Nor mov'd at Glories breath,   80
Which Shadow-like on wings of Time doth glide;
So Malice to disarme,
And conquere hastie Wrath,
As to doe good to those that Worke your harme:
To hatch no base Desires   85
Or Gold or Land to gaine,
Well pleas'd with what by Vertue one acquires,
To have the Wit and Will
Consorting in one Straine,
Than what is good to have no higher skill.   90
Never on Neighbours well,
With Cocatrices Eye
To looke, and make an others Heaven your Hell;
Not to be Beauties Thrall,
All fruitlesse Love to flie,   95
Yet loving still a Love transcending all.
A Love which while it burnes
The Soule with fairest Beames,
In that uncreated Sunne the Soule it turnes,
And makes such Beautie prove,   100
That (if Sense saw her Gleames?)
All lookers on would pine and die for love.
Who such a life doth live,
Yee happie even may call,
Ere ruthlesse Death a wished end him give,   105
And after then when given,
More happie by his fall,
For Humanes, Earth, enjoying Angels, Heaven.
Swift is your mortall Race,
And glassie is the Field,   110
Vaste are Desires not limited by Grace;
Life a weake Tapper is,

l. 92   Cocatrices Eye. The cockatrice or basilisk killed with a glance; it was a
        symbol of evil.
l. 112 Tapper. Candle.

Then while it light doth yeeld
Leave flying joyes, embrace this lasting Blisse.
This when the Nimph had said,   115
Shee div'd within the Flood,
Whose Face with smyling Curles long after staid.
Then Sighes did Zephyres presse,
Birdes sang from every Wood,
And Ecchoes rang, this was true Happinesse.   120

Hymne v

AN HYMNE OF THE
FAIREST FAIRE

AN HYMNE OF THE NATURE, ATRIBUTES,
AND WORKES OF GOD

I feele my Bosome glow with wontlesse Fires,
Rais'd from the vulgar prease my Mind aspires
(Wing'd with high Thoghts) unto his praise to clime,
From deepe Eternitie who call'd foorth Time;
That Essence which not mov'd makes each thing move,   5
Uncreat'd Beautie all-creating Love:
But by so great an object, radient light,
My Heart appall'd, enfeebled restes my Sight,
Thicke Cloudes benighte my labouring Ingine,
And at my high Attempts my Wits repine.   10
If thou in mee this sacred Rapture wrought,
My Knowledge sharpen, Sarcells lend my thought;
Grant mee (Times Father, world-containing King)
A Pow'r, of Thee in pow'rfull Layes to sing,
That as thy Beautie in Earth lives, Heaven shines,   15
So it may dawne, or shadow in my Lines.
    As farre beyond the starrie walles of Heaven,
As is the loftiest of the Planets seven

l. 2   *prease.* Press, crowd.
l. 9   *Ingine.* Mind.
l. 12 *Sarcells.* Wings.

117

Sequestred from this Earth, in purest light,
Out-shining ours, as ours doth sable Night,   20
Thou, All-sufficient, Omnipotent,
Thou ever-glorious, most excellent,
GOD various in Names, in Essence one,
High art enstalled on a golden Throne,
Out-reaching Heavens wide Vastes, the Bounds of nought,   25
Transcending all the Circles of our Thought:
With diamantine Scepter in thy Hand,
There thou giv'st Lawes, and dost this World command,
This world of Concords rais'd unliklie-sweete,
Which like a Ball lyes prostrate to thy Feete.   30
    If so wee may well say (and what wee say,
Heere wrapt in flesh, led by dimme Reasons ray,
To show by earthlie Beauties which wee see
That spirituall Excellence that shines in Thee,
Good Lord forgive) not farre from thy right Side,   35
With curled Lockes *Youth* ever doth abide;
Rose-cheeked *Youth*, who garlanded with Flowres,
Still blooming, ceasleslie unto thee powres
Immortall Nectar, in a Cuppe of Gold,
That by no darts of Ages Thou grow old,   40
And as ends and beginnings Thee not clame,
Successionlesse that Thou bee still the same.
    Neare to thy other side resistlesse *Might*,
From Head to Foote in burnisht Armour dight,
That ringes about him, with a waving Brand,   45
And watchfull Eye, great Sentinell doth stand;
That neither Time nor force in ought impaire
Thy workmanshippe, nor harme thine Empire faire,
Soone to give Death to all againe that would
Sterne *Discord* raise which thou destroy'd of old;   50
Discord that Foe to order, Nurse of Warre,
By which the noblest things dimolisht are:
But (Catife) Shee no Treason doth devise,
When *Might* to nought doth bring her enterprise,
Thy All-upholding *Might* her Malice raines,   55

l. 27   *diamantine.* Made of diamonds.
l. 53   *Catife.* Captive, wretch.

And her in Hell throwes bound in iron Chaines.
    With Lockes in waves of Gold that ebbe and flow
On ivorie necke, in Robes more white than Snow,
Truth stedfastlie before thee holdes a Glasse,
Indent'd with Gemmes, where shineth all that was,   60
That is, or shall bee: heere, ere ought was wrought,
Thou knew all that thy Pow'r with Time forth-brought,
And more, Things numberlesse which thou couldst make,
That actuallie shall never beeing take:
Heere, thou beholdst thy selfe, and (strange) dost prove,   65
At once the Beautie, Lover and the Love.
    With Faces two (like Sisters) sweetlie faire,
Whose Blossomes no rough Autumne can impaire,
Stands *Providence*, and doth her lookes disperse
Through everie Corner of this Universe: 70
Thy *Providence* at once which generall Things
And singulare doth rule, as Empires Kings;
Without whose care this world (lost) would remaine,
As Shippe without a Maister in the Maine,
As Chariot alone, as Bodies prove   75
Depriv'd of Soules by which they bee, live, move.
    But who are They which shine thy Throne so neare?
With sacred countenance, and looke severe,
This in one hand a pondrous Sword doth hold,
Her left stayes charg'd with Ballances of Gold;   80
That with Browes girt with Bayes, sweete-smiling Face,
Doth beare a Brandon, with a babish grace
Two milke-white Winges him easilie doe move,
O Shee thy *Justice* is, and this thy *Love*!
By this thou brought this Engine great to light,   85
By that it fram'd in Number, Measure, Weight,
That destine doth reward to ill and good;
But Sway of *Justice* is by *Love* with-stood,
Which did it not relent and mildlie stay,
This World ere now had had its funerall Day.   90
    What Bands (enclustred) neare to these abide,
Which into vaste *Infinitie* them hide?

l. 82 *Brandon.* Torch.
    babish. Childish.

Infinitie that neither doth admit,
Place, Time, nor Number to encroach on it:
Heere *Bountie* sparkleth, heere doth *Beautie* shine,   95
Simplicitie, more white than Gelsemine,
Mercie with open wings, ay-varied *Blisse*,
Glorie, and *Joy*, that *Blisses* darling is.
    Ineffable, All-pow'rfull GOD, All-free,
Thou onelie liv'st, and each thing lives by Thee,   100
No Joy, no, nor Perfection to Thee came
By the contriving of this Worlds great Frame;
Ere Sunne, Moone, Starres beganne their restlesse race,
Ere paint'd with purple Light was Heavens round Face,
Ere Aire had Clouds, ere Clouds weept down their showrs, 105
Ere Sea embraced Earth, ere Earth bare Flowres,
Thou happie liv'd; World nought to Thee supply'd,
All in thy selfe thy selfe thou satisfy'd:
Of Good no slender Shadow doth appeare,
No age-worne tracke, in Thee which shin'd not cleare;   110
Perfections Summe, prime-cause of everie Cause,
Midst, end, beginning, where all good doth pause.
Hence of thy Substance, differing in nought
Thou in Eternitie thy Sonne foorth brought,
The onelie Birth of thy unchanging Minde,   115
Thine Image, Paterne-like that ever shin'd,
Light out of Light, begotten not by Will,
But Nature, all and that same Essence still
Which thou thy selfe; for thou dost nought possesse
Which hee hath not, in ought nor is hee lesse   120
Than Thou his great Begetter; of this Light,
Eternall, double, kindled was thy Spright
Eternallie, who is with Thee the same,
All-holie Gift, Embassadour, Knot, Flame:
Most sacred, Triade, O most holie One,   125
Unprocreat'd Father, ever-procreat'd Sonne,
Ghost breath'd from both, you were, are, aye shall bee
(Most blessed) Three in One, and One in Three,
Uncomprehensible by reachlesse Hight,

l. 96 *Gelsemine*. Jasmine.
l. 98 *Blisses*. In text, 'Blesses'.
l. 122 *Spright*. Spirit.

And unperceived by excessive Light.   130
So in our Soules, three and yet one are still,
The Understanding, Memorie, and Will;
So (though unlike) the Planet of the Dayes,
So soone as hee was made begate his Rayes,
Which are his Of-spring, and from both was hurl'd   135
The rosie Light which comfort doth the World,
And none fore-went an other: so the Spring,
The Well-head, and the Streame which they foorth bring,
Are but one selfe-same Essence, nor in ought
Doe differ, save in order, and our Thought   140
No Chime of time discernes in them to fall,
But three distinctlie bide one Essence all.
But these expresse not Thee; who can declare
Thy beeing? Men and Angels dazel'd are:
Who force this Eden would with wit or sence,   145
A Cherubin shall finde to barre him thence.
      Alls Architect, Lord of this Universe,
Wit is ingulph'd that would thy greatnesse pierce;
Ah! as a Pilgrime who the *Alpes* doth passe,
Or *Atlas* Temples crown'd with winters glasse,   150
The ayrie *Caucasus*, the *Apennine*,
Pyrenès cliftes where Sunne doth never shine,
When hee some heapes of Hilles hath over-went,
Beginnes to thinke on rest, his Journey spent,
Till mounting some tall Mountaine hee doe finde,   155
More hights before him than hee left behinde:
With halting pace, so while I would mee raise
To the unbounded Circüits of thy praise,
Some part of way I thought to have o're-runne,
But now I see how scarce I have begunne,   160
With wonders new my Spirits range possest,
And wandring waylesse in a maze them rest.
      In those vaste Fieldes of Light, etheriall Plaines,
Thou art attended by immortall Traines
Of Intellectuall Pow'rs, which thou brought forth   165
To praise thy Goodnesse, and admire thy Worth;
In numbers passing other Creatures farre,

l. 133   *Planet of the Dayes.* The sun.

121

Since most in number noblest Creatures are,
Which doe in Knowledge us no lesse out-runne,
Than Moone doth Starres in light, or Moone the Sunne;   170
Unlike, in Orders rang'd and manie a Band,
(If Beautie in Disparitie doth stand?)
Arch-Angels, Angels, Cherubes, Seraphines,
And what with name of Thrones amongst them shines,
Large-ruling Princes, Dominations, Powres,   175
All-acting Vertues of those flaming Towres:
These fred of Umbrage, these of Labour free,
Rest ravished with still beholding Thee,
Inflam'd with Beames which sparkle from thy Face,
They can no more desire, farre lesse embrace.   180
    Low under them, with slow and staggering pace
Thy hand-Maide *Nature* thy great Steppes doth trace,
The Source of second Causes, golden Chaine
That linkes this Frame, as thou it doth ordaine;
Nature gaz'd on with such a curious Eye   185
That Earthlings oft her deem'd a Deitye.
By *Nature* led those Bodies faire and greate
Which faint not in their Course, nor change their State,
Unintermixt, which no disorder prove,
Though aye and contrarie they alwayes move;   190
The Organes of thy Providence divine,
Bookes ever open, Signes that clearelie shine,
Times purpled Maskers, then doe them advance,
As by sweete Musicke in a measur'd Dance.
Starres, Hoste of heaven, yee Firmaments bright Flowrs,   195
Cleare Lampes which over-hang this Stage of ours,
Yee turne not there to decke the Weeds of Night,
Nor Pageant-like to please the vulgare Sight,
Great Causes sure yee must bring great Effectes,
But who can descant right your grave Aspects?   200
Hee onlie who You made deciphere can
Your Notes, Heavens Eyes, yee blinde the Eyes of Man.
    Amidst these saphire farre-extending Hights,
The never-twinkling ever-wandring Lights

l. 176 *Umbrage.* Shade.
l. 183 *golden Chaine.* The great chain of being, God's scale of created things.
l. 204 *The . . . Lights.* The planets.

Their fixed Motions keepe; one drye and cold,   205
Deep-leaden colour'd, slowlie there is roll'd,
With Rule and Line for times steppes measur'd even,
In twice three Lustres hee but turnes his Heaven.
With temperate qualities and Countenance faire,
Still mildelie smiling sweetlie debonnaire,   210
An other cheares the World, and way doth make
In twice sixe Autumnes through the Zodiacke.
But hote and drye with flaming lockes and Browes
Enrag'd, this in his red Pavillion glowes:
Together running with like speede if space,   215
Two equallie in hands atchieve their race;
With blushing Face this oft doth bring the Day,
And usheres oft to statelie Starres the way,
That various in vertue, changing, light,
With his small Flame engemmes the vaile of Night.   220
Prince of this Court, the Sunne in triumph rides,
With the yeare Snake-like in her selfe that glides;
Times Dispensator, faire life-giving Source,
Through Skies twelve Posts as hee doth runne his course,
Heart of this All, of what is knowne to Sence   225
The likest to his Makers Excellence:
In whose diurnall motion doth appeare
A Shadow, no, true pourtrait of the yeare.
The Moone moves lowest, silver Sunne of Night,
Dispersing through the World her borrow'd light,   230
Who in three formes her head abroad doth range,
And onelie constant is in constant Change.
     Sad Queene of Silence, I neere see thy Face,
To waxe, or waine, or shine with a full grace,
But straight (amaz'd) on Man I thinke, each Day   235
His state who changeth, or if hee find Stay,
It is in drearie anguish, cares, and paines,
And of his Labours Death is all the Gaines.

l. 205   *one drye and cold.* Saturn.
l. 208   *twice three Lustres.* Thirty years: a luster is a period of five years.
l. 211   *An other.* Jupiter.
l. 214   *This in his red Pavillion.* Mars.
l. 217   *this oft doth bring the Day.* Venus.
l. 220   *With his small Flame.* Mercury.

Immortall Monarch, can so fond a Thought
Lodge in my brest? as to trust thou first brought   240
Heere in Earths shadie Cloister wretched Man,
To sucke the Aire of woe, to spend Lifes span
Midst Sighes and plaints, a stranger unto Mirth,
To give himselfe his Death rebuking Birth?
By sense and wit of Creatures Made King,   245
By sense and wit to live their Underling?
And what is worst, have Eaglets eyes to see
His owne disgrace, and know an high degree
Of Blisse, the Place, if thereto hee might clime,
And not live thralled to imperious Time?   250
Or (dotard) shall I so from Reason swerve,
To deeme those Lights which to our use doe serve,
(For thou dost not them need) more noblie fram'd
Than us, that know their course, and have them nam'd?
No, I neere thinke but wee did them surpasse   255
As farre, as they doe Asterismes of Glasse,
When thou us made; by Treason high defil'd,
Thrust from our first estate wee live exil'd,
Wandring this Earth, which is of Death the Lot,
Where he doth use the Pow'r which he hath got,   260
Indifferent Umpire unto Clownes and Kings,
The supreme Monarch of all mortall things.
    When first this flowrie Orbe was to us given
It but in place disvalu'd was to Heaven,
These Creatures which now our Soveraignes are,   265
And as to Rebelles doe denounce us warre,
Then were our Vassalles, no tumultuous Storme,
No Thunders, Quakings, did her Forme deforme,
The Seas in tumbling Mountaines did not roare,
But like moist Christall whispered on the Shoare,   270
No Snake did met her Meads, nor ambusht lowre
In azure Curles beneath the sweet-Spring Flowre;
The Nightshade, Henbane, Naple, Aconite,
Her Bowels then not bare, with Death to smite

l. 256 *Asterismes.* Constellations, stars.
l. 264 *disvalu'd.* Not of equal value.
l. 271 *met.* Measure.
l. 273 *Nightshade . . . Aconite.* All poisonous plants.

Her guiltlesse Brood; thy Messengers of Grace,   275
As their high Rounds did haunte this lower Place:
O Joy of Joyes! with our first Parents Thou
To commune then didst daigne, as Friends doe now:
Against thee wee rebell'd, and justly thus,
Each Creature rebelled against us,   280
Earth, reft of what did chiefe in her excell,
To all became a Jaile, to most a Hell,
In Times full Terme untill thy Sonne was given,
Who Man with Thee, Earth reconcil'd with Heaven.
    Whole and entire all in thy Selfe thou art,   285
All-where diffus'd, yet of this *All* no part,
For infinite, in making this faire Frame,
(Great without quantitie) in all thou came,
And filling all, how can thy State admit,
Or Place or Substance to be voide of it?   290
Were Worlds as many, as the Raies which streame
From Heavens bright Eyes, or madding Wits do dreame,
They would not reele in nought, nor wandring stray,
But draw to Thee, who could their Centers stay;
Were but one houre this World disjoyn'd from Thee,   295
It in one houre to nought reduc'd should bee,
For it thy shaddow is, and can they last,
If sever'd from the Substances them cast?
O only blest, and Author of all blisse,
No Blisse it selfe, that all-where wished is,   300
Efficient, exemplarie, finall Good,
Of thine owne Selfe but onely understood;
Light is thy Curtaine, thou art Light of Light,
An ever-waking Eye still shining bright,
In-looking all, exempt of passive powre,   305
And change, in change since Deaths pale shade doth lowre.
All Times to thee are one, that which hath runne,
And that which is not brought yet by the Sunne,
To thee are present, who dost alwayes see
In present act, what past is or to bee.   310
Day-livers wee rememberance doe losse
Of Ages worne, so Miseries us tosse,
(Blinde and lethargicke of thy heavenly Grace,
Which sinne in our first Parents did deface,

125

And even while Embryones curst by justest doome)   315
That wee neglect what gone is, or to come:
But thou in thy great Archieves scrolled hast
In parts and whole, what ever yet hath past,
Since first the marble wheeles of Time were roll'd,
As ever living, never waxing old,   320
Still is the same thy Day and Yesterday,
An un-divided *Now*, a constant *Ay*.
    O King, whose Greatnesse none can comprehend,
Whose boundlesse Goodnesse doth to all extend,
Light of all Beautie, Ocean without ground,   325
That standing flowest, giving dost abound,
Rich palace, and Indweller ever blest,
Never not working ever yet in Rest;
What wit cannot conceive, words say of Thee,
Heere where as in a Mirrour wee but see,   330
Shadowes of shadowes, Atomes of thy Might,
Still owlie eyed when staring on thy Light,
Grant that released from this earthly Jaile,
And fred of Clouds which heere our Knowledge vaile,
In Heavens high Temples, where thy Praises ring,   335
I may in sweeter Notes heare Angels sing.

Hymne vi

A PRAYER FOR MANKINDE

Great GOD, whom wee with humble Thoughts adore,
Eternall, infinite, Almightie King,
Whose Dwellings Heaven transcend, whose Throne before
Archangells serve, and Seraphines doe sing;
Of nought who wrought all that With wondring Eyes   5
Wee doe behold within this spacious Round,
Who makes the Rockes to rocke, to stand the Skies,
At whose Command Clouds dreadfull Thunders sound:
Ah! spare us Wormes, weigh not how wee (alas!)
(Evill to our selves) against thy Lawes rebell,   10
Wash of those Spots which still in Mindes cleare Glasse
(Though wee be loath to looke) wee see to well.
Deserv'd Revenge, O doe not doe not take,
Doe thou revenge what shall abide thy blow?
Passe shall this World, this World which thou didst make,   15
Which should not perish till thy Trumpet blow.
What Soule is found whom Parents Crime not staines?
Or what with its owne Sinne destaind is not?
Though Justice Rigor threaten (ah) her Raines
Let Mercy guide, and never bee forgot.   20
    Lesse are our Faults farre farre than is thy Love,
O What can better seeme thy Grace divine,
Than They that plagues deserve thy Bounty prove,
And where thou showre mayst Vengeance faire to shine?
Then looke and pittie, pittying forgive   25
Us guiltie Slaves, or Servants, now in thrall,
Slaves, if (alas) *thou looke how wee doe live;*
Or doing ill Or doing nought at all?
Of an ungratefull Minde a foule Effect!
But if thy Giftes which amplie heretofore   30
Thou hast upon us powr'd thou dost respect,
Wee are thy Servants, nay, than Servants more;
Thy Children, yes, and Children dearely bought,
But what strange Chance us of this Lot bereaves,
Poore worthles Wights how lowlie are wee brought,   35
Whom Grace made Children Sinne hath turned Slaves?

Sinne hath turn'd Slaves, but let those Bands Grace breake,
That in our Wrongs thy Mercies may appeare,
Thy Wisedome not so meane is, Pow'r so weake,
But thousand wayes they can make Worlds thee feare.   40
    O Wisedome boundlesse; O miraculous Grace!
Grace, Wisdome which make winke dimme Reasons Eye,
And could Heavens King bring from his placelesse Place,
On this ignoble Stage of Care to die:
To dye our Death, and with the sacred Streame   45
Of Bloud and Water, guishing from his Side,
To put away each odious act and Blame,
By us contriv'd, or our first Parents Pride.
Thus thy great Love and Pitty (heavenly King)
Love, Pitty, which so well our Losse prevent,   50
Of Evill it selfe (loe!) could all Goodnesse bring,
And sad Beginning cheare with glad Event.
O Love and Pitty! ill-knowne of these Times.
O Love and Pittie! carefull of our neede,
O Bounties! Which our execrable Crimes   55
(Now numberlesse) contend neere to exceed.
Make this excessive Ardour of thy Love,
So warme our Coldnesse, so our Lifes renew,
That wee from sinne, Sinne may from us remove,
Wit may our will, Faith may our Wit subdue.   60
Let thy pure Love burne up all worldly Lust,
Hells pleasant Poison killing our best part,
Which makes us joye in Toyes, adore fraile Dust
In stead of Thee, in Temple of our Heart.
    Grant when at last our Soules these Bodies leave,   65
Their loathsome Shops of Sinne, and Mansions blinde,
And Doome before thy royall Seat receave,
They may a Saviour, not a Judge thee finde.

SONNETS

i

TO SIR WILLIAM ALEXANDER

Though I have twice beene at the Doores of *Death*,
And twice found shoote those Gates which ever mourne,
This but a lightning is, Truce tane to Breath,
For late borne Sorrowes augure fleete returne.
Amidst thy sacred Cares, and courtlie Toyles,   5
Alexis, when thou shalt heare wandring Fame
Tell, *Death* hath triumph'd o're my mortall Spoyles,
And that on Earth I am but a sad Name;
If thou e're helde mee deare, by all our Love,
By all that Blisse, those Joyes Heaven heere us gave,   10
I conjure Thee, and by the Maides of *Jove*,
To grave this short Remembrance on my Grave.
    Heere *Damon* lyes, whose Songes did some-time grace
    The murmuring *Eske*, may Roses shade the place.

l. 5   *sacred Cares, and courtlie Toyles.* Alexander worked with King James on a
       translation of the Psalms, and was an official at court.
l. 6   *Alexis.* Alexander.
l. 11 *Maides of Jove.* The Muses.
l. 13 *Damon.* Drummond.

ii

IN PIOUS MEMORIE OF
EUPHEMIA KYNINGHAME

Who

Died the 23 of Julie, 1616.

This Beautie faire, which *Death* in Dust did turne,
And clos'd so soone within a Coffin sad,
Did, passe like Lightning, like to Thunder burne;
So little Life, so much of Worth, it had.
Heavens but to show their Might heere made it shine,   5
And when admir'd, then in the Worlds Disdaine
(O Teares, O Griefe!) did call it backe againe,
Lest Earth should vaunt Shee kept what was Divine.
What can wee hope for more? what more enjoy?
Since fairest Things thus soonest have their End,   10
And, as on Bodies Shadowes doe attend,
Since all our Blisse is follow'd with Annoy?
    Yet Shee's not dead, She lives where She did love,
    Her Memorie on Earth, Her Soule above.

iii

I feare to me such fortune be assignd
As was to thee, who did so well deserve,
Brave HAKERSTOWNE, even suffred here to sterve
Amidst basse minded freinds, nor true, nor kind.
Why were the fates and furies thus combind,   5
Such worths for such disasters to reserve?
Yet all those evills never made the suerve
From what became a well resolved mind;
For swelling Greatnesse never made the smyle,
Dispising Greatnesse in extreames of want;   10
O happy thrice whom no distresse could dant!

l. 3 *Hakerstowne.* Col. James Halkerstone.
l. 7 *the suerve.* Thee swerve.

130

Yet thou exclaimed, ô Time! ô Age! ô Isle!
Where flatterers, fooles, baudes, fidlers, are rewarded,
Whilst Vertue sterves unpittied, unregarded.

iv

First in the orient raign'd th' assyrian kings,
To those the sacred persian prince succeeds,
Then he by whom the world sore-wounded bleeds,
Earths crowne to Greece with bloodie blade he brings;
Then Grece to Rome the Raines of state resignes: 5
Thus from the mightie Monarche of the Meeds
To the west world successivelie proceeds
That great and fatall period of all things;
Whilst wearied now with broyles and long alarmes,
Earths maiestie her diademe layes downe   10
Before the feet of the unconquered crowne,
And throws her selfe (great Monarch) in thy armes.
   Here shall she staye, fates have ordained so,
   Nor has she where nor further for to goe.

ll. 1-5 *First . . . resignes.* The four empires or monarchies of world history, see
   Notes.
l. 3 *Then he.* Alexander.
l. 6 *the mightie Monarch.* Darius.
   Meeds. Medes.
l. 12 *great Monarch* God: Christianity was regarded as heir to the fourth mon-
   archy of Rome.

v

All good hath left this age, all trackes of shame,
Mercie is banished and pittye dead,
Justice from whence it came to heaven is fled,
Relligion maim'd is thought an idle Name.
Faith to distrust and malice hath given place,   5
Envie with poysond teeth hath freindship torne,
Renowned knowledge lurkes, despisd, a scorne,
Now it is evill all evill not to embrace.

There is no life save under servile Bandes,
To make Desert a Vassall to their crimes   10
Ambition with Avarice joyne Handes;
O ever-shamefull, O most shamelesse Tymes!
    Save that Sunnes light wee see, of good heare tell,
    This Earth wee courte so much were verye Hell.

vi

Doth then the world goe thus, doth all thus move?
Is this the Justice which on Earth wee find?
Is this that firme decree which all doth bind?
Are these your influences Powers above?
Those soules which Vices moodye Mistes most blind,   5
Blind Fortune blindlie most their friend doth prove:
And they who Thee (poore Idole) Vertue love
Plye like a feather toss'd by storme and wind.
Ah! (if a Providence doth swaye this all?)
Why should best Mindes groane under most distresse,   10
Or why should pryde Humilitie turne Thrall,
And injuryes the Innocent oppresse?
    Heavens hinder, stope this fate, or grante a Tyme
    When Good maye have as well as Bad their prime.

THE ENTERTAINMENT of the High and Mighty Monarch, Prince CHARLES, King of great Brittaine, France and Ireland, into his ancient and Royall Citie of Edenbourgh, the 15 of June 1633.

[The king is greeted by various tableaux on his way into the city, and is addressed by Caledonia, the Muses, a selection of classical deities, and the sun and the moon.]

JOVE

Delight of heaven, sole honour of the earth,
Jove (courting thine ascendant) at thy birth
Proclaimed thee a King, and made it true,
That Emperies should to thy worth be due,
He gave thee what was good, and what was great,   5
What did belong to love, and what to state,
Rare gifts whose ardors turne the hearts of all,
Like tunder when flint attomes on it fall;
The *Tramontane* which thy faire course directs,
Thy counsells shall approve by their effects;   10
Justice kept low by grants, and wrongs, and jarres,
Thou shalt relieve, and crowne with glistering starres,
Whom nought save law of force could keepe in awe
Thou shalt turne Clients to the force of law,
Thou armes shalt brandish for thine owne defence,   15
Wrongs to repell, and guard weake innocence,
Which to thy last effort thou shalt uphold,

l. 8   *tunder.* Tinder.
l. 9   *Tramontane.* The pole-star, thus, the guiding light.

As Oake the Ivy which it doth infold;
All overcome, at last thy selfe orecome,
Thou shalt make passion yield to reasons doome: 20
For smiles of fortune shall not raise thy mind,
Nor dismall most disasters turne declin'd,
True *Honour* shall reside within thy Court,
Sobrietie, and *Truth* there still resort,
Keepe promis'd faith thou shalt, Supercheries   25
Detest, and beagling Marmosets despise,
Thou, others to make rich, shalt not make poore
Thy selfe, but give that thou mayst still give more;
Thou shalt no Paranymph raise to high place,
For frizl'd locks, quaint pace, or painted face;   30
On gorgeous rayments, womanising toyes,
The workes of wormes, and what a Moth destroyes,
The Maze of fooles, thou shalt no treasure spend,
Thy charge to immortality shall tend,
Raise *Pallaces*, and *Temples* vaulted high,   35
Rivers ore arch, of hospitality,
Of Sciences the ruin'd Innes restore,
With walls and ports incircle *Neptunes* shore,
To new found worlds thy Fleets make hold their course,
And find of *Canada* the unknowne Sourse,   40
People those Lands which passe *Arabian* fields
In fragrant Wood and Muske which *Zephyre* yields;
Thou fear'd of none, shalt not thy people feare,
Thy peoples love thy greatnesse shall up-reare,
Still rigour shall not shine, and mercy lower,   45
What love can doe thou shalt not doe by power,
New and vast taxes thou shalt not extort,
Load heavy those thy bounty should support,
By harmlesse *Justice* graciously reforme,
Delighting more in calme then roaring storme,   50

l. 25   *Supercheries.* Frauds.
l. 26   *beagling Marmosets.* Spying monkeys.
l. 29   *Paranymph.* Bridesmaid; hence, probably, effeminate creature.
l. 32   *workes of wormes.* Silks.
l. 33   *Maze.* Delusion.
l. 37   *Innes.* Colleges.
l. 40   *Canada.* The St Lawrence river.

Thou shalt governe in *peace* as did thy *Sire*,
Keepe, save thine owne, and kingdomes new acquire,
Beyond *Alcides* Pillars, and those bounds
Where *Alexanders* fame till now resounds,
Till thou the greatest be among the Greats;   55
Thus heavens ordaine, so doe decree the Faits.

l. 53   *Alcides Pillars.* Pillars of Hercules at the straits of Gibraltar.

THE SONG OF THE MUSES

At length we see those eyes,
   which cheere both over earth and skies,
Now ancient *Caledon*
   thy beauties highten, richest robes put on,
   and let young joyes to all thy parts arise.   5

Here could thy Prince still stay,
   each moneth should turne in May,
We need not starre nor Sunne,
   save him to lengthen dayes and joyes begunne,
   sorrow and night to farre climes hast away.   10

Now Majestie and Love
   combin'd are from above,
Prince never Scepter swayd
   lov'd subjects more, of subjects more obey'd,
   which may indure whilst heavens great orbs do move.   15

Joyes did ye alwayes last,
   lifes sparke ye soone would wast,
Griefe followes sweet delight,
   as day is shaddowed by sable night,
   yet shall remembrance keep you still, when past.   20

l. 3   *Caledon.* Caledonia, Scotland.

SATIRICAL VERSES

i

The scottish kirke the English church doe name,
The english church the Scotes a kirke doe call;
Kirke and not church, church and not kirke, O shame!
Your kappa turne in chi, or perishe all:
Assemblies meet, post Bishopes to the court;   5
If these two Nationes fight, its strangeres sport.

ii

A CHARACTER OF THE ANTI-COVENANTER, OR MALIGNANT

Would yee know these royall knaves
Of free Men would turne us slaves;
Who our Union doe defame
With Rebellions Wicked Name?
Read these Verses, and yee il spring them,   5
Then on Gibbetes straight cause hing them.
They complaine of sinne and follye,
In these tymes so passing hollye
They their substance will not give,
Libertines that we maye live;   10
Hold that people too too wantom,
Under an old king dare cantom.
They neglecte our circular Tables,
Scorne our actes and lawes as fables,
Of our battales talke but meeklye,   15

l. 12   *cantom.* Canton, hence secede.

With sermones foure content them weeklye,
Sweare King Charles is neither Papist,
Armenian, Lutherian, Atheist;
But that in his Chamber-Prayers,
Which are pour'd 'midst Sighs and Tears,   20
To avert God's fearful Wrath,
Threatning us with Blood and Death,
Persuade they would the Multitude,
This King too holy is and good.
They avouch we'll weep and groan   25
When Hundred Kings we serve for one,
That each Shire but Blood affords
To serve the Ambition of young Lords,
Whose Debts ere now had been redoubled,
If the State had not been troubled.   30
Slow they are our Oath to swear,
Slower for it Arms to bear;
They do Concord love and Peace,
Would our Enemies embrace,
Turn Men Proselytes by the Word   35
Not by Musket, Pike, and Sword.
They Swear that for Religion's Sake
We may not massacre, burn, sack;
That the Beginning of these Pleas
Sprang from the ill-sped ABC's;   40
For Servants that it is not well
Against their Masters to Rebel;
That that Devotion is but slight
Doth force men first to swear, then fight;
That our Confession is indeed   45
Not the *Apostolick CREED*,
Which of Negations we contrive,
Which *Turk* and *Jew* may both subscrive;
That Monies should Men's Daughters marry,
They on frantick War miscarry,   50
Whilst dear the Souldiers they pay,
At last who will snatch all away,
And as Times turn worse and worse,
Catechise us by the Purse;
That Debts are paid with bold stern Looks,   55

137

That Merchants pray on their Compt-books;
That Justice, dumb and sullen, frowns
To see in Croslets hang'd her Gowns;
That Preachers ordinary Theme
Is 'gainst Monarchy to declaim;   60
That since Leagues we began to swear,
Vices did ne're so black appear;
Oppression, Blood-shed, ne're more rife,
Foul Jars between the Man and Wife;
Religion so contemn'd was never,   65
Whilst all are raging in a Fever.
They tell by Devils and some sad Chance
That that detestable League of *France*,
Which cost so many Thousand Lives,
And Two Kings by Religious Knives,   70
Is amongst us, though few descry;
Though they speak Truth, yet say they Lye.
Hee that sayes that night is night,
That halting folk walk not upright,
That the owles into the spring   75
Doe not nightingalles outsing;
That the seas wee can not plough,
Plant strawberryes in the raine-bow;
That waking men doe not sound sleep,
That the fox keepes not the sheep;   80
That alls not gold doth gold appeare,
Believe him not although hee sweere.
To such syrenes stope your eare,
Their societyes forbeare.
Tossed you may be like a wave,   85
Veritye may you deceave;
True fools they may make of you;
Hate them worse than Turke or Jew.
Were it not a dangerous Thing,
Should yee againe obey the king,   90
Lordes losse should souveraigntie,
Souldiours haste backe to Germanie,
Justice should in your Townes remaine,

l. 58   *Croslets.* Corslets, armour.

138

Poore Men possesse their own againe,
Brought out of Hell that word of plunder   95
More terrible than divell and Thunder,
Should with the Covenant flye away,
And charitye amongst us stay?
When yee find those lying fellowes,
Take and flowere with them the Gallowes;   100
On otheres yee maye too laye hold,
In purse or chestes if they have Gold.
Who wise or rich are in the Nation,
Malignants are by protestation.
Peace and plentie should us nurish,   105
True religion with us flourish.

l. 100 *flowere.* Decorate.

Against the king, sir, now why would yee fight?
Forsooth because hee made mee not a knight.
And yee my lordes, why arme yee against Charles?
Because of lordes hee would not make us Earles.
Earles, why lead you forth these angrye bandes?   5
Because wee will not quite the churches landes.
Most hollye church-Men, what is your intent?
The king our stipendes largelie did augment.
Commones, to tumult thus how are yee driven?
Our priestes say fighting is the way to Heaven.   10
Are these just cause of Warre, good Bretheren, grante?
Him Plunder! hee nere swore our covenant.
      Give me a thousand covenants, I'll subscrive
Them all, and more, if more yee can contrive
Of rage and malice; and let evrye one   15
Blake treason beare, not bare Rebellione.
I'll not be mockt, hist, plunder'd, banisht hence
For more yeeres standing for a . . . prince.
The castells all are taken, and his crown,
The sword and sceptre, ensignes of Renown,   20
With the lieutenant fame did so extoll,

And all led captives to the Capitoll;
I'll not die Martire for any mortall thing,
It's enough to be confessour for a king.
Will this you give contentment, honest Men?   25
I have written Rebelles, pox upon the pen!

iv

ENCOMIASTIKE VERSES BEFORE A BOOK
ENTITLED *FOLLIES*

At ease I red your Worke, and am right sorrye
It came not forth before *Encomium Morie*,
Or in the dayes when good king James the first
Carowsd the Horses spring to quench his thirst;
I durst have given my Thombe and layed a wager   5
Thy Name had grac't the chronicle of Jhon Major.
Had thou liv'd in the dayes of great Augustus,
(Hence, vulgare dotards, hence, unlesse yee trust us)
Thy Workes (with geese) had kept the Capitole,
And thou for ever been a happy soule,   10
Thy statue had been raisd neare Claudianus,
And thou in court liv'd equall with Sejanus.
Cornelius Tacitus is no such Poet,
Nor Livie; I'll say more ere that I goe yet.
Let all that heare doe weare celestiall bonnetes   15
Lyke thyne (they cannot write four-squared sonnetes)
Which shine like to that Mummye brought from Venice,
Or like the french kings relicks at Saint Denis.
It is a matter of regrate and pittie
Thou art not read into that famous citie   20
Of Constantine, for then the Turckes and Tartares
Had drunke with us, and like to ours worne gartares;

l. 1 *At ease.* On the privy(?).
l. 2 *Encomium Morie. Encomium Moriae* or *The Praise of Folly* by Erasmus.
l. 3 *king James.* James I of Scotland.
l. 4 *the Horses spring.* The spring Hippocrene, used by Pegasus and sacred to the Muses.
l. 6 *Jhon Major.* The Scots historian.
l. 17 *Mummye.* A dark medicinal compound.

And the strange Muphetees and hard Mameluckes
Had cut their beardes, and got by hart thy Bookes.
If any them detract, though hee were Xenaphon,   25
Thou shalt have such revenge as ere was tane of one,
From this our coast unto the Wall of China,
Where Maides weare narrow shoes; thou hast been a
Man for envie, though such forsooth was Horace,
Yet thou no lesse dost write than hee, and soare ass   30
As farre in this our tongue as any Latines,
Though some doe reade their verse, that ware fine satines;
Romes latest wonder, great Torquato Tasso,
Writing, to thee were a pecorious asse, hoe!
Now, to conclude, the nine Castalian lasses   35
Their Maidenheades thee sell for fannes and glasses.

l. 34 *pecorious.* Rich.
l. 35 *the nine Castalian lasses.* The Muses.

v

FOR A LADYES SUMMONDS OF NONENTREE

Kite.
Summond not mee to enter, there's no doubt
These twice foure yeares and more I have beene out,
And I it not denie; I did you wrong
At first, but since could not come in for throng.
Counts, knights, and Gentilles so hanted your Roome   5
Then your kinsmen, yeomen, and evrye Groome.
Why should I pressed? What? should I beene there
Where Brother Nepheu were so familiare?
And that with his French page sore-galled lord
Whom our east-Neighboures brought unto accord?   10
When all are gone and desolate's the place
Yee will mee enter, altred is your case;

Nonentree. Non-entry: a term in Scots law applied to land rights, here given a
    sexual connotation.
l. 5 *Gentilles.* Gentlemen.
l. 7 *pressed.* Precede?

141

Now it no more is like unto that thing
That earst it was than a gate is like a Ring:
Looke how a Medow ere that it be shorne   15
And when its hay with cartes and carrs all worne
Doth differ from it selfe; or as a way
Which was untrode unbarber'd yeasterday
Is not it selfe when cattells feet it goare
So is not yours the thing it was before.   20
As is that hole in which to save an host
The valiant Curtius himselfe madlie lost.
Is it not now? or like that ship of Drackes
That sail'd all seas, and now standes full of lackes,
Or like those Wells which turne in iron or stone   25
Any good tymber that is in them Thrown.
A candle-sticke though of Silver when some light
Hath brunt into its socked some darke night
Doth turne so furious hote that who would trie
A new light there of needes his light must frie.   30
Thou something was when lying thee behind
That Lord laught at thy Mother braking wind
And was surprisd; or when thy hand betrayd
Unto thy Dildo thy soft Madenhead.
And when thy bloudlesse Husband rod from home   35
And some rode after and tooke up his Roome.
Unhappy Kite, doth not thy breath stinke worse
Than that strong matter which Nature doth force
From a turn'd Gutt, and though it sent perfum
Thats but some stronger ordure to consume.   40
And(foole) though thou a Bonnet ware of Haire
Is not thy spotted Skull as Uglie bare
As thy paintd cheeke? Thy Haires were stronglie stout
Each one did tyre a Man ere it came out.
Are not the Twinnes now of thy withered brest   45

l. 22   *Curtius.* Curtius to save Rome jumped into a chasm which opened in
        front of the Forum.
l. 23   *Drackes.* Sir Francis Drake's.
l. 25   *those Wells.* Petrifying wells.
ll. 38–9   *that strong matter.* Ambergris?
l. 43   *The Haires* . . . Alluding to the belief that with each act of sexual intercourse
        a hair fell out.

(Which some tyme like Parnassus raisd each crest)
Like sodden Haggises, and thy drye skin
Like to those Bagges that Saffrons put with in.
Let your geometrike foot-man serve your turne
Or the porter whom last yeere yee did burne   50
Or your learnd childrens Tutor, who well can
Teach any Woman to decline to man,
That will himselfe a diphthongue turne with you
Pox on them if they tell what e're yee doe.
Its onlie hee alone sees both the poles   55
And shall see yours like to two hills of Moles
Which are grown one, though late they lookt aside
Now onlie interjectiones them divide.
Let mee alone, and force mee not to enter
If Hell be into earth its in your Center.

l. 48   *those Bagges* . . . Bags stained yellow.
l. 50   *burne.* Infect.

vi

If of the dead save good nought should be said
Hee'll get no Epitaph who heere is layd,
Hee overturned churches, did confound
The heaven and earth, threw monumentes to ground,
Disdaind and scorned all memorialls   5
Of antique ages and for funeralles
- Or worthye Men, Hee suffered not a Tombe
To enclose their bones: nor any Temple hold
Their sad remembrances: nor would heare told
That Husbandes and their Wyves one Quire contain'd,   10
That Sacred places by the Saintes were stain'd,
That Ravens their corses rather should consume
Ere to church burialls they should presume.
He filld the age hee livd in with strange dreames,
Now the posteritie gives him anathemes,   15
Detesteth his remembrance, and doth pray
Hee never rise more in the letter day.

l. 15   *anathemes.* Curses.

143

PROSE

A CYPRESSE GROVE

Though it hath beene doubted, if there bee in the Soule such imperious and superexcellent Power, as that it can, by the vehement and earnest working of it, deliver knowledge to an other without bodilie Organes, and by onelie[1] Conceptions and Ideas produce reall Effects; yet it hath beene ever, and of all, held, as infalible and most certaine, that it often (either by outward inspiration or some secret motion in it selfe) is Augure of its owne Misfortunes, and hath shadowes of approaching Dangers presented unto it before they fall forth. Hence so manie strange Apparitions and signes, true Visions, uncouth heavinesse, and causelesse languishings: Of which to seeke a reason, unlesse from the sparkling of GOD in the Soule, or from the God-like sparkles of the Soule, were to make Reason unreasonable, by reasoning of things transcending her reach.

Having when I had given my selfe to rest in the quiet Solitarinesse of the Night, found often my imagination troubled with a confused feare, no, sorrow or horror, which interrupting Sleepe, did astonish my Senses, and rouse mee, all appalled and transported in a sudden Agonie and amazednesse; of such an unaccustomed Perturbation, not knowing, nor beeing able to dive into any apparent cause, carried away with the streame of my (then doubting) Thoughts, I beganne to ascribe it, to that secret fore-knowledge and presaging power of the profeticke Minde, and to interpret such an Agonie to bee to the Spirit, as a sudden faintnesse and universall wearines useth to bee to the Bodie, a signe of following Sicknesse, or, as Winter Lightninges, Earth-quakes, and Monsteres prove to Common-wealthes and great Cities, Herbingers[2] of wretched events, and Emblemes of their hidden Destinies.

Heereupon, not thinking it strange if whatsoever is humaine should befall mee, knowing how Providence over-commeth Griefe, and discountenances Crosses: And that as wee should not despaire in Evills which may happen us, wee should not bee too confident, nor too much leane to those goods wee enjoye, I beganne to turne over in my remembrance all that could afflict miserable Mortalitie, and to fore-cast everie accident which could beget gloomie and sad apprehensions, and with a maske of horrour shew it selfe to humaine eyes. Till in the end (as by unities and points Mathematicians are brought to great numbers, and huge greatnesse) after manie fantasticall glances of the woes of Mankind, and those encombrances which follow upon life, I was brought to thinke, and with amazement, on the last of humaine Terrors, or as one tearmed it, the last of all dreadfull and terrible evils *Death*: For to easie Censure it would appeare, that the Soule, if it can fore-see that divorcement which it is to have from the Bodie, should not without great reason bee thus over-grieved, and plunged in inconsolable and un-accustumed Sorrow; considering their neare Union, long Familiaritie and Love, with the great Change, Paine, uglinesse, which are apprehended to bee the inseperable attendants of Death.

They had their beeing together, partes they are of one reasonable Creature, the harming of the one is the weakning of the working of the other; what sweete contentments doeth the Soule enjoye by the senses, They are the Gates and Windowes of its Knowledge, the Organes of its Delight? If it bee tideous to an excellent Player on the Lute to endure but a few Monethes[3] the want of one, how much more must the beeing without such noble Tooles and Engines bee plaintfull to the Soule? And, if two Pilgrimes, which have wandred some little peece of ground together, have an hearts-griefe when they are neare to parte, what must the sorrow bee at the parting of two so loving Friendes and never-loathing Lovers as are the Bodie and Soule?

Death is the sade Estranger of acquantance, the eternall Divorcer of Mariage, the Ravisher of the Children from their Parentes, the stealer of Parents from the Children, the Interrer of Fame, the sole cause of Forgetfulnesse, by which the living talke of those gone away as of so manie Shadowes, or fabulous Paladines[4]: all Strength by it is enfeebled, Beautie turned in deformitie and rottennesse, Honour in contempt, Glorie into basenesse, it is the unreasonable breaker off of all the actions of Vertue; by which wee enjoye no more the sweete pleasures on Earth, neither contemplate the statelie revolutions of the Heavens; Sunne perpetuallie setteth, Starres never rise unto us; It in one moment depriveth us of what with so great toyle and care in manie yeeres wee have heaped together: By this are Successions of Linages cut short, Kingdomes left Heirelesse, and greatest States orphaned: It is not overcome by Pride, smoothed by gawdie Flatterie, tamed by Intreaties, bribed by Benefites, softned by Lamentations, diverted by Time, Wisedome, save this, can alter and helpe anie thing.

By Death wee are exiled from this faire Citie of the World; it is no more a World unto us, nor wee anie more People into it. The Ruines of Phanes,[5] Palaces, and other magnificent Frames, yeeld a sad Prospect to the Soule: And how should it consider the wracke of such a wonderfull Maister-piece as is the Bodie without Horrour?

Though it cannot well and altogether bee denyed but that Death naturallie is terrible and to bee abhorred; it beeing a Privation of life, and a not beeing, and everie privation beeing abhorred of Nature and evill in it selfe, the feare of it too beeing ingenerate universalie in all Creatures; yet I have often thought that even naturallie, to a Minde by onelie Nature resolved and prepared, it is more terrible in conceite than in veritie, and at the first glance than when well pryed into; and that rather by the weakness of our Fantasie, than by what is in it; and that the marble Colours of obsequies, weeping, and funerall pompe (with which wee our selves limne[6] it forth) did adde much more Gastlinesse unto it than otherwayes it hath. To averre[7] which conclusion when I had recollected my over-charged spirits I began thus with my selfe.

If on the great Theater of this Earth, amongst the numberlesse number of Men, *To die* were onelie proper to thee and thine, then undoubtedlie thou hadst reason to grudge at so severe and partiall a Law. But since it is a necessitie, from the which never an Age by-past hath beene exempted, and unto which these which bee, and so manie as are to come, are thralled (no consequent of life beeing more common and familiar) why shouldst thou, with unprofitable and nothing availing stubburnnesse, oppose to so unevitable and necessarie a Condition? This is the high-way of mortalitie, our generall Home: behold, what millions have trode it before thee, what multitudes shall after thee, with them which at that same instant runne! in so universall a Calamitie (if Death be one) private complaints cannot bee heard: With so manie royall Palaces, it is small lose to see thy poore Caban burne. Shall the Heavens stay their ever-rolling Wheeles (for what is the motion of them but the motion of a swift and ever-whirling wheele, which twinneth[8] forth and againe up-windeth our life?) and hold still Time, to prolong thy miserable dayes, as if the highest of their working were to doe homage unto thee? Thy Death is a peece of the order of this *All*, a part of the Life of this World; for while the world is the world, some creatures must dye, and others take life. Eternall things are raised farre above this Orbe of generation and corruption, where the first Matter, like a still-flowing and ebbing Sea, with diverse

Waves, but the same Water, keepeth a restlesse and never-tyring Current; what is below in the Universality of the kind, not in it selfe, doeth abide; *Man* a long line of yeeres hath continued, *This Man* everie hundreth is swipt away. This aire-encircled Globe is the sole Region of Death, the Grave, where everie thing that taketh life must rotte, the Listes of Fortune and Change, onelie glorious in the inconstancie and varying Alterationes of it; which though manie, seeme yet to abide one, and being a certaine entire one, are ever manie. The never-agreeing bodies of the elementall Brethren[9] turne one in another, the Earth changeth her countenance with the Seasons, some-times looking colde and naked, other tymes hote and flowrie: Nay, I can not tell how, but even the lowest of those celestiall Bodies, that Mother of Moneths,[10] and Empresse of Seas, and moisture, as if shee were a Mirrour of our constant mutabilitie, appeareth (by her great nearnesse unto us) to participate of our alterations, never seeing us twice with that same Face, now looking blacke, than[11] pale and wanne, sometimes againe in the perfection and fulnesse of her beautie shining over us. Death heere no lesse than Life doth acte a part; the taking away of what is olde beeing, the making way for what is young. This Earth is as a Table Booke,[12] and men are the Notes, the first are washen out, that new may be written in. They which forewent us did leave a Roome for us, and should wee grieve to doe the same to these which should come after us? who beeing admitted to see the exquisite Rarities of some Antiquaries Cabinet is grieved, all viewed, to have the Courtaine drawen, and give place to new Pilgrimes? And when the LORD of this Universe hath shewed us the various wonders of his amazing Frame, should wee take it to heart, when hee thinketh time to dislodge? This is his unalterable and unevitable Decree; as wee had no part of our will in our entrance into this Life, wee should not presume of anie in our leaving it, but soberlie learne to will that which hee wills, whose verie willing giveth beeing to all that it wills, and adoring the Orderer, not repine at the Order and Lawes, which allwhere, and all-wayes, are so perfectlie established, that who would essay to alter and amend anie of them, hee should either make them worse, or desire thinges beyond the levell of possibilitie: all that is necessarie and convenient for us they have bestowed upon us, and freelie granted, and what they have not bestowed nor granted us, neither is it necessarie, nor convenient that wee should have it.

If thou doest complaine, that there shall bee a time in the which thou shalt not bee, why doest thou not too grieve, that there was a time in the which thou wast not, and so that thou art not as olde, as that enlifening Planet of Time? For, not to have beene a thousand yeeres before this moment, is as much to bee deplored, as not to bee a thousand after it, the effect of them both beeing one: that will bee after us which long long ere wee were was. Our Childrens children have that same reason to murmure that they were not young men in our dayes, which wee now, to complaine that wee shall not be old in theirs. The Violets have their time, though they empurple not the Winter, and the Roses keepe their season, though they discover not their beautie in the Spring.

Empires, States, Kingdomes, have by the Doome of the Supreame providence their fatall Periods, great Cities lye sadlie buried in their dust, Artes and Sciences have not onelie their Ecclipses, but their wainings and deathes; the gastlie Wonders of the World, raised by the ambition of Ages, are overthrowne and trampled; some Lights above (deserving to bee intitled Starres) are loosed and never more seene of us; the excellent fabrike of this Universe it selfe shall one day suffer ruine, or a change like a ruine, and poore Earthlings thus to bee handled complaine!

But is this Life so great a good, that the lose of it should bee so deare unto Man? if it be? the meanest creatures of Nature thus bee happie, for they live no lesse than hee: If it bee so great a felicitie, how is it esteemed of man himselfe at so small a rate, that for so poore gaines, nay, one disgracefull Word, hee will not stand to loose it? What excellencie is there in it, for the which hee should desire it perpetuall, and repine to bee at rest, and returne to his olde Grand-mother Dust? Of what moment are the Labours and Actions of it, that the interruption and leaving off of them should bee to him so distastfull, and with such grudging lamentations received?

Is not the entring into Life weaknesse? the continuing Sorrow? in the one hee is exposed to all the injuries of the Elementes, and like a condemned Trespasser (as if it were a fault to come to light) no sooner borne than fast manacled and bound, in the other hee is restlesslie, like a Ball, tossed in the Tinnise-court of this world; when hee is in the brightest Meridiane of his glorie, there needeth nothing to destroy him, but to let him fall his owne hight: A reflexe of the Sunne, a blast of winde, nay, the glance of an Eye is sufficient to undoe Him: Howe can that be anie great matter, of which so small instrumentes and slender actions are maisters?

His Bodie is but a Masse of discording humours, composed and elemented by the conspiring influences of superior Lights,[13] which though agreeing for a trace of tyme, yet can never be made uniforme and keept in a just proportion. To what sickenesse is it subject unto, beyond those of the other sensitive Creatures? no parte of it beeing which is not particularlie infected and afflicted by some one, nay, everie part with many, yea, so many, that the Maisters of that Arte can scarce number or name them. So that the life of diverse of the meanest Creatures of Nature, hath with great reason by the most Wise, beene preferred to the naturall life of Man: And wee should rather wonder how so fragill a matter should so long endure, than how so soone dissolve, and decay.

Are the Actiones of the most part of men, much differing from the Exercise of the Spider, that pitcheth toyles, and is tapist,[14] to pray on the smaller Creatures, and for the Wearing of a scornefull Webbe eviscerateth it selfe manie dayes, which when with much Industerie finished, a little Puffe of Winde carrieth away both the worke and the worker? Or are they not, like the playes of Children? Or (to hold them at their highest rate) as is a May-Game, a Maske, or what is more earnest, some studie at Chesse? Everie day wee rise and lye downe, apparrell our Bodies and disapparrell them, make them Sepulchers of dead Creatures, wearie them, and refresh them; which is a Circle of idle Travells, and Laboures (like *Penelopes* Taske)[15] unprofitablie renewed. Some time wee are in a Chase after a fading Beautie; now wee seeke to enlarge our Boundes, increase our Treasure, living poorelie, to purchase what wee must leave to those wee shall never see, or (happelie)[16] to a Foole, or a prodigall Heire; raised with the wind of Ambition, wee courte that idle name of Honour, not considering how They mounted aloft in the highest Ascendant of earthlie Glorie, are but tortured Ghostes, wandring with golden Fetters in glistering Prisones, having Feare and Danger their unseparable Executioners, in the midst of Multitudes rather guarded than regarded. They whom opacke[17] imaginations, and inward Thoughtfulnesse, have made wearie of the worlds Eye, though they have withdrawne themselves from the course of Vulgare Affaires, by vaine Contemplationes, curious Searches, thinke their life away, are more disquieted, and live worse than others, their Wit beeing too sharpe to give them a true taste of present Infelicities, and to agravate their woes; while they of a more shallow and blunt Conceit, have want of Knowledge and Ignorance of themselves, for a remedie and Antidote against all the Greevances and incombrances of Life.

What *Camelion*,[18] what *Euripe*,[19] what *Raine-bow*, what *Moone* doth change so oft as Man? hee seemeth not the same person in one and the same day, what pleaseth him in the Morning, is in the Evening distastfull unto him. Yong hee scorneth his childish Conceits, and wading deeper in Yeeres (for Yeeres are a Sea, into which hee wadeth untill he drowne) hee esteemeth his Youth unconstancie, Rashnesse, Follie; Old, hee beginneth to pittie himselfe, plaining because hee is changed, that the World is changed, like those in a Ship, which when they launce from the Shore, are brought to thinke the Shore doeth flie from them. Hee hath no sooner acquired what hee did desire, but hee beginneth to enter into new Cares, and desire what hee shall never bee able to acquire. When hee seemeth freed of evill in his owne estate, hee grudgeth and vexeth himselfe at the happinesse and fortunes of others. Hee is pressed with Care for what is present, with Griefe, for what is past, with Feare for what is to come, nay, for what will never come; And as in the Eye one Teare draweth another after it, so maketh hee one Sorrow follow upon a former, and everie day lay up stuffe of Griefe for the next.

The Aire, the Sea, the Fire, the Beasts bee cruell Executioners of Man; yet Beastes, Fire, Sea and Aire, are pittifull to Man in comparison of man, for moe[20] men are destroyed by men, than by them all. What Scornes, Wrongs, Contumelies, Imprisonmentes, Torments, Poysons receiveth Man of Man? What Ingines and new workes of Death are daylie found out by Man against man? What Lawes to thrall his Libertie, Fantasies and Bugbeares, to infatuate and inveigle his reason? Amongst the Beastes is there anie that hath so servile a Lot in anothers behalfe as Man, yet neither is content, nor hee who raigneth, nor hee who serveth?

The halfe of our Life is spent in Sleepe; which hath such a resemblance to Death, that often it separates the Soule from the Bodie, and teacheth it a sort of beeing above it, making it soare beyond the Spheare of sensuall Delightes, and attaine to Knowledge, unto which, while the Bodie did awake, it dared scarce aspire. And who would not rather than remaine chained in this loathsome Galley of the World, Sleepe ever (that is dye) having all thinges at one stay, bee free from those Vexationes, Disasteres, Contempts, Indignities, and manie manie Anguishes, unto which this Life is envassalled and made thrall? and, well looked unto, our greatest Contentment and Happinesse heere seemeth rather to consist in an absence of Miserie, than in the enjoying of any great Good.

What have the dearest Favorites of the World, created to the Paternes of the fairest Ideas of Mortalitie to glorie in? Is it Greatnesse? Who can bee great on so small a Round as is this Earth, and bounded with so short a course of time? How like is that to Castles or imaginarie Cities raised in the Skies by chaunce-meeting Cloudes? or to Gyantes modelled (for a sport) of Snow which at the hoter lookes of the Sunne melt away and lye drowned in their owne moisture? Such an impetuous Vicissitude towseth[21] the Estate of this World! Is it Knowledge? But wee have not yet attained to a perfect Understanding of the smallest Flower, and why the Grasse should rather bee greene than red. The Element of Fire is quite put out, the Aire is but Water rarified, the Earth is found to move, and is no more the Center of the Universe, is turned into a Magnes;[22] Starres are not fixed, but swimme in the etheriall Spaces, Cometes are mounted above the Planetes; Some affirme there is another World of men and sensitive Creatures, with Cities and Palaces in the Moone; the Sunne is lost, for, it is but a Light made of the conjunction of manie shining Bodies together, a Clift in the lower Heavens, through which the Rayes of the highest defuse themselves, is observed to have Spots; Thus, Sciences by the diverse Motiones of this Globe of the Braine of Man, are become Opiniones, nay, Errores, and leave the Imagination in a thousand Labyrinthes. What is all wee knowe compared with what wee knowe not? Wee have not yet agreed about the chiefe Good and Felicitie. It is (perhaps) artificiall Cunning, how manie Curiosities bee framed by the least Creatures of Nature (who like a wise Painter showeth in a small Pourtrait more ingine[23] than in a great) unto which the industrie of the most curious Artizanes doeth not attaine? Is it Riches? What are they, but the Idoles of Fooles, the casting out of Friendes, Snares of Libertie, Bandes to such as have them, possessing rather than possessed, Mettalles which Nature hath hidde (fore-seeing the great Harmes they should occasion) and the onelie Opinion of Man, hath brought in estimation? They are like to Thornes which laid on an open hand are easilie blowne away, and wound the closing and hard-gripping, Prodigalls mis-spend them, Wretches mis-keepe them; when wee have gathered the greatest aboundance, wee our selves can enjoye no more of them, than so much as belonges to one man: They take not away Want, but occasione it, what great and rich men doe by others, the meaner and more contented sort doe by themselves. Will some talke of our pleasures? It is not (though in the Fables) told out of purpose, that *Pleasure* beeing called up to Heaven, to disburthen her selfe and become more light, did heere leave her Apparrell, which *Sorrow* (then naked, forsaken, and wandring) finding, did afterwards attire her selfe with: And if wee would say the truth of most of our Joyes, wee must confesse them to bee but disguised Sorrowes; Remorse ever ensueth[24] them, and (beeing the Heires of Displeasure) seldome doe they appeare, except Sadnesse and some wakning Griefe hath reallie preceded and fore-went them. Will some Ladies vaunt of their Beautie? That is but Skin-thicke of two Senses onelie knowne, short even of marble Statues and Pictures; not the same to all Eyes, dangerous to the Beholder, and hurtfull to the Possessour, an Enemie to Chastitie, a Frame made to delight others more than those which have it, a superficiall Varnish hiding Bones and the Braines, thinges fearefull to bee looked upon: Growth in Yeares doeth blast it, or Sicknesse, or Sorrow preventing[25] them; Our Strength, matched with that of the unreasonable Creatures, is but Weaknesse. All wee can set our eyes upon in these intricate mazes of Life is but Alchimie, vaine Perspective, and deceiving Shadowes, appearing farre other wayes afarre off, than when enjoyed, and looked upon at a neare Distance. O! who if before hee had a beeing, hee could have knowledge of the manie-fold Miseries of it, would enter this woefull Hospitall of the World, and accept of life upon such hard conditiones?

If Death bee good, why should it bee feared? and if it bee the worke of Nature, how should it not bee good? for, Nature, is an Ordinance Disposition and Rule, which GOD hath established in creating this Universe, as is the Lawe of a King, which can not erre: For, how should the Maker of that Ordinance erre? Sith in Him there is no impotencie and weaknesse, by the which hee might bring forth what is unperfect, no perversenesse of Will, of which might proceede any vicious action, no Ignorance, by the which hee might goe wrong in working; beeing most Powerfull, most Good, most Wise, nay, All-Wise, All-Good, All-Powerfull: Hee is the first Orderer, and marshelleth everie other Order, the highest Essence, giving Essence to all other thinges, of all Causes the Cause: Hee worketh powerfullie, bounteouslie, wiselie, and maketh Nature (his artificiall Organ) doe the same. How is not Death of Nature? Sith what is naturallie generate, is subject to Corruption, and sith such an Harmonie (which is Life) arising of the mixture of the foure Elementes, which are the ingredientes of our Bodies, can not ever endure; the contrarieties of their qualities (as a consuming rust in the baser Metalles) beeing an inward cause of a necessarie dissolution. O of fraile and instable Thinges the constant, firme, and eternall Order! For even in their changes they keepe ever universall auncient and uncorruptible Lawes.

Againe, how can Death bee evill; sith it is the Thaw of all these vanities which the Frost of Life bindeth together? If there bee a Sacietie[26] in Life, then must there not bee a Sweetenesse in Death? Man were an intollerable thing, were hee not mortall; The Earth were not ample enough to containe her Of-spring, if none dyed: in two or three Ages (without Death) what an unpleasant and lamentable Spectacle were the most flowrishing Cities? For, what should there bee to bee seene in them, save Bodies languishing and courbing[27] againe into the Earth, pale disfigured Faces, Skelitones in steade of Men? And what to bee heard, but the Exclamationes of the Yong, Complaintes of the Old, with the pittifull cryes of sicke and pining Persons? there is almost no infirmitie worse than Age.

If there bee anie evill in Death, it would appeare to bee that Paine and torment, which wee apprehend to arise from the breaking of those strait Bands which keepe the Soule and Bodie together; which, sith not without great struggling and motion, seemeth to prove it selfe vehement and most extreame. The Senses are the onelie cause of paine, but before the last Trances of Death they are so brought under, that they have no (or verie little) strength, and their strength lessening the strength of Paine too must bee lessened. How should wee doubt but the weakenesse of Sense lesseneth Paine, sith wee know, that weakned and maimed partes which receive not nourishment, are a great deale lesse sensible than the other partes of the Bodie: And see, that olde strengthlesse, decrepit Persons leave this World almost without paine, as in a Sleepe? If Bodies of the most sound and wholesome constitution bee these which most vehementlie feele paine, it must then follow that they of a distempered and crasie[28] Constitution, have least feeling of Paine; and by this reason, all weake and sicke Bodies should not much feele Paine; for if they were not distempered and evill complexioned, they would not bee sicke. That the *Sight, Hearing, Taste, Smelling*, leave us without Paine, and un-awares, we are undoubtedlie assured: And why should wee not thinke the same of the *Feeling*? That, by which wee are capable of Feeling, is the vitall Spirits animated by the Braine, which in a Man in perfect Health, by veines and arteres[29] are spred and extended through the whole bodie, and hence it is that the whole Bodie is capable of paine: But, in dying Bodies wee see, that by pauses and degrees those partes which are furthest removed from the Heart, become cold, and beeing deprived of naturall heate, all the paine which they feele, is that they doe feele no paine. Now, even as ere the sicke bee aware, the vitall Spirits have with-drawne themselves from the whole extension of the Bodie, to succour the Heart (like distressed Citizens which finding their Walles battered downe, flie to the defence of their Cittadell) so doe they abandonne the Heart without any sensible touch: As the flame, the Oyle failing, leaveth the Weeke, [30] or as the light the Aire which it doeth invest. As to those shrinking motions, and convultions of Sinewes and Members, which appeare to witnesse great paine, let one represent to himselfe the Stringes of an high-tuned Lute, which breaking, retire to their naturall windings, or a peece of Ice, that without any out-ward violence, cracketh at a Thaw: No otherwise doe the Sinewes of the Bodie, finding themselves slacke and unbended from the Braine, and their wonted labours and motions cease, struggle, and seeme to stirre themselves, but without either paine or sense. Sowning [31] is a true pourtrait of Death, or rather it is the same, beeing a Cessation from all action, motion, and function of Sense and Life: But in Sowning there is no paine, but a silent rest, and so deepe and sound a sleepe, that the naturall is nothing in comparison of it; What great paine then can there bee in Death, which is but a continued Sowning, a sweete ignorance of Cares, and a never againe returning to the workes and dolorous felicitie of Life? The wise and all provident Creator hath made Death by many signes of paine appeare terrible, to the effect, that if Man, for reliefe of miseries and present evills, should have unto it recourse, it beeing (apparantlie) a worser, hee should rather constantlie indure what hee knoweth, than have refuge unto that which hee feareth and knoweth not, the Terrours of Death seeme the Gardianes of Life.

Now although Death were an extreame Paine, sith it comes in an Instant, what can it bee? why should wee feare it? for, while wee are, it commeth not, and it beeing come, wee are no more. Nay, though it were most painefull, long continuing, and terrible-uglie, why should wee feare it? Sith Feare is a foolish passion but where it may preserve; but it can not preserve us from Death, yea, rather Feare maketh us to meete with that which wee would shunne, and banishing the Comfortes of present Contentmentes bringeth Death more neare unto us: That is ever terrible which is unknowne; so doe little Children feare to goe in the darke, and their Feare is increased with Tales.

But that (perhaps) which anguisheth Thee most, is to have this glorious Pageant of the World removed from Thee, in the Prime and most delicious Season of thy life; for, though to dye bee usuall, to dye young may appeare extraordinarie. If the present Fruition of these things bee unprofitable and vaine, what can a long Continuance of them bee, If God had made Life happier, hee had also made it longer? Stranger and newe Halcyon, why wouldst thou longer nestle amidst these unconstant and stormie Waves? Hast thou not alreadie suffred enough of this World, but thou must yet endure more? To live long, is it not to bee long troubled? But number thy Yeares, which are now (   ) and thou shalt find, that where as ten have over-lived Thee, thousands have not attained this age. One yeare is sufficient to behold all the magnificence of Nature, nay, even one Day and Night; for more, is but the same brought againe: This Sunne, that Moone, these Starres, the varying Dance of the Spring, Summer, Autumne, Winter, Is that verie same which the golden Age did see. They which have the longest time lent them to live in, have almost no part of it at all, measuring it, either by that space of time which is past, when they were not, or by that which is to come: Why shouldst thou then care, whether thy Dayes bee manie, or few, which when prolonged to the uttermost, prove, paralel'd with Eternitie, as a Teare is to the Ocean? To dye young, is to doe that soone, and in some fewer dayes, which once thou must doe; it is but the giving over of a Game that (after never so manie hazardes) must bee lost. When thou hast lived to that Age thou desirest, or one of *Platos* yeares,[32] so soone as the last of thy dayes, riseth above thy Horizon, thou wilt then as now demand longer Respite, and expect more to come, the oldest are most unwilling to dye. It is Hope of long life, that maketh Life seeme short. Who will behold, and with the eyes of judgement behold, the manie Changes depending on humaine affaires, with the afterclaps of Fortune, shall never lament to dye yong. Who knoweth what alterations and sudden disasters, in outward estate, or inward contentments, in this Wildernesse of the World, might have befallen him who dyeth yong, if hee had lived to bee olde? Heaven, fore-knowing imminent harmes, taketh those which it loveth to it selfe, before they fall foorth: Death in Youth is like the leaving a supperfluous Feast, before the drunken Cups be presented and walke about. Pure and (if wee may so say) Virgine Soules carrie their bodies with no small Agonies, and delight not to remaine long in the dregs of humane corruption, still burning with a desire to turne backe to the place of their Rest; for this World is their Inne, and not their Home. That which may fall foorth everie houre, can not fall out of time. Life is a Journey in a dustie Way, the furthest Rest is Death, in this some goe more heavilie burthened, than others:

Swift and active Pilgrimes come to the end of it in the Morning, or at Noone, which Tortoyse-paced Wretches, clogged with the fragmentarie rubbige[33] of this World, scarce with great travell crawle unto at Mid-night. Dayes are not to bee esteemed after the number of them, but after the goodnesse: more Compasse maketh not a Spheare more compleate, but as round is a little, as a large Ring; nor is that Musician most praiseworthie who hath longest played, but hee in measured Accents who hath made sweetest Melodie; to live long hath often beene a let[34] to live well. Muse not how many yeares thou mightst have enjoyed Life, but how sooner thou mightst have lossed it; neither grudge so much that it is no better, as comfort thy selfe that it hath beene no worse: let it suffice that thou hast lived till this day; and (after the course of this World) not for nought; thou hast had some smiles of Fortune, favours of the worthiest, some friendes, and thou hast never beene disfavoured of the Heaven.

Though not for Life it selfe, yet that to after-worlds thou mightst leave some Monument that once thou wast, happilie in the cleare light of Reason, it would appeare that Life were earnestly to be desired: for sith it is denyed us to live ever (said one) let us leave some worthy Remembrance of our once heere beeing, and drawe out this Spanne of Life to the greatest length and so farre as is possible. O poore Ambition! to what (I pray Thee) mayst thou concreded[35] it? Arches and stately Temples, which one Age doth raise, doth not another raze? Tombes and adopted Pillars, lye buried with those which were in them buried: Hath not Avarice defaced, what Religion did make glorious? All that the hand of man can upreare, is either over-turned by the hand of man, or at length by standing and continuing consumed: as if there were a secret opposition in Fate (the unevitable Decree of the Eternall) to controule our industry, and conter-checke all our devices and proposing. Possessions are not enduring, Children lose their Names, Families glorying (like Marigolds in the Sunne) on the highest top of Wealth and Honour (no better than they which are not yet borne) leaving off to bee. So doeth Heaven confound, what wee endeavour by Labour and Arte to distinguish. That Renowne by Papers,[36] which is thought to make men immortall, and which nearest doth approach the Life of these eternall Bodies above, how slender it is, the very word of Paper doth import; and what is it when obtained, but a flowrish of Words, which comming Tymes may scorne? How many millions never heare the Names of the most famous Writers, and amongst them to whom they are known, how few turne over their Pages, and of such as doe, how many sport at their Conceits, taking the Verity for a Fable, and oft a Fable for Veritie, or (as wee doe Pleasants)[37] use all for recreation? Then the arising of more famous, doth darken, put downe, and turne ignoble the Glorie of the former, being held as Garments, worne out of fashion. Now when thou hast attained what Praise thou couldst desire, and thy fame is emblazoned in many Stories, never after to bee either shadowed or worne out, it is but an Eccho, a meere Sound, a Glow-worme, which seene a farre, casteth some cold beames, but approached is found nothing, an imaginarie happinesse, whose good dependes on the opinion of others. Desert and Vertue for the most part want Monuments and Memorie, seldome are recorded in the Volumes of Admiration, nay, are often branded with Infamie, while Statues and Trophees are erected to those, whose names should have beene buried in their dust, and folded up in the darkest clowds of oblivion: So doe the rancke Weeds in this Garden of the World choacke and over-run the swetest Flowres. Applause, whilst thou livest, serveth but to make Thee that faire Marke against which Envye and Malice direct their Arrows, and when thou art wounded, all Eyes are turned towards thee (like the Sunne which is most gazed on in an Ecclipse) not for Pittie or Praise but Detraction; at the best, it but resembleth that Siracusianes Spheare of Christall[38] not so faire as fraile: and, borne after thy death, it may as well bee ascribed, to some of those were in the Trojan Horse, or to such as are yet to bee borne an hundreth yeares hereafter, as to Thee, who nothing knowes, and is of all unknowne. What can it availe thee to bee talked of, whilst thou art not? Consider in what Bounds our Fame is confined, how narrow the Listes are of humane Glorie, and the furthest shee can stretch her winges. This Globe of the Earth and water, which seemeth huge to us, in respect of the Universe, compared with that wide wide Pavillion of Heaven, is lesse than little, of no sensible quantitie, and but as a Point: for the Horizon which boundeth our sight, devideth the Heaven as in two halfes, having alwaies sixe of the Zodiacke Signes above, and as many under it, which if the Earth had any quantitie compared to it, it could not doe. More, if the Earth were not as a point, the Starres could not still in all parts of it appeare to us as of a like greatnes; for where the Earth raised it selfe in Mountaines, wee beeing more neare to Heaven, they would appeare to us of a greater quantity, and where it is humbled in Vallies, wee beeing further distant, they would seeme unto us lesse: But the Starres in all partes of the Earth appearing of a like greatnesse, and to every part of it, the Heaven imparting to our sight the halfe of its inside, wee must avouch it to bee but as a Point. Well did One compare it to an Ant-hill, and men (the Inhabitants) to so manie Pismires,[39] and Grashoppers, in the toyle and varietie of their diversified studies. Now of this small indivisible thing, thus compared, how much is covered with Waters? how much not at all discovered? how much un-inhabited and desart? and how many millions of millions are they, which share the remnant amongst them, in Languages, Customes, divine Rites differing, and all almost to others unknowne? But let it bee granted that Glorye and Fame are some great matter, are the life of the dead, and can reach Heaven it selfe, sith they are oft buried with the honoured, and passe away in so fleet a Revolution of time, what great good can they have in them? How is not Glorie temporall, if it increase with yeares and depend on time? Then imagine mee (for what cannot Imagination reach unto?) one could bee famous in all times to come, and over the whole World present, yet shall hee bee for ever Obscure and ignoble to those mightie Ones, which were onely heere-tofore esteemed famous, amongst the Assyrians, Persians, Romans. Againe, the vaine Affectation of man is so suppressed, that though his workes abide some space, the Worker is unknowne: the huge Egyptian Pyramides, and that Grot in *Pausilipo*,[40] though they have wrestled with Time, and worne upon the vaste of dayes, yet are their Authores no more known, than it is knowne by what strange Earth-quackes, and Deluges, Iles were divided from the Continent, or Hilles bursted foorth of the Vallies. Dayes, Monthes, and Yeares, are swallowed up in the great Gulfe of Tyme (which puts out the eyes of all their Glorie) and onelie a fattall oblivion remaines: Of so manie Ages past, wee may well figure to our selves some likelie Apparances, but can affirme little Certaintie.

But (my Soule) what aileth thee, to bee thus backward and astonished, at the remembrance of Death, sith it doth not reach Thee, more than Darknesse doth those farre-shinning Lampes above? Rouse thy selfe for shame, why shouldst thou feare to bee without a Bodie, sith thy Maker, and the spirituall and supercelestiall Inhabitantes have no Bodies? Hast thou ever seene any Prisoner, who when the Jaile Gates were broken up, and hee enfranchised and set loose, would rather plaine and sit still on his Fetters, than seeke his freedome? Or any Mariner, who in the midst of Stormes arriving neare the Shore, would launch forth againe unto the Maine, rather than stricke Saile and joyfullie enter the leas[41] of a save Harbour? If thou rightlie know thy selfe, thou hast but small cause of anguish; for, if there bee any resemblance of that which is infinite, in what is finite (which yet by an infinite imperfection is from it distant) If thou bee not an Image, thou art a Shadow of that unsearchable Trinitie, in thy three essentiall Powers, Understanding, Will, Memorie; which though three, are in Thee but one, and abiding one, are distinctly three: But in nothing more comest thou neare that Soveraigne Good, than by thy Perpetuitie, which who strive to improve,[42] by that same doe it prove: Like those that by arguing themselves to bee without all reason, by the verie arguing, show how they have some. For, how can what is whollie mortall more thinke upon, consider, or know that which is immortall, than the Eye can know Soundes, or the Eare discerne of Coloures; if none had Eyes, who would ever dispute of light or shadow? And if all were deafe, who would descant of Musicke? To Thee nothing in this visible world is comparable; thou art so wonderfull a Beautie, and so beautifull a Wonder, that if but once thou couldst be gazed upon by bodily Eyes, every heart would be inflamed with thy love, and ravished from all servile basenesse and earthlie desires. Thy being dependes not on Matter; hence by thine Understanding dost thou dyve into the being of everie other thing; and therein art so pregnant, that nothing by Place, Similitude, Subject, Time, is so conjoyned, which thou canst not separate; as what neither is, nor any wayes can exist, thou canst faine, and give an abstract being unto. Thou seemest a World in thy selfe, containing Heaven, Starres, Seas, Earth, Floodes, Mountaines, Forestes, and all that lives: Yet rests thou not satiate with what is in thyselfe, nor with all in the wide Universe (because thou knowest their defects) untill thou raise thy selfe, to the contemplation of that first illuminating Intelligence, farre above Time, and even reaching Eternitie it selfe, into which thou art transformed, for, by receiving thou (beyond all other thinges) art made that which thou receivest. The more thou knowest the more apt thou art to know, not being amated[43] with any object that excelleth in predominance, as Sense by objectes sensible. Thy Will is uncompellable, resisting Force, daunting Necessitie, despising Danger, triumphing over Affliction, unmoved by Pittie, and not constrained by all the toyles and disasters of Life. What the Artes-Master of this Universe is in governing this Universe, thou art in the Bodie; and as hee is whollie in everie part of it, so art thou whollie in everie part of the Bodie: Like unto a Mirrouer,[44] everie small parcell of which a parte, doeth represent and doe the same, what the whole did enteire and together. By Thee Man is that Hymen of eternall and mortall thinges, that Chaine, together binding unbodied and bodilie Substances, without which the goodlie Fabricke of this World were unperfect. Thou hast not thy beginning from the fecunditie, power, nor action of the elementall qualities, beeing an immediate Master-piece of that great Maker: Hence hast Thou the Formes and Figures of all thinges imprinted in Thee from thy first originall. Thou onelie at once art capable of contraries, of the three partes of Time,[45] Thou makest but one, thou knowest thy selfe so separate, absolute, and diverse an essence from thy Bodie, that Thou disposest of it as it pleaseth Thee, for in Thee there is no passion so weake which mastereth not the feare of leaving it. Thou shouldst bee so farre from repining at this separation, that it should bee the chiefe of thy desires; Sith it is the passage, and meanes to attaine thy perfection and happinesse. Thou art heere, but as in an infected and leprous Inne, plunged in a flood of humours, oppressed with Cares, suppressed with Ignorance, defiled and destained with Vice, retrograd in the course of Vertue; Small thinges seeme heere great unto Thee, and great thinges small, Follie appeareth Wisedome and Wisedome Follie. Fred of thy fleshlie Care, thou shalt rightlie discerne the beautie of thy selfe, and have perfect Fruition of that All-sufficient and All-suffizing Happinesse, which is GOD himselfe; to whom thou owest thy beeing, to Him thou owest thy well beeing; Hee and Happinesse are the same. For, if GOD had not Happinesse, Hee were not GOD, because Happinesse is the highest and greatest Good: If then GOD have Happinesse, it can not bee a thing differing from Him, for, if there were any thing in Him differing from Him, Hee should bee an Essence composed and not simple. More, what is differing in any thing, is either an accident or a part of it selfe; In GOD Happinesse can not bee an accident, because Hee is not subject to any accidents; if it were a part of Him (since the part is before the whole) wee should bee forced to grant, that something was before GOD. Bedded and bathed in these earthlie ordures,[46] thou canst not come neare this soveraigne Good, nor have any glimpse of the farre-off dawning of his un-accessible Brightnesse, no, not so much as the eyes of the Birds of the night have of the Sunne. Thinke then by Death, that thy Shell is broken, and thou then but even hatched; that thou art a Pearle, raised from thy Mother, to bee enchaced in Gold, and that the death-day of thy bodie, is thy birth-day to Eternitie.

Why shouldst thou bee feare-stroken? and discomforted, for thy parting from this mortall Bride, thy Bodie; sith it is but for a tyme, and such a tyme, as shee shall not care for, nor feele any thing in, nor thou have much neede of her? Nay, sith thou shalt receive her againe, more goodlie and beautifull, than when in her fullest Perfection thou enjoyed her; beeing by her absence made like unto that Indian Christall, which after some Revolutions of Ages, is turned into purest Diamond. If the Soule bee the Forme of the Bodie, and the Forme seperated from the Matter of it, can not ever so continue, but is inclined and disposed to bee reunited thereinto; What can let and hinder this desire, but that some time it bee accomplished, and obtaining the expected end, rejoyne it selfe againe unto the Bodie? The Soule separate hath a desire, because it hath a will, and knoweth it shall by this reunion receive Perfection: too, as the Matter is disposed, and inclineth to its Forme when it is without it, so would it seeme that the Forme should bee towards its Matter in the absence of it. How is not the Soule the Forme of the Bodie, sith by it it is, sith it is the beginning and cause of all the actions and functions of the Bodie: For though in excellencie it passe everie other Forme, yet doeth not that excellencie take from it the Nature of a Forme. If the abiding of the Soule from the Bodie bee violent, then can it not bee everlasting, but have a regresse: How is not such an estate of beeing and abiding not violent to the Soule, if it bee naturall to it to bee in its Matter, and (seperate) after a strange manner, many of the powers and faculties of it (which never leave it) are not duelie exercised? This Union seemeth not above the Horizon of naturall reason, farre lesse impossible to bee done by GOD: and though Reason can not evidentlie heere demonstrate, yet hath shee a mistie and groping notice. If the Bodie shall not arise, how can the onelie and Soveraigne Good bee perfectlie and infinitlie good? For, how shall Hee be just, nay, have so much justice as man, if he suffer the evill and vicious to have a more prosperous and happie life, than the followers of Religion and Vertue, which ordinarlie useth to fall forth in this life? For, the most wicked are Lords and Gods of this Earth, sleeping in the lee port of Honour, as if the spacious habitation of the World had beene made onelie for them, and the Vertuous and good, are but forlorne cast-awayes, floting in the surges of distresse, seeming heere either of the Eye of Providence not pittied, or not reguarded: beeing subject to all dishonours, wrongs, wrackes; in their best estate passing away their dayes (like the Dazies in the Field) in silence and contempt. Sith then Hee is most good, most just, of necessitie, there must bee appointed by Him an other time and place of retribution, in the which there shall be a Reward for living well, and a Punishment for doing evill, with a life where-into both shall receive their due; and not onelie in their Soules divested, for, sith both the parts of man did acte a part in the right or wrong, it carrieth great reason with it, that they both (inteire man) bee araigned before that high Justice, to receive their owne: Man is not a Soule onlie, but a Soule and Bodie, to which either Guerdon[47] or punishment is due. This seemeth to bee the Voice of Nature in almost all the Religions of the World; this is that generall Testimonie, charactered in the minds of the most barbarous and salvage[48] people; for, all have had some roving Guesses at Ages to come, and a Glow-worme light of another life, all appealing to one generall Judgement Throne. To what else could serve so many expiations, sacrifices, prayers, solemnities, and misticall Ceremonies? To what such sumptuous Temples, and care of the dead? to what all Religion? If not to showe, that they expected a more excellent manner of being, after the Navigation of this life did take an end. And who doeth denie it, must denie that there is a Providence, a GOD; confesse that his worshippe, and all studie and reason of vertue are vaine; and not believe that there is a World, are creatures, and that Hee Himselfe is not what Hee is.

But it is not of Death (perhaps) that we complaine, but of Tyme, under the fatall shadow of whose winges, all things decay and wither: This is that Tyrant, which executing against us his diamantine[49] lawes, altereth the harmonious constitution of our Bodies, benuming the Organes of our knowledge, turneth our best Senses sencelesse, makes us loathsome to others, and a burthen to our selves; Of which evills Death releiveth us. So that, if wee could bee transported (O happy colonie!) to a place exempted from the Lawes and conditiones of Time, where neither change, motion, nor other affection of materiall and corruptible things were, but an immortall, unchangeable, impassible, all-sufficient kinde of life, it were the last of things wisheable, the tearme and center of all our Desires. Death maketh this transplantation; for the last instant of Corruption, or leaving off of any thing to bee what it was, is the first of Generation, or being of that which succeedeth; Death then beeing the end of this miserable transitory life, of necessity must bee the beginning of that other all excellent and eternall: And so causeleslie of a vertuous Soule it is either feared or complained on.

As those Images were limned[50] in my minde (the morning Starre now almost arising in the East) I found my thoughts in a mild and quiet calme; and not long after, my Senses one by one forgetting their uses, began to give themselves over to rest, leaving mee in a still and peaceable sleepe; if sleepe it may bee called, where the Minde awaking is carried with free wings from out fleshlie bondage? For heavy lids, had not long covered their lights, when mee thought, nay, sure I was, where I might discerne all in this great *All*; the large compasse of the rolling Circles, the brightnesse and continuall motion of those Rubies of the Night, which (by their distance) heere below can not bee perceived; the silver countenance of the wandring Moone, shining by anothers light, the hanging of the Earth (as environed with a girdle of Christall) the Sunne enthronized in the midst of the Planetes, eye of the Heavens, Gemme of this precious Ring the World. But whilst with wonder and amazement I gazed on those celestiall Splendors, and the beaming Lampes of that glorious Temple (like a poore Countrieman brought from his solitarie Mountaines and Flockes, to behold the magnificence of some great Citie) There was presented to my sight a Man, as in the spring of His yeares, with that selfe same Grace, comelie feature, majesticke Looke which the late (   )[51] was wont to have: on whom I had no sooner fixed mine eyes, when (like one Planetstroken) I become amazed: But Hee with a milde demeanour, and voyce surpassing all humane sweetnesse appeared (mee thought) to say,

What is it doth thus paine and perplexe thee? Is it the remembrance of Death, the last Period of wretchednesse, and entrie to these happie places; the Lanterne which lighteneth men to see the Misterie of the blessednesse of Spirites, and that Glorie which transcendeth the Courtaine of things visible? Is thy Fortune below on that darke Globe (which scarce by the smalnesse of it appeareth here) so great, that thou art heart-broken and dejected to leave it? What if thou wert to leave behinde thee a (   )[52] so glorious in the eye of the World (yet but a mote of dust encircled with a pond) as that of mine, so loving (   )[53] such great Hopes, these had beene apparant occasions of lamenting, and but apparant? Dost thou thinke thou leavest Life too soone? Death is best young; things faire and excellent, are not of long indurance upon Earth. Who liveth well, liveth long; Soules most beloved of their Maker are soonest releeved from the bleeding cares of Life, and with almost a sphericall swiftnesse wafted through the Surges of Humane miseries. Opinion (that great Enchantresse and Peiser[54] of things, not as they are, but as they seeme) hath not in any thing more, than in the conceit of Death, abused[55] Man: Who must not measure himselfe, and esteeme his estate, after his earthlie being, which is but as a dreame: For, though hee bee borne on the Earth, hee is not borne for the Earth, more than the Embryon for the mothers wombe. It plaineth to bee releeved of its bands, and to come to the light of this World, and Man waileth to bee loosed from the Chaines with which hee is fettered in that Valley of vanities: it nothing knoweth whither it is to goe, nor ought of the beauty of the visible works of God, neither doth Man of the magnificence of the intellectuall World above, unto which (as by a Mid-wife) hee is directed by Death. Fooles, which thinke that this faire and admirable Frame, so variouslie disposed, so rightly marshalled, so strongly maintained, enriched with so many excellencies, not only for necessity, but for ornament and delight, was by that Supreme Wisedome brought forth, that all things in a circulary course, should bee and not bee, arise and dissolve, and thus continue, (as if they were so many Shadowes careleslie cast out and caused by the encountring of those superiour celestiall Bodies, changing onelie their fashion and shape, or fantasticall Imageries, or shades of faces into Christall) But more They, which beleeve that Hee doth no other-wayes regard this his worke than as a Theater, raised for bloudy Sword-playeres, Wrastlers, Chasers of timorous and Combatters of terrible Beastes, delighting in the daily torments Sorrowes distresse and Miserie of Mankind. No, no, the Eternall Wisedome, did make Man an excellent Creature, though hee faine would, unmake himselfe, and returne unto nothing: And though hee seeke his felicity among the reasonlesse Wights, he hath fixed it above. Hee brought him into this world as a Master to a sumptuous well-ordered and furnished Inne, a Prince to a populous and rich Empirie, a Pilgrime and Spectator to a Stage full of delightfull Wonders and wonderfull Delightes. And as some Emperour or great Monarch, when hee hath raised any stately City, the worke beeing atchieved, is wont to set his Image in the midst of it, to bee admired and gazed upon: No otherwise did the Soveraigne of this World, the Fabricke of it perfected, place Man (a great Miracle) formed to his owne Paterne, in the midst of this spacious and admirable Citie, by the divine splendor of his Reason to bee an Interpreter and Trunchman[56] of his Creation, and admired and reverenced by all his other Creatures. GOD containeth all in Him, as the beginning of all, Man containeth all in Him, as the midst of all; inferiour things bee in Man more noblie than they exist, superiour thinges more meanely, celestiall thinges favour him, earthly thinges are vassaled unto him, hee is the knot and Band of both; neither is it possible but that both of them have peace with Man, if Man have peace with Him who made the Covenant betweene them and Him. Hee was made that hee might in the Glasse of the World behold the infinite Goodnesse, Power, Magnificence, and Glorie of his Maker, and beholding know, and knowing Love, and loving enjoy, and to hold the Earth of him as of his Lord Paramount, never ceasing to remember and praise Him. It exceedeth the compasse of Conceit, to thinke that that Wisedome which made everie thing so orderlie in the partes, should make a confusion in the whole, and the chiefe Master-piece; how bringing forth so manie excellencies for Man, it should bring forth Man for basenesse and miserie. And no lesse strange were it, that so long life should bee given to Trees, Beastes, and the Birds of the Aire, Creatures inferiour to Man, which have lesse use of it, and which can not judge of this goodlie Fabricke, and that it should bee denyed to Man: Unlesse there were another manner of living prepared for him, in a Place more noble and excellent.

But alas! (said I) had it not beene better that for the good of his Countrie A (   )[57] endued with so many peerlesse Giftes, had yet lived upon Earth: How long will yee (replyed hee) like the Ants, thinke there are no fairer Palaces, than their Hills; or like to pore-blind[58] Moles, no greater light, than that little which they shunne? As if the Maister of a Campe, knew when to remove a Sentinell, and Hee who placeth Man on the Earth, knew not how long hee had neede of him? Life is a Governement and Office, wherein Man is so long continued, as it pleaseth the Installer; of the administration and charge of which, and what hath passed during the tyme of his Residence, hee must rander an account, so soone as his Tearme expyreth, and hee hath made Roome for others. As mens Bodies differ in stature, which none can make more long or short after their desire; So doe they varie in that length of Tyme which is appointed for them to live upon the Earth. That Providence which prescriveth Causes to everie Event, hath not onlie determined a definite and certaine number of dayes, but of actions, to all men, which they can-not goe beyond.

Most (   )[59] then (answered I) Death is not such an evill and paine, as it is of the Vulgare esteemed. Death (said hee) nor painefull is, nor evill (except in contemplation of the cause) beeing of it selfe as in-different as Birth; Yet can it not bee denyed, but amidst those Dreames of earthlie pleasures, the uncouthnesse of it, with the wrong apprehension of what is unknowne in it, are noysome; But the Soule sustained by its Maker, resolved, and calmlie retired in it selfe, doeth find that Death (sith it is in a moment of Time) is but a short, nay, sweete Sigh; and is not worthie the remembrance, compared with the smallest dram of the infinite Felicitie of this Place. Heere is the Palace Royall of the Almightie KING, in which the uncomprehensible comprehensiblie manifesteth Himselfe; in Place highest, in Substance not subject to any corruption or change, for it is above all motion, and solide turneth not; in Quantitie greatest, for, if one Starre, one Spheare bee so vast, how large, how hudge in exceeding demensions, must those boundes bee, which doe them all containe? In Qualitie most pure and Orient,[60] Heaven heere is all but a Sunne, or the Sunne all but a Heaven. If to Earthlinges the Foote-stoole of GOD, and that Stage which Hee raised for a small course of Tyme, seemeth so Glorious and Magnificent; How highlie would They prize (if they could see) his eternall Habitation and Throne? and if these bee so dazeling, what is the sight of Him, for whom, and by whom all was created? of whose Glory to behold the thousand thousand part, the most pure Intelligences are fully satiate, and with wonder and delight rest amazed; for the Beauty of His light and the Light of his Beauty are uncomprehensible. Heere doth that earnest appetite of the Understanding, content it selfe, not seeking to know any more; For it seeth before it, in the vision of the Divine essence (a Mirour in the which not Images or shadowes, but the true and perfect Essence of every thing created, is more cleare and conspicuous, than in it selfe) all that is knowne or understood: And where as on Earth our senses show us the Creator by his Creatures, heere wee see the Creatures by the Creator. Heere doth the Will pause it selfe, as in the Center of its eternall rest, glowing with a fervent Affection of that infinite and all-sufficient Good; which beeing fully knowne, cannot (for the infinite motives and causes of love which are in Him) but bee fully and perfectly loved: As hee is onely true and essentiall Bountie so is Hee onelie essentiall and true Beauty, deserving alone all love and admiration, by which the Creatures are onely in so much faire and excellent, as they participate of his Beauty and excelling Excellencies. Heere is a blessed Company, every one joying as much in anothers Felicity, as in that which is proper, because each seeth another equallie loved of GOD; Thus their distinct joyes are no fewer, than the Co-partners of the joye: And as the Assemblie is in number answerable to the large capacitie of the Place, so are the Joyes answerable to the numberlesse number of the Assemblie. No poore and pittifull Mortall, confined on the Globe of Earth, who hath never seene but Sorrow, or interchangablie some painted superficiall Pleasures, and had but Guesses of contentment, can rightlie thinke on, or be sufficient to conceive the tearmelesse Delightes, of this Place. So manie Feathers move not on Birdes, so manie Birds dint not the Aire, so manie Leaves tremble not on Trees, so manie Trees grow not in the solitarie Forestes, so manie Waves turne not in the Ocean, and so manie graines of Sand limit not those Waves; as this triumphant Court hath varietie of Delights, and Joyes exempted from all comparison. Happinesse at once heere is fullie knowne and fullie enjoyed, and as infinite in continuance as extent. Heere is flourishing and never-fading Youth without Age, Strength without Weaknesse, Beautie never blasting, Knowledge without Learning, Aboundance without Lothing, Peace without Disturbance, Participation without Envy, Rest without Labour, Light without rising or setting Sunne, Perpetuitie without Momentes, for Time (which is the Measure of Motion) did never enter in this shining Eternitie. Ambition, Disdaine, Malice, difference of Opinions, can not approach this Place, resembling those foggie mists, which cover those Lists of sublunarie things. All Pleasure, paragon'd with what is heere, is paine, all Mirth Mourning, all Beautie Deformitie: Here one dayes abiding is above the continuing in the most fortunate Estate on the Earth manie yeeres, and sufficient to contervaile[61] the extreamest tormentes of Life. But, although this Blisse of Soules bee great, and their Joyes many, yet shall they admit addition, and bee more full and perfect, at that long wished and generall Reunion with their Bodies.

Amongst all the wonders of the great Creator, not one appeareth to bee more wonderfull, nor more dazell the Eye of Reason (replied I) than that our Bodies should arise, having suffered so manie changes, and Nature denying a returne from Privation to a Habit.

Such power (said hee) beeing above all that the Understanding of Man can conceave, may well worke such wonders; For, if Mans understanding could comprehend all the Secrets and Counselles of that Eternall Maiestie it would of necessity bee equall unto it. The Author of Nature, is not thralled to the Lawes of Nature, but worketh with them, or contrarie to them, as it pleaseth Him: What Hee hath a will to doe, Hee hath power to performe. To that Power, which brought all this round *All* from nought, to bring againe in one instant any Substance which ever was into it, unto what it was once, should not be thought impossible; For, who can doe more, can doe lesse: and His power is no lesse, after that which was by Him brought forth is decayed and vanished, than it was before it was produced; beeing neither restrained to certaine limits, or Instrumentes, or to any determinate and definite manner of working: where the power is without restraint, the work admitteth no other limits, than the workers will. This World is as a Cabinet to GOD, in which the small things (how ever to us hide and secret) are nothing lesse keeped, than the great. For, as Hee was wise and powerfull to create, so doth His Knowledge comprehend His own Creation; yea, every change and variety in it, of which it is the verie Source. Not any Atome of the scattered Dust of Mankinde, though dayly flowing under new Formes, is to him unknowne: and His Knowledge doth distinguish and discerne, what once His power shall awake and raise up. Why may not the Artsmaster of the World, like a Molder, what hee hath framed in divers Shapes, confound in one Masse, and then severally fashion them againe out of the same? Can the Spagericke[62] by his Arte restore for a space to the dry and withered Rose, the naturall Purple and Blush: And cannot the Almightie raise and refine the body of Man, after never so many alterations in the Earth? Reason her selfe findes it more possible for infinite power, to cast out from it selfe a finite world, and restore any thing in it, though decayed and dissolved, to what it was first; than for Man a finit peece of reasonable miserie, to change the forme of matter made to his hand: the power of GOD never brought forth all that it can, for then were it bounded and no more infinit. That Time doth approach (O haste yee Times away) in which the Dead shall live, and the Living bee changed, and of all actions the Guerdon[63] is at hand; Then shall there bee an end without an end, Time shall finish, and Place shall bee altered, Motion yeelding unto Rest, and another World of an Age eternall and unchangeable shall arise: Which when Hee had said (mee thought) Hee vanished, and I all astonished did awake.

NOTES

1. *onelie.* Mere.
2. *Herbingers.* Forerunners.
3. *Monethes.* Months.
4. *Paladines.* Knights of Charlemagne, heroes of romance.
5. *Phanes.* Temples.
6. *limne.* Paint or decorate.
7. *averre.* Verify.
8. *twinneth.* Spins.
9. *elementall Brethren.* Earth, air, fire, water.
10. *Moneths.* Months.

11. *than*. Then.
12. *Table Booke*. Memorandum book.
13. *superior Lights*. Sun, moon, and planets.
14. *pitcheth toyles, and is tapist*. Spins webs and is hidden.
15. *Penelopes Taske*. Weaving endlessly at her loom.
16. *happelie*. By chance.
17. *opacke*. Opaque, obscure.
18. *Camelion*. Chameleon.
19. *Euripe*. Euripus, a strait or sea-channel with violent and uncertain currents.
20. *moe*. More.
21. *towseth*. Disorders.
22. *Magnes*. Magnet.
23. *ingine*. Wit, genius.
24. *ensueth*. Follows.
25. *preventing*. Coming before.
26. *Sacietie*. Satiety.
27. *courbing*. Bending.
28. *crasie*. Diseased.
29. *arteres*. Arteries.
30. *Weeke*. Wick.
31. *Sowning*. Swooning.
32. *Platos yeares*. The "perfect" year at the end of a cycle of 25,000 years.
33. *rubbige*. Rubbish.
34. *let*. Hindrance.
35. *concreded*. Entrust.
36. *Papers*. Literature.
37. *Pleasants*. Clowns.
38. *Siracusianes Spheare of Christall*. The sphere of Archimedes, a model of the heavens.
39. *Pismires*. Ants.
40. *that Grot in Pausilipo*. The tunnel or cave of Posilipo near Naples.
41. *leas*. Protection.
42. *improve*. Disprove.
43. *amated*. Dismayed.
44. *Mirrouer*. Mirror.
45. *three partes of Time*. Past, present, and future.
46. *Ordures*. filths.
47. *Guerdon*. Reward.
48. *Salvage*. Savage.
49. *Diamantine*. Consisting of diamonds, diamond-hard.
50. *limned*. Painted, depicted.
51. *the late (   )*. Probably Henry, Prince of Wales, d. 1612.
52. *(   )*. Kingdom(?).
53. *(   )*. Subjects(?).
54. *Peiser*. One who weighs.
55. *Abused*. Deceived.
56. *Trunchman*. Interpreter.
57. *(   )*. Prince.

58. *pore-blind*. Near-blind.
59. (   ). Gracious Prince.
60. *Orient*. Radiant.
61. *contervaile*. Counterbalance.
62. *Spagericke*. Alchemist.
63. *Guerdon*. Reward.

A SPEECH ON TOLERATION

Sir, amongst the many blessings your Subjectes enjoye under this your Governement, this is not the least, that for the well[1] of your Majestie, and the publicke good of the Kingdome, the meanest of your Subjectes may freelie open his minde and declare his opinione unto you his Soveraigne. And if ever there was a time in which grave, good and sound counsell should be delivered to your Majestie it is this, and the difficultyes of the Commonwealth doe now require it. Not ever in matteres of advice and consultatione can wee embrace and follow what is most reasonable, and what according to Lawes, Justice, Equitie should be, but what necessitye driveth us unto, and what is most convenient for the present time to be, and what wee may well and fairlie accomplish and bring to passe.

The Estate of your Kingdome is troubled with diversitie of opiniones concerning Religione; It is to be wished that the one onlie true Religion were in the heartes of all your Subjectes (Since diversitie of opiniones of Religione and heresies, are the verie punishment of God almightie upon men for their horrible vices and roring Sinnes. And when Men forsake his feare and true obedience, God abandoneth them to their owne opiniones and fantasies in Religion: out of which arise partialityes, factiones, divisiones, strife, intestine discords, which burst forth into civill warres, and in short time bring Kingdomes and Commonwealthes to their last Periodes). But matteres arising to such a hight and disorder, as by all appearances they are like to advance in this Kingdome, the number of the Sectaryes[2] daylie increasing, without dissimulating my thoughts to your Majestie, the preservation of the People being the supresme[3] and principall Law which God almightie hath enjoyned to all Princes, I hold it more expedient to give place to the exercise of both Religions, than under pretence and shadow of them to suffer the commone peace of your Subjectes to be torne in pieces. What can wisdome (Sir) advise yow to doe with these Separatists? Either they must be tollerated for a time or they must altogether be removed, and that by death or banishment? So soon as a Prince beginneth to spoyle, banish, kill, burne his people, for matters abstract from sence and altogether spirituall, hee becometh as it were a plague unto them. It is an errour of state in a Prince, for an opinione of pietie to condemne to death the adhereres to new doctrine. For, the constancie and patience of those who voluntarilie suffer all temporall miseryes and death it selfe for matteres of faith, stirre up and invite numberes, who at first and before they had suffered were ignorant of their faith and doctrine, not onlie to favour their cause but to embrace their opiniones; Pity and commiseration opening the gates: thus their Beleefe spredeth it selfe abroad, and their number daylie encreaseth. It is a no less errour of State to banish them: Banished Men are so manie Ennemyes abroad, reddye upon all occasiones to invade their native Countrie, to trouble the peace and tranquillitye of your Kingdome.

To take armes against Sectaries and Separatists will be a great enterprise, a matter hard and of many dangeres: Religione can not be preached by Armes; the first Christianes detested that forme of proceeding: Force and compulsion may bring forth Hypocrites, not true Christianes. If there be any heresie amongst your people, this wound is in the Soule; our Soules being spirituall Substances upon which fire and iron can not worke, they must be overcome by spirituall armes: Love the Men and pittye their erroures? Who can laye upon a Man a necessitie to beleeve that which hee will not beleeve, or what hee will beleeve, or doth beleeve, not to beleeve. No Prince hath such power over the Soules and thoughts of Men, as hee hath over their Bodyes. Now to ruine and extirpate all those Sectaryes, what will it prove else than to cut off one of your armes, to the great prejudice of your Kingdome and weakening of the State? They daylie encreasing in number, and no Man being so miserable and meane, but that hee is a member of the State?

The more easie manner and nobler way were to tollerate both Religiones, and graunt a place to two Churches in the Kingdome till it shall please almightie God to reunite the mindes of your Subjectes, and turne them all of one will and opinione: Be content to keepe that which yee may, Sir, since yee can not that which yee would.

It is a false and erroneous opinione, that a Kingdome can not subsiste which tollerateth two Religiones: Diversitie of Religion shooteth not up societye, nor barreth civill conversatione amongst Men. A litle time will make persones of different Religiones contracte such acquaintance, custome, familiaritie together, that they will be

175

intermixted in one Cittye, familie, yea mariage bed, State and Religione haveing nothing commoan. Why (I praye) may not two Religiones be suffered in a State (till by some sweet and easie meanes they be reduced to a right governement) since in the Church (which should be unione it selfe and of which the Romane Church much vanteth) all-most infinit Sectes and kyndes of Monkes are suffered; differing in their Lawes, Rules of governement, fashiones of living, dyet, apparell, maintenance and opiniones of perfectione, and who sequestree themselves from our publike unione? The Romane Empyre had its extensione, not by similitud and likenesse of Religione. Different Religiones, providing they enterprise or practise no thing against the politike Lawes of the Kingdome, maye be tollerated in a State.

The Murtheres, massacres, Battailles, which arise and are like daylie to encrease amongst Christians, all which are undertaken for Religione, are a thousand times more execrable, and be more open plaine flat impietie, than this libertye of diversitie of Religiones with a quiet peace can be injust: for as much as the greatest part of those who flesh themselves in bloud and slaughter, and overturne by armes the peace of their Neighboures (whom they should love as themselves) spoyling and ravaging lyke famished Lyones, sacrifice their Soules to the infernall Poweres without further hopes or meanes of recoverye, and comming bake, when those otheres are in some way of Repentance.

In seeking libertie of Religione, these Men seeke not to beleeve any thing that may come in their Braines; but to use Religione according to the first Christiane institutiones, serving God and obeying the Lawes under which they were borne.

That Maxime so often echoed amongst the Church-Men of Rome, that the Chase and following of Heretikes is more necessarye than that of Infidelles, is well applyed for the inlarging and increasing the dominiones, Souveraignitie, and power of the Pope, but not for the amplifying and extending of the Christiane Religione, and the Well and benefite of the Christian common wealth.

Kingdomes and Souveraignities should not be governed by the Lawes and interests of Priests, and Church-men, but according to the exigencie, need, and as the case requireth of the publick well, which often is necessitated to passe and tolerate some defectes and faults. It is the duetye of all Christian Princes to endevoure and take paines that their Subjectes embrace the true faith, as that semblablye and in even partes they observe all Gods commandements, and not more one commandement than another. Notwithstanding when a vice can not be extirpate and taken away without the ruine of the State, it would appeare to humane judgements that it should be suffered: Neither is there a greater obligatione, bond, necessitye of Law, to punish here-tickes more than fornicatores, which yet for the peace and tranquillitye of the State are tollerated and passed over. Neither can a greater inconveniencie and harme follow if wee shall suffer men to live in our Commonwealth who beleeve not nor embrace not all our opiniones. In an Estate manye thinges are for the time tollerated, because they can not without the totall ruine of the State be sudainlie amended and reformed.

These men are of that same nature and condition of which wee are; they worshippe as wee doe one God, they beleeve those very same holye Recordes; wee both aime at salvatione, wee both feare to offend God, wee both set before us one happinesse. The difference betwixt them and us hangeth on this one point, that they having found abuses in our Church, require a Reformation: Now shall it be said for that wee runne diverse wayes to one end, understand not rightlie otheres language, wee shall pursue otheres with fire and sword, and extirpate otheres from the face of the Earth. God is not in the bitter divisione and alienatione of affectiones, nor the raging flames of seditiones, nor in the Tempestes of the turbulent whirl-windes of contradictiones and disputationes, but in the calme and gentle breathinges of peace and concord. If any wander out of the high way, wee bring him to it again, if any be in darkenesse, wee show him light, and kill him not; in musicall instruments if a string jarre and be out of tone, wee doe not freetinglie breake it, but leasurelie veere it about to a concord: and shall wee be so churlish, cruell, uncharitable, so wedded to our own superstitious opiniones, that wee will barbarouslye banish, kill, burne those who, by love and sweetnesse wee might reddilye winne and recall againe?

Let us win and demerite these men by reasone, let them be cited to a free councell, it may be they shall not be proven heretickes, neither that they maintaine opiniones condemned by the auncient Councelles. Let their Religion be compared and paraleled with the Religion of the first age of the Church.

Shall wee hold this people worse then the Jewes, which yet have their Synagogues at Rome it selfe? Let them receave instructiones from a free and lawful Councell, and forsake their erroures, when they shall be clearlie and fairlie demonstrate unto them. Heresie is an errour in the fundamentall Grounds of Religion, Shisme intendeth a resolutione in separatione: Let a good Councell be convocated, and see if they be reddye or not to reunite themselves to us.

That which they beleeve is not evill, but to some it will appearre they beleeve not enough, and that there is in them rather a defect of good than anye habit of evill. Other pointes when they shall be considdered, shall be found to consiste in externall ceremonyes of the Church rather than in substance of doctrine, or what is essentiall to Christianitie. These men should be judged before condemned, and they should be heard before they be judged. Which being hollelye and uprightlie done, wee shall find it is not our Religiones, but our private interestes and our passiones which troubleth us; and the State.

NOTES

1. *well.* Weal, well-being.
2. *Sectaryes.* Members of a sect.
3. *supresme.* Supreme.

IRENE

A REMONSTRANCE FOR CONCORD, AMITIE AND LOVE, AMONGST HIS MAJESTIES SUBJECTES

As pilgrimes wandring in the Night by the inconstant glances of the Moone, when they behold the Morning gleames; as Marineres after Tempestes on the seas at their arrivall in save Harboures; as those that are perplexed and taken with some uglie visiones and affrightmentes in their Slumberes when they are awaked, and calmelie roused up: So did this Kingdome, State, no whole Isle, amidest those Suspiciones, Jelousies, Surmises, Terroures more than Pannicall, after the late declaration of the Kings Majestie, find themselves surprised and over-reached with unexpected and unexpressable Joyes. Religion was murning, Justice wandring, Peace seeking whither to flie; a strange hideous grime pale shadow of a new Governement was begune to crawle abroad, putting up an hundreth heades. Mens courages were growing hote, their hatred kindled; all either drawing the Swordes, or laying their handes upon them. The Ennemie was designed the Country, the Quarrell, differences of Opiniones. Townes were pestered with Guardes of armed Citizenes, the countrey and villages thralled with dormant Musteres: The danger seemed great, the feare was greater, all expected the Prince would enter the listes, and so hee did; meane Thinges must yeeld unto the more noble, *Vicit amor Patriae*;[2] that same wind which gathered the Clowdes did dissipate them. Hee not onlie giveth way to our zeale, graciouslie assenting to all our desires, but condescendeth, yea commandeth that our own write should be current and embraced by all his Subjectes: to humaine eyes a perfect conclusion of our wretched distractiones. Let Fame of this Prince praise his other Vertues, wee should never forget in this his unparalelled prudence and clemencie.

The Prince knew that warre was the verye scourge of God upon a People, the ruine of Mankynd and the figure of Hell to come, of which no good Prince, (except for high and grievous offences) will be the Causer; That Princes use to invade the Territoryes of their ennemyes and not their native countreyes; That Warres amongst compatriotes for the most part end in the overthrow and wrack of the State, as it happened to the Romaine Empire by the warres of Constantine against Licinius. That amongst disagreeing Subjectes who ever should winne the Prince should losse; That Rigour made not Men change their Mindes, but oftner turning them desperate made them more wilfull in their opiniones; That the lawes of Reasone should governe the power of a Prince; that the people are as children and hee their father, they as a flocke hee their Pastour; That the preservation of subjectes is the cheif and principall law God and Nature imposed on Princes; That *Principi non minus turpe multa supplicia quam Medico multa funera*;[3] That Strength and Valour over-come openlie, but that the noblest Victorie is by secret mining the hart, by loyaltie, trust, clemencie, mercie; That the love of the people is the surest Guarde of a Prince, to which all his Endeavoures should tend.

These have beene his ordinarie Meditationes, this the dailie exercise of his life; about this when otheres were sleeping was hee waking; when otheres in quietnesse hee was in cares; and when wee were stubborne and restie[4] to come to him hee hath come to us: So carefull hath hee beene to intertaine peace amongst his Subjectes and with them.

All haile most sacred Peace, which though a stranger and yongling amongst other Nationes, yet art a Denized,[5] and as old as the Sybilles amongst us of great Bretaigne! Were it not for thee, the calm shades of Churches and Universityes should be transformed in pavilliones and campes of Horrour, the Nobilitie and Gentrye sequestrated from their delightfull sport and recreationes at home, should be thralled to the bondage, burthenes and dangeres of spoyle, rapine, turmoyles and bloud: Were it not for Thee, the citizen in steed of his magnifick Porches and marble Walkes, with his children and beloved should be driven to measure the wayles Pathes of his ruinated countrey, and wander amongst the terroures of his slaughtered acquaintances and fellow-Burgesses. The Merchant should abandon his Trafficke; the Husband-man, broken with the heavie loades of the insolent Souldeour, had turned his acres in leas, his sythes and ploughes in swordes, speares and ammunition, and evrye state were it not for thee had mortallye suffered. . . .

[Love is the basis of the commonwealth; the first law of the state is obedience. Leagues and covenants usurp the rights of princes. Self-interest is inimical to peace, war to religion.]

How great so ever yee be (abandoned to your own presumption) or what ever faire pretences yee make a show of, how ever yee varnish your actiones, who labour to eclipse the Prince in his Favoures and bountie from shining on his people, or vaile the peoples love towards their Soveraigne, and put the Multitud in feare that yee your selves maye rule the State: Thinke yee may a while thus dallye but never safelye and securelie long hold out against your Prince, and that how ever Princes maye be constrained and content to beare saille for a tyme yet that they are sure paye-Maisteres in the end. Studie reconciliation, and learne that honorable retraites are no wayes inferiour to brave charges. A Princes estate deeplie rooted by tyme and power, by reverence and respect, and established by a succession of many kinges is not so easilie undermined as yee beleeve, neither will your delusiones and trickes by the Nimblenesse of your handes plucke it up. Bee what yee seeme, or seeme not what yee are not: If yee would doe justice unto otheres, beginne at your selves! Impietie is no zeale, Crueltie no valour, Craft and Deceit no true prudence, open and violent oppression and robberyes, or your plundering, no faire Stratagemes, Sedition and Rebellion no good service to a King. If the Prince holdes not his crown of you but of God (who distributeth honoures as it seemeth best unto him) and the aunccient lawes of his Kingdome; If his crown be not by election, but by a lineall Succession; If hee be not a conditionall Prince but an absolute Souveraigne; If hee be lawfullye invested, anointed and crowned: Why should yee servantes give a law to your Maister? What Honoures, Richesse, Greatnesse, yee enjoye, yee have all from your Kinges, his auncestoures, and yee owe him all subjection, service, obedience. Who assume and usurpe the rightes of their souveraigne, the lawes of God and Men proclaime worthye of Death. Good Princes should be obeyed, yea, evill Princes should be tollerated. God who raised Kinges above you, holdeth himselfe wronged in their wronges, and revengeth the injuries done unto them. Though they should in some thinges goe beyond their dutyes, they are not to be judged by their Subjectes; for no power within their dominiones is superiour to theirs. What can yee purchase by some few Monethes libertie of dauncing to your own shadowes, in new Magistracies, offices of State, imaginarie and fantasticall counsilles, landskippes of Common Wealthes, and an icye Grandeur, erected by your selves to impaire and derogate to souveraignitie, to dissolve governement, but a part of a Tragicomedie? Yes, lesse, for some playeres have personated and acted the partes of Kinges, Magistrates, Counselloures all the dayes of their lives. Such who are taken and enamoured with false praises, are ordinarlie affrayed and stand in aw of false Scornes. Yee, who now walke so statlie, and in the postures and habites of Princes, contemning your equalles and betteres, when the Monarch shall over-come this Ecclipse, yee maye be found to reassume your first Garmentes, and (perhaps) more torne than when yee put them off. When yee have reached your last aymes, what have yee done, but put out the fire which yee should have stirred up, dissolved the memberes which yee should have fastened together? Kingdomes are preserved by the reputation, fame, renown of their Princes: This is their strongest Guarde in Peace and surest Garrisones in Warre. So soone as a Prince beginneth to be despized and falleth in contempt by misgovernement, hee is deposed by it as well as by death: either his kingdome by forraine invasiones or intestine dissensiones is ransaked. But how manye changes will interviene, what hazardes be interposed, between your ambitious aymes, and the accomplishing of them? What battailles shall be fought, what blood spent, an age shall not put an end to these quarrelles? Confusion followes where obedience leaves. What conquest can a Subject make against his Souveraigne, where the warre is insurrection, and the Victorie high treasone? It was fatall to the one Brutus[6] to banish kinges, and to the other[7] to stabe Caesare, but it was also fatall that the first killed his two sonnes, and the other with that same dager himselfe. It was fatall to the Duck of Guise and his Brother[8] to ligue the french Romanistes against their king, and advance their ambition by that tempeste of Popularitie: But it was also fatall to them after a deserved death to be consumed in flames, deprived both of Tombe and Buriall. The climactericke[9] and period of the monarchicall Governementes of Europe is not yet come, and when, or if ever, it shall come, yee who are Nobles shall perish with it: For, the commones (then all Princes) will not suffere in their Statutes, Edictes, Ordinances any longer *I*, but *Wee*. In distribution and parting of honoures, offices, richesse, landes, they will proceed after an arithmeticall proportion, and not a geometricall: Townes will close their Gates upon you, and yee may some day expect a Sicilian even song[10]. . . .

Now yee People, to whom dayes present seeme ever worst, who extolle and praise the former ages yee never knew or remembered, and condemne and despise the present tyme, though yee know not the disease of it: that thinke thinges to come more certaine than thinges seeme; who take the Shadow for the Bodye, the Maske for the Face, the Smoake for the Fire, Lyes for Veritie, Veritie for Lyes: Who whom yee blesse this day the next day yee execrate; whose insolencyes in advantage over otheres in tyme of your power and rage is beyond all boundes, and whose basenesse, when brought under and thralled is unexpressable: Who are ever made the fewell of Sedition under colour of Devotion. When yee caste off, and refuse the gracious and easie yoakes of your Princes, yee are charged and beare the heavie Burthenes of State-impostures, Usurperes and Tyrantes, who to compasse and attaine their secret designes leave no exaction, oppression, crueltie, unpractised upon you: make you spend your lives and fortunes to purchasse confusion, and make you liable to the most intollerable kynd of slaverye, that is to be slaves to your fellow subjectes, paye them intollerable Taxes, Loanes, Pole-monies, and odious Excises. People! endeavoure to honour God and beleeve in him, and next God, love and respect your Prince and souveraigne Magistrate, embrace and accepte from him and his counsell what is good and agreeable to reasone, for these love you. Follow not the counseles and instructiones of factious and mutinous Men, who desire no thing else but to worke themselves in action and imploymentes by your overthrow, for these hate you. The Sheepheard and the Butcheur have both a care of Sheep, but their endes are farre different; the care of the Sheepheard is to feed them and keep them upon faire pasturages; the Butcheurs care is to kill and bring them to the Shambles.[11] When yee are led and governed by your Kinges, yee are in the handes of your Sheepheardes, but when yee are seduced by other pretended Governoures, yee are in the handes of Butcheures, for the end of their governing you is bloud and Civill Warres. People! beleeve in God, Men are untrue, and the best of them but spirituall forges of Tyrannie. God onlie doth command what is good for you, God will not have anye naturall dutye broken amongst you: obedience of Children to Parentes, of Servantes to their Maisters, of Citizenes to Magistrates, of Subjectes to their Princes; Religion came not down from heaven, to banish the Virtues found upon the earth, nor to demolish the most admirable worke reasone hath produced and brought forth, humaine Societyes. And if men active in mischeif, shall prove any thing, though by miracles, contrarye to this, their miracles are false delusiones, and their instructiones guilded lyes: God made peace for you and Heaven, but yee for your selves make warre and Hell. Questione not the thrones of Kinges, revive not your old equalityes of Nature, Authoritie is that chaine which linketh you together; lend not your strength to kill your selves, and make you weaker; cast not your selves in a voluntarye servitude; turne not your selves in a statelesse State. What gaine yee by your enterchange of Warre for Peace? When did yee ever prospere by resisting and opposing the lawfull authoritie of your Princes? Your seduceres constraine you to wed their quarrelles, beare the charges of their Warres, to plye your Backes to them to ascend the Stages of their ambition, avarice and revenge: But they forget to tell you that if the stage, overlayd by too much Weight, shall fall, they shall tumble headlong down, and yee remaine miserablie bruised. When a tyme shall come wherein yee shall be constrained to abhorre these Men, turne your hatred and spite against them, and with the price of their Bloud, redeeme your own lives, buy your pardones and absolutiones. Then to your destructione shall they and yee together find, what it importeth to pull the Scepter from your Souveraigne, and wrest the Sword out of the hand of the lawfull Magistrate. Samuell cap. 15 v. 23. *For Rebellion is as the Sinne of Witchcraft, and Stubborness is as iniquitye and Idolatrie.* Everye factious cause is weake. . . .

Yee lightes of the World, examples of Holiness and all Vertues, you living libraryes of Knowledge, Sanctuaryes of Goodnesse, looke upon the weakenesse and fragilitie of Mankynd! The Bodyes of Common wealthes are alreddye turned in Skeletones, the Cityes in Sepulcheres, the fieldes in Shambles, the Trees in Gibbetes. Pittye humaine Race, spare the bloud of Man: the earth is druncke with it, the Watteres empurpled, the aire empoysoned, and all by you, for, who give advice and counsell for the performing of evill actiones, cause them, and doe these actiones themselves: and they who command them and approve them when done are beyond the actores guilty. . . . Hollie chaine betwixt Heaven and Earth, how art thou profaned? How long sall ambition, æmulation, avarice, malice, revenge make a cloake of thee to their most irreligeous endes? If wee must fight for Thee, have wee not milliones of infidelles to pursue, and that bloudie race of Hottoman, which possesseth the fairest boundes and dearest pledges of Christianitie of all the earth? But for what great matteres concerning thee would wee now launce forth into a sea of Bloud? Nor for renewing thy Beautie, not for supporting thy Glorie, not for propagation of thee amongst the sun-brunt Nationes of the south, or the farre east or north, or westerne Wildernesses: But for taking from thee what thou hast manye ages since purchased; for turning thee as naked as when thou first appeared in this World; for quintessencing[12] and alambiking[13] thee, and using thee as alchimists doe gold, which they turne often in sophisticate powderes. Sacred Race, have yee no remorse when yee enter in the cabinetes of your own hartes and there for finest arras[14] and pourtraites find milliones of christianes represented unto you, disfigured, massacred, butchered, made havock of, in all the fashiones, the imaginationes of wicked mankynd could devise? For the maintaining of those opiniones and problemes, which yee are conscious to your selves, are but Centaures children,[15] the imaginationes and fantasies of your own braines; concerning which yee would argue, and chyde one another, but never shed one Unce of your bloud? Have yee no remorse, that by your rhethoricke under pretence of pietie and devotion yee persuade a populace to cast off that obedience they have sworne to their native Kinges, arise in armes against them, breath no thing but Spoyle, Vengeance and Rebellion, undermining closelye the foundationes of States and removing those propes upon which Empyres and Governementes stand? Is bloud the tribute of your endevoures, the misteryes of your hollye Wordes, when yee preach Mens bodyes to the Warres, their goodes to Taxe, their freedome to Bondes? What can yee expect by your perpetuall innovationes but to put truth to silence? Our Maister said hee sent out his apostles as Sheep amongst Wolves, but now of manye Church-men it maye be said they come out as Wolves in the midst of Sheep: that for breed they have given stones to their children, and for fishes serpentes.

The propes, stayes, maister-beames of Religion being faith, hope and charitie, meekenesse, patience and humilitie; to substitute for them and put in their places, pryde, lust, rage, deceite, robberyes, avarice, blasphemyes, crueltyes, oppression, dissentiones, with all the other Vices and Corruptiones of the life of man, which are the consequences and necessarye sequelles of Warre, is not this to overthrow and undermine the excellent and admirable frame of Religion? Which is not to be found amidst the clattering and horroure of armes, and men thristing to dye their handes in others bloud? When yee strive to make creation lesse and privation infinit, and make life yeeld up it selfe to be put out before this frame of Nature be decayed, when for the observing and tracing some Shadows of the first table of the law (matteres disputable) yee care not reallie to breake and transgresse all the second table, as if wronges and mischeefes done to men were approved service done to the almightie God: When yee turn Trumpettes of Sedition, make furye give lawes, and banish all lawes of dutie: When yee seeke your happinesse amongst armes, that is, in the midst of ambition and tumultes; When yee beget and nurse Jelousyes in Princes, and contempt in subjectes, dissention in familyes, wranglings in schooles, and mutinyes in armyes, ruines of noble houses, corruption of bloud, confiscation of estates, torturing of bodyes, anxious entangling and perplexing of consciences: Do yee not scorne in effect, that which in outward show and appearance yee so highlie extolle and reverence? and tell the World how bravelie so ever yee maske and flowrishe in Wordes, yee beleeve not your own discourses, and that your hartes are farre farre distant from your Mouthes. How can the voice of the lambe be heared or understood amidst the noyse and howling of wolves, which belsh no thing but Bloud . . . ?

[Abandon extremism, tolerate difference of opinion, practice Christian goodness. Take the universe as your model of order.]

The Souveraigne creator of this All making no thing but in order, and order not being but where there is a difference and diversitie; yea, not onlie this Universe in generall, but there is no creature in it, not a bodye, not a simple that is not composed and existing with some diversitye. Gemmes, gold, the mineralles, the elementes existe not pure: the planetes have a motion contrarye to the first moveable:[16] yet is there a perfect harmonie in all this great frame and a discording Concord maketh all the parcelles of it delightfull. Of the diversitie and varietie which is in this World ariseth that beautie so wonderfull and amazing to our eyes. In architecture diversitie doth not destroy Uniformitie: the limmes of a noble fabricke may be correspondent enough, though they be various. Wee find not two persones of one and the same shape, figure and lineamentes of the Face, lesse of the same conditiones, qualityes, humoures, though they be of the selfe same parentes, and why doe wee seeke to find men all of one thought and one opinion in formalityes and matteres disputable? or, if they shall be found dissonant and disagreeing from the vulgarlie receaved opiniones, or erroures, why should wee by our fancye and law of Power banish, proscribe, designe or expose them to slaughter? Why should wee onlye honour and respect these of our opiniones as our freindes, and carrye our selves towards otheres as if they were beastes and trees, nay as our ennemyes? Were it not more seemelye and meet to make a difference between men according to their Vice or Vertue? There be manye wicked men of our profession, and a great number of good and civill men of other professiones, *Suadenda est Religio non imperanda*:[17] The consciences of men neither should nor will be forced by the violence of iron or fire, nor will soules be compelled to beleeve that which they beleeve not; they are not drawne nor subdued but by reasone, nor persuaded but by evidence and faire demonstrationes. In this disease of spirites the true appeale is to that Judge that evrye Spirit knowes, for all men maye Erre. Religion is made barbarous when it is onlie set for rapine and murther, and to proscribe and confiscate the lives and goodes of those who professe it not. O the madnesse of Mankynd that had rather trouble and torment himselfe and otheres than enjoye a sweet and peaceable rest! had rather burne his own house, than not have his Neighboures set on fire! Happye Cittye sayeth Sybilla[18] that heareth but the voyce of one Herauld; unhappye wee amidst our manye and diverse contentiones, furious polimickes, endlesse variances, contraverses, brawlinges, debates and quarrelles. When shall we leave off to wed other mens fancyes, when shall wee adhere to reall substances, and leave deluding shadowes? When shall wee cherish Concord and Peace, love one another in those degrees wee have beene reddye to prosecute otheres with malice and hatred, obeye and be beloved of our Princes, and such whom God hath placed to governe and have authoritie over us? O tymes beyond the reach of enjoying and onlie within the infinit power of Wishing! Then shall that divine power which for evrye mans particulare and the general offences of this Kingdome hath taken away our judgement and understanding, and out of his Justice blindfolded us, restore them againe unto us, and grant us light and sight to see and discerne our erroures. Then like Men cured of Madnesse, wee shall be strucken with astonishment to consider our tragicall extravagancyes and the terroures and fits of our frenzies; Then shall wee know our charmes and hate our Charmeres: Then better taught, and of more sound discretion and sence wee shall know, embrace and follow that which is necessarye and convenient for our Well and saftye: *Glory shall dwell in our land, mercie and truth shall meet together, righteousnesse and peace shall kisse one another.*[19]

Most gracious Souveraigne, how thy prudence hath beene great, thy Goodnesse without Example! The further wee are distant from thy presence the more bountifullie hast thou daigned to glaunce upon us and give us the fairer aspect of thy Vertues. Thou hast pittyed our Weaknesse, thou hast not answered our Stubburnesse; knowing the best way to be revenged of our insolencies was, not to be like unto us. What couldest thou have done more, what shouldest thou have done lesse, for that distracted and distressed countrey, in which thou wast borne? And now Sir (if ever this paper shall have the happinesse to kisse your royal handes?) as yee have hitherto graciouslie cast an eye upon her,[20] disdaine not to listen to these her humble supplicationes and last groanes: Behold her prostrate at your feet, come to exhibite and shew forth her woefull estate and condition.

Manye (sayeth shee) have beene my Miseryes, manye my Sorrowes; The open invasiones of forraneres in auncient tymes, the secret plotes and conspiracyes of myne own thereafter: The beholding of my Sanctuaryes defaced, my Temples equalled with the ground, my Townes ransacked: my painfull Strugglinges under the bondage of most terrible Governoures, tolerating what their malice could invent, or their boldnesse attempte; the calamityes of a rigourous and pittilesse Heaven; the Barbarous deadlye fewdes of myne inhabitantes amongst themselves at home, the slaughteres and destructions of them amongst stranger Nationes abroad. But no aggrievance, no chance, no disaster hath so perplexedlie incumbred me, and cast mee down, as, that the manye merites, benefaites, favoures of your blessed father forgot, the graciousnesse, the goodnesse of your self despised, in the midst of your ingagementes in the neighboure Warres and troubles of Europe, my Nurcelinges (distaining themselves with ingratitude) should have adventured to leave in the Mindes of their race and posteritie a suspition, that they did take their bloud and descent from men branded with any marke of Lese-Majestie[21] or Rebellion. Alas Sir they have not knowen about what they have beene disquieting themselves, what should have been the event of their rash proceedinges! This hath beene in them a Sideration,[22] the blasting of some unhappie influence, deserving rather pitie than punishment. And though againe despising the healthfull counselles of their freindes, they should rejecte your favoures, refuse foolishlie your gracious offeres, continue in their stubbornesse, and essaye to runne headlong to their perdition: prove not your Power against them: shake them not, for in a litle tyme they will decline and fall. Their confusion and disorderes will bring them back, and by a revolution at last reduce them to their wonted dutye and order: dissention winneth ground at first, but good counsell acquireth strength with tyme. Cure their sickenesse by the indulgent meanes of clemencie, not by the Severitie of Justice: Sith the one evill amendeth not another, vanquish and subdue them by mercie. The impregnable forteresse of a Prince is the love of his Subjectes, which doth onlie arise from the height of his clemencie, and this excesse of meekenesse is in him a kynd of Justice. . . .

Turne not mee Sir (your countrey) in a Shambles, a desert Wildernesse, a Sepulcher, a Monument of desolation. By that dutye and reverence yee ow to God Allmightie, who placed you to represent Him upon Earth; By the ashes and memoryes of so manye Kinges your predicessoures, who heere so peaceablye raigned; by that Charitie which is due to mee your native countrey. If there be no King so good as your self? If there be no people which more dearly love their Kinges (how ever now in an aigue?) than this? If they have lost any thing of what they faine to be libertie (which is onlie a Power to doe what is convenient) restore it unto them: change their troubles in rest, their miseryes in prosperitie, their dissensiones in Concord and Peace: which out of that Chaos wherein they now struggle, that Labyrinth wherein they are like to intangle and losse themselves, shall releeve and winde them out and repaire evrye thing to its first lustre and beautie. So God shall be served, you of all obeyed, and your desolate countrey preserved from those manye Woes and dangeres which threaten Her.

NOTES

1. *Irene.* Irene was a goddess of peace.
2. *Vicit . . .* Love of the country has conquered.
3. *Principi . . .* For a Prince many punishments are no less shameful than many funerals for a doctor.
4. *restie.* Sluggish, indolent.
5. *Denized.* Denizen, a citizen.
6. *the one Brutus.* Junius Brutus.
7. *the other.* Marcus Brutus.
8. *the Duck of Guise and his Brother.* Henri, Duc de Guise and Lous, Cardinal de Guise, murdered by the orders of Henri III in 1588. They were leaders of the Holy League.
9. *climactericke.* The critical period or fatal time.
10. *Sicilian even song.* The occupying French were massacred by the Sicilians in 1282, the signal being the vespers bell. Hence, a bloody insurrection.
11. *Shambles.* Slaughter-house.
12. *Quintessencing.* Reducing to the purest and most essential part.
13. *alambiking.* Distilling.
14. *arras.* A rich tapestry (showing figures and scenes).
15. *Centaures children.* Monsters.
16. *the first moveable.* The primum mobile of Ptolemaic astronomy; the tenth sphere placed next to God in His eleventh heaven.
17. *Suadenda . . .* Religion should be a matter of persuasion, not compulsion.

18. *Sybilla.* The prophetess of the *Oracula Sibylina.*
19. *Glory shail dwel¹ . . . Psalms* 85, 9–10.
20. *her.* Scotland. The editor of *Works* (1711) supplies "your Ancient Kingdom"
21. *Lese-Majestie.* An offence against the sovereign; treason.
22. *Sideration.* A sudden paralysis.

A LETTER ON THE
TRUE NATURE OF POETRY,
ADDRESSED TO DR. ARTHUR JOHNSTON

To his much honoured freind M. Arthur Jhonston
physician to the king

It is more praise-worthie in noble and excellent Things to know some
thing, though litle, than in meane and ignoble matteres to have a
perfect knowledge. Amongst all those rare ornamentes of the Mind of
man, poesy hath had a most eminent place, and beene in high esteeme,
not onlye at one tyme and in one climate, but during all tymes and
through those partes of the World where any ray of humanitie and
civilitie hath shined. So that shee hath not unworthelie deserved the
name, of the Mistresse of humaine life, the height of Eloquence, the
Quientessence of knowledge, the lowd Trumpet of fame, the langage
of the Godes. There is not any thing endureth longer: Homers Troy
hath out-lived manye Republikes, and both the Roman and Grecian
Monarchyes. Shee subsisteth by her selfe, and after one demeanour
and countenance her beautie appeareth to all ages. In vaine have some
men of late (Transformeres of evrye thing) consulted upon her reform-
ation, and endevured to abstracte her to Metaphysicall Ideas, and
Scholasticall Quiddityes, denuding her of her own Habites and those
ornamentes with which shee hath amused the World some thousand
yeeres. Poesie is not a Thing that is yet in the finding and search, or
which may be other wise found out, being all reddye condescended
upon by all Nationes, and as it were established *iure Gentium*,[1] amongst
Greekes, Romaines, Italienes, French, Spaniardes. Neither doe I thinke
that a good piece of poesie, which Homer, Virgill, Ovid, Petrach,
Bartas, Ronsard, Boscan, Garcilasso (if they were alife, and had that
langage) could not understand, and reach the sense of the writer.
Suppose these men could find out some other new Idea like poesie, it
should be held as if Nature should bring forth some new animal,
Neither Man, Horse, Lyon, Dog, but which had some Memberes of

all, if they had beene proportionablie and by right Symmetrie set together. What is not like the ancientes and conforme to those Rules which hath beene agreed unto by all tymes, maye(indeed) be some thing like unto poesie, but it is no more Poesie than a Monster is a Man. Monsteres breed admiration at the first, but have ever some strange loathsomnesse in them at last. I Denye not but a Mulet is more profitable than some horses, yet it is neither horse nor asse, and yet it is but a Mulet. There is a taile told of a poore Miserable fellow accused of Bestialitie, and hee at his araignment confessed that it was not out of any evill intention hee had done it, but onlie to procreate a Monster with which (having no thing to sustaine his life) hee might winne his bread, going about the countrey. For the like cause it may be thought these men found out ther new poesie differing from the matteres, manners, Rules of former ages: either they did not see the Way of poesie or were affrayd to enter it. The Verses of Camillus Quernus as they are imitated by Strada seeme verye plausible and to admiration to some, but how farre they are off right poesie Children may guesse. These Mens new conceptiones aproach nearer his, than to the Majestie and statlinesse of the great Poetes. The contempte and undervaluing of Verses hath made men spare their travaile in adorning manye of them but poesie, as it hath over-come ignorance, at last will over-come Envie and contempte. This I have beene bold to write unto you not to give you any instruction, but to manifeste myne Obedience to your Request.

NOTE

1. *iure Gentium.* By the law of nations natural law.

APPENDIX

MEMORIALLS

Anno 1606 the 3 of September being Tusday I first arrived in france. the 6 thereafter came to Paris. The 10 of aprill 1607 I came to Burges in Berrye there remained till agust 1608.

Anno 1608 the 13 of November about twelfe a clocke in the night not 20 miles from Scarsbrough returning to Scotland by the rencount- 5 ring of a ship in the broad sea I was in great Danger to have been drowned. the one ship braking the shroudes of the other and shee bursting her at the keelle. this happened the 23 of my age. Upon a Tusday.

Tusday the 21 of Agust 1610 about Noone by the Death of my 10 father began to be fatall to mee the 25 of my age

The 19 of March 1610 was fatall to mee 25 of my age. at Harbattle Castell neare Annicke. By Roaveres[?]

The 5 of Agust 1604 the 19 of my age was fatall to mee. by the Bonfires. 15

The moneth of November 1620 was fatall to mee by a sort of pleurisie on my right side which continued eight weekes

The 29 of September 1621 as I was at supper with Sir Alexander Drummond of Carnok in the Hall of Carnok I evanished in a sown almost dead. 20

The 29 of Maye 1622 I was made Burgeose of Hadingtoun.

The 12 of March 1625 I suspected my selfe to have been poysoned

The 28 of November 1626 by the falling from a high stare I was in danger of my life.

The 8 December 1626 I was made Burgeose of Edenbenbrough [sic] 25 solemlye with a Banquet which began in the lower councell house at 7 in the after-Noone and continued till almost ten of cloke my Burgeose Ticket given mee in gold letteres.

The 3 of februarye 1629 I contracted a collik which turned in a fievre at Sterling which continued with mee 20 Dayes in which I was 30

193

almost dead. I stayed in my chamber 5 weekes. in which tyme I wrot the pageantes for King Charles.

The first of September 1629 was a disastrous day to mee by a blow on my right hand.

the 6 of June 1630 by the fall of a horse I almost broke my collar bone. 35

The 28 of februarye 1631 was fatall to mee by miscarying of a horse over coalepits

The 9 of Januarye 1631 was fatall. but happye.

The 16 of October 1631 I was made Burgeos of the Canongate with the viscount Sterlin. 40

The 19 of September 1632 at one in the morning the horrible paine of the collike came to mee and continued 18 houres, beginning to relent at 6 afternoone. the 21 at 5 after-noone it beganne againe and continued till till [sic] 4 in the morning more terrible than Death.

The 11 of februarye 1633 I was made Burgeos of lythgow with the 45 Lord of Traquare.

The 21 of May 1634 about ten of the evning was fatall to mee by lossing many obligationes which interest mee above 3000 markes.

In the Moneth of June 1635 all my litle children were sicke of the small poxes and one dyed. 50

The 12 of Julie 1636 after Midnight the collik and stone surprised mee, the paine of all paines and continued in extremitie 12 houres. a fievre continued with mee and paine till the 13 of August the after noone of which day I voyded a great gravell Stone.

anno 1602 in the Moneth of September by reading Heliodorus and 55 other Bookes the 17 yeere of my age I had a paine in myne eyes for the space of eight dayes that I was altogether barred of seeing.

The 21 of aprile 1637 I first knew what the Gutte was, it continued 14 dayes on my right foot.

The 7 of September 1637 my face swelled and my left eye was in 60 a danger of closing. a small fievre accompanyed with a pricking of the face, keeping me from sleep many nightes.

9 of September 1639 I escaped a fearfull wandring in the night by the providence almightie going alone thorough mosse and colpites.

The 30 of Januarye 1640 Elizabeth Logan contract⟨ed?⟩ a cold 65 and fievre which continued with her till the 8 of March.

1640. the 25 of december I contracted a cold with a fievre which continued five dayes and then turned in a Gutte upon my left foot. the great Toe.

1641 in March I contracted a Goute in my right foote and the 70 distellation continued in a sort of Tootheach, after which it invaded my left eare, with grea⟨t⟩ paine arising on the Temple of my head eight dayes I never sleeped. full of fearfull resveryes. I feare it turne in an apoplexie.

In September the 6 day 1646. I contracted a goute which removed 75 from one parte to an other.

The 6 of august 1647 fryday by the fall of a horse I almost broke my collar bone left side.

[The journal continues in the hand of Drummond's eldest son, Sir William Drummond.]

The 4 of december 1649 my fathere dyed of a sort of gravell. . . .

NOTES

l. 3   *Burges*. Bourges.
l. 11   *fatall*. Disastrous.
l. 13   *Annicke*. Alnwick.
l. 13   *Roaveres*[?]. Rovers, robbers.
l. 19   *sown*. Swoon.
l. 21   *Burgeose*. Burgess.
l. 30   *fievre*. Fever.
l. 32   *the pageantes . . . The Entertainment.*
l. 37   *coalepits*. Drummond had coal on his land.
l. 40   *viscount Sterlin*. Sir William Alexander was made Viscount Stirling on September 4, 1630.
l. 45   *lythgow*. Linlithgow.
l. 46   *the Lord of Traquare*. John Stewart, Earl of Traquair. He was one of the king's privy councillors in 1633.
l. 58   *Gutte*. Gout.
l. 65   *Elizabeth Logan*. Drummond's wife.
l. 71   *distellation*. A defluxion of rheum, a catarrh.
l. 73   *resveryes*. Reveries.

NOTES

[These are additional to the explicatory footnotes]

The texts

Unless otherwise stated, the text used is that of L. E. Kastner's Scottish Text Society edition (Edinburgh, 1913). The textual problems raised by Drummond's poetry are complex: his early work appeared in a number of editions, and besides correcting between editions Drummond corrected between impressions of the same edition, even going to the length of having correction slips printed and pasted into the text. Kastner lists all variants; the text he provides seems as close as possible to the text that Drummond finally settled upon.

Sources and models

The bulk of modern scholarship on Drummond has been devoted to establishing his indebtedness to a wide variety of foreign and domestic models. For the imitative nature of his poetry, see the editorial notes by W. C. Ward in the Muses Library edition of his poems (London, 1894), and Kastner's notes in the *S.T.S.* edition. A notable recent addition to our knowledge of Drummond's sources is R. D. S. Jack's "Drummond: the major Scottish sources," *Studies in Scottish Literature*, VI (1968), 36–46. For the imitative nature of *A Cypresse Grove* see again Kastner; M. A. Rugoff, "Drummond's debt to Donne," *PQ*, XVI (1937), 85–88; G. Smith, "The influence of Sir John Hayward and Joshua Sylvester upon Drummond's *Cypresse Grove*," *PQ*, XXVI (1947), 69–80; M. P. McDiarmid, "The Spanish Plunder Of William Drummond of Hawthornden," *MLR*, XLIV (1949), 17–25. R. C. Wallerstein's "The style of Drummond in its relation to his translations," *PMLA*, XLVII (1933), 1090–1107, is a balanced discussion of the degree to which Drummond transformed his originals.

Drummond's language

It is worth remembering while reading Drummond that his knowledge of English, as distinct from Scots, was acquired from books. He did want to be read as an *English* writer, one of "the Muses of Albion," but his desire and his achievement did not match. He tried to master English pronunciation and English usage but was not always successful: what appears as an awkwardness, reading in English, may be smooth or forceful in Scots.

Drummond's first poetry was in fact written in Scots, and his own customary language was Scots. The early notes in his manuscripts use the "qu" and the Scots "y" spellings, his vocabulary is Scots, his constructions Scots. Ask is "speir," kept is "keppit," wished is "villit" etc.

In his published work Drummond attempted to erase Scotticisms, but occasional examples survived his vigilance, some spellings and particularly some pronunciations. The latter, of course, are of importance in his poetry. In the textual notes I have only explained and drawn attention to Scots usage that is no longer current; I believe that readers will have little difficulty with Drummond's language.

One other Scots trait of his vocabulary: Drummond, especially in his prose, borrows and adapts many words from the French, or uses the French form of the English word. Thus he has "fievre" for fever, "supresme" for supreme, "resveryes" for reveries, "souveraigne" for sovereign.

Teares on the Death of Moeliades

This, Drummond's first published work, was first printed in 1613. It was included in the same year in *Mausoleum*, a collection of epitaphs on the death of Prince Henry, who had died in November, 1612, in his eighteenth year. Moeliades or Meliades, according to Drummond in his note to the poem, was the name that Henry adopted for his knightly sports, being an anagram of *Miles a Deo* (soldier from God).

Poems

The *Poems* came out first in a trial edition (probable date 1614). The 1616 edition, besides the poems of The First Part and The Second Part (printed here in their entirety) included *Teares on the Death of Moeliades*, the "Urania" or spiritual poems, and a collection of madrigals and epigrams. Sonnet vii. Here and elsewhere in Drummond's work is the expression of the neo-Platonic doctrine that all earthly beauty is but the pale reflection of heavenly beauty.

Madrigals and Epigrams

The bulk of these were attached to the *Poems* (1616), though a few here are from the suppressed edition of 1614(?) and Edward Phillip's posthumous edition (1656).

Forth Feasting

James VI returned to Scotland in May, 1617, and later the same year Drummond published his poem in celebration of the visit.

Flowres of Sion

Flowres of Sion was first published in 1623, with a second edition coming out in 1630. The text here includes all the poems with the exception of the unfinished "The Shadow of the Judgement" and three occasional sonnets. Incorporated in *Flowres* are most of the "Urania" section of the *Poems* (1616).

Flowres is a characteristic verse meditation on standard religious themes: contemplation of the vanity of human achievement, Christ's life and death as remedy and one true hope, and the Christian's happiness in adoration of the works and wonders of God. Without relying upon the precise and intricate structure recommended by some Catholic authorities, Drummond does seem to base his organization on the Catholic three-fold meditational process: first memory of the Christian predicament, then understanding of the Christian solution, then finally adoration of God who planned the mystery. The three parts of the imaginative meditation, Memory, Understanding and Will (or Love), were the proper approach to the Trinity, Father, Son, and Holy Ghost. They were moreover the three essential parts of the human soul as Drummond makes clear in *A Cypresse Grove*: "thou art a Shadow of that unsearchable Trinitie, in thy three essentiall Powers, Understanding, Will, Memorie; which though three, are in Thee but one, and abiding one, are distinctly three. . . ."

Sonnet xiv. Drummond uses several emblems or emblematic figures throughout these poems. The pelican who plucks her breast to feed her young, and the phoenix who rises again from the fire are both symbols of Christ. There is other less obvious emblematic imagery: the rose within a briar, the Christian as seafarer, life as a shadow.

Hymn v, ll. 160 *et seq*. Here follows a conventional description of the renaissance cosmos, arranged in its appropriate order descending from God: first the angels in their ranks (ll. 173–6), then the great chain of being (ll. 181–6) which begins with the heavenly bodies and the planets in their order (Saturn, Jupiter, Mars, Venus and Mercury; ll. 205–20).

Sonnets

Sonnets i and ii were published in Drummond's lifetime; the others were printed posthumously.

Sonnet ii. This poem is taken from a half-sheet printed to commemorate Euphemia Cunningham, to whom Drummond is said to have been betrothed. According to the dedication Euphemia "in the Prime of Her Youth died the 23. of Julie, 1616." Under a dedication to Jane, Countess of Perth, Drummond re-printed the sonnet with little alteration in *Flowres of Sion* (1623).

Sonnet iii. Nothing is known about the subject of this sonnet. The mood of the poem is characteristic of Drummond's middle age.

Sonnet iv. The medieval interpretation of world history as the history of the four monarchies or empires of Assyria, Persia, Greece and Rome was still popular in Drummond's time. The four monarchies were seen as matching the prophecy of Daniel (*Daniel*, Chap. VII), and many Protestants forecast the imminent dissolution of the fourth monarchy, the Church of Rome (heir to the Roman empire) and the establishment of God's kingdom on earth. In his poem Drummond is more particularly referring to Sir William Alexander's *Monarchicke Tragedies*, four plays on the four monarchies.

The Entertainment

Drummond was the chief (if not the only) script-writer and organizer of the pageant that was held to entertain King Charles on his visit to Edinburgh in 1633. *The Entertainment* was published the same year. Drummond records in his "Memorialls" (see the Appendix) that he actually wrote the pageant four years earlier, in February 1629, during a bout of illness.

Satirical Verses

These were not published in Drummond's lifetime.
i "The scottish kirke . . ." Kastner believes this to be a reference to the proceedings of the General Assembly of 1638.

198

ii *A Character of the Anti-Covenanter.* Drummond had little time for the Covenant, although he was certainly forced to sign it.

iv *Encomiastike verses.* The subject of this work is unknown.

v *For a ladyes summonds.* Previously unpublished. The original is in Drummond's hand in the Hawthornden MSS (N.L.S. MS 2062, ff. 193r–195r).

vi "If of the dead . . ." Previously unpublished. The original is in Drummond's hand in the Hawthornden MSS (N.L.S. MS 2062, f. 91r). It was probably written during the 1640s.

A Cypresse Grove

In its first version this essay was called *A Midnight's Trance* (printed 1619), a title which acknowledged Drummond's model as the so-called *Dream of Cicero* (the *Somnium Scipionis*), and placed it in the tradition of midnight meditations on death and the inevitable transitoriness of life. Reflecting his wide variety of sources (see my summary in *The Library,* pp. 29–30), Drummond offers a variety of attitudes from Stoicism to Christian reassurance.

The essay is organized as a loose series of exercises using the three-fold meditational system (see the note on the *Flowres of Sion*): first the subject is considered from the Memory, then the Understanding, then the Will (or Love). Thus after a brief introduction Drummond begins "I beganne to turne over in my remembrance . . ." before proceeding three paragraphs later to an understanding, "Though it cannot well and altogether bee denyed but that Death naturallie is terrible. . . ." The process is repeated numerous times, coming to a resolution when the dreamer, with the coming of the dawn, finds his thoughts calm in contemplation of God and His works, of "all in this great All."

A Cypresse Grove was published with the *Flowres of Sion* in 1623, and again in 1630.

A Speech on Toleration

This passage is taken from Drummond's *The History of Scotland* (first edition 1655). One of the privy councillors is addressing James V; the year is 1540 at the time of the first disturbances of the reformation.

Drummond re-worked this speech several times during the 1630s, and it was certainly intended as a comment upon the troubles of his own time. When the councillor finishes speaking, the history continues: "But the King followed not this opinione. . . ."

My text is based on the fair copy in the Hawthornden MSS (N.L.S. MS. 2057, ff. 202–8). This is a draft in a secretary's hand, with corrections in Drummond's own hand.

The title is supplied from the Hawthornden MSS.

Irene

This posthumously published pamphlet was written in late 1638 as an attempt to respond to and perhaps resolve the political crisis of that year. The National Covenant had been signed in March, and negotiations between the Covenanters and the Marquis of Hamilton, the representative of Charles I, had been going on all summer. By September the king had been forced in the face of civil war to agree to the demands of the Covenanters: episcopacy was to be severely limited and the presbyterian kirk would be allowed to govern itself. Drummond's *Irene* congratulates the king on the wisdom of compromise, and yet warns his fellow-countrymen of the serious dangers of disobedience and insurrection. Considering the events of the following twelve years, Drummond's warnings may seem prophetic.

Drummond held a conventional middle-of-the-road view of monarchy: he did not agree with James VI's version of divine right (as set out in the *Basilicon Doron*) nor did he agree with George Buchanan's theory of the right of a people to depose their sovereign (stated in *De Jure Regni apud Scotos*). He reiterates several times in his essay that commonplace of renaissance political philosophy: "No Guard so sure as Love unto a Crowne" (*Forth Feasting*, l. 246).

My text is based on a draft in Drummond's hand in the Hawthornden MSS (N.L.S. MS. 2058, ff. 149r-186r). This is probably not the copy which went to the printer of the *Works* (1711) but it is a better text than given in that wretched edition.

The extracts printed here represent rather more than half the pamphlet.

A Letter on The True Nature of Poetry

This letter is included here as an important statement of Drummond's critical position. Dr Johnston was court physician to King Charles, and an accomplished Latin poet. The letter is an affirmation of the solid conservatism of Drummond's taste in poetry: John Donne and his school may be the object of the attack upon "metaphysical ideas and scholastical quiddities." It was probably written in the 1630s.

My text is taken from the draft copy in the Hawthornden MSS (N.L.S. MS. 2061, ff. 39r-40r).

"Memorialls"

This is the complete text of a brief journal begun by Drummond probably in his late twenties, and continued by him until shortly before his death. (The unpublished manuscript from which it is taken also includes some genealogical notes, and some additions made by Drummond's son William.)

The manuscript is now in Dundee University Library. I have expanded contractions, and normalized "u" and "v", but otherwise transcribed Drummond's text as it is.